Assessing Organizational Performance in Higher Education

BARBARA A. MILLER

JB JOSSEY-BASS

Assessing Organizational Performance in Higher Education

BICENTENNIAL
1807
WILEY
2007
BICENTENNIAL

John Wiley & Sons, Inc.

Copyright © 2007 by John Wiley & Sons, Inc. All rights reserved.

Published by Jossey-Bass
A Wiley Imprint
989 Market Street, San Francisco, CA 94103-1741   www.josseybass.com

Jossey-Bass books and products are available through most bookstores. To contact Jossey-Bass directly call our Customer Care Department within the U.S. at 800-956-7739, outside the U.S. at 317-572-3986, or fax 317-572-4002.

Jossey-Bass also publishes its books in a variety of electronic formats. Some content that appears in print may not be available in electronic books.

Library of Congress Cataloging-in-Publication Data

Miller, Barbara A., 1943-
Assessing organizational performance in higher education /
Barbara A. Miller ; foreword by Suzanne Swope.
    p. cm.
Includes bibliographical references and index.
ISBN-13: 978-0-7879-8640-7 (pbk.)
ISBN-10: 0-7879-8640-2 (pbk.)
1. Universities and colleges--United States--Evaluation.
2. Universities and colleges--United States--Administration. I. Title.
LB2331.63.M55 2007
378.1'07--dc22   2006022688
Printed in the United States of America

FIRST EDITION

10 9 8 7 6 5 4 3 2 1

CONTENTS

TABLES, FIGURES, EXHIBITS, AND WORKSHEETS

EXHIBITS

WORKSHEETS

FOREWORD

Anyone interested in the survival of higher education realizes that the industry is going through a profound change. Just like manufacturing and health care before it, higher education must face the reality that costs, new technologies, and changing customer expectations create pressures on the industry. Anyone who works in colleges or has a stake in their success will find this book of great interest. Quality education in all its manifestations is crucial to the survival of democracy, as well as to the industry itself.

Peter Drucker, a longtime authority in management, proposed in *Management Challenges for the 21st Century* (1999) that we may need to stop thinking from a perspective of managing the work of people and begin managing for performance. To be effective, we must define customers' values and their decision-making processes regarding their income distribution. Management must organize and evaluate the entire operational process, focusing on results and performance.

No one knows these principles better as they relate to higher education than Barbara A. Miller (formerly Lembcke). She has served as an administrative leader, teacher, researcher, and consultant in private and public universities. Her breadth of perspective and knowledge about systems—how they are defined, measured, evaluated, and changed—are extensive. Miller's broadly based higher education background, combined with her teaching and administrative experience, makes her insights and analysis extremely valuable for those of us serving a variety of roles in the institution as well as those in evaluation positions as stakeholders outside the organization.

Assessing Organizational Performance in Higher Education embraces assessment at the organizational, program, and process levels and evaluates the work from a perspective rooted in systems thinking. Readers will be able to identify major work processes, the significance of these processes in producing quality outcomes, and the strategies necessary for continuous improvement. The book complements the body of literature on assessment, providing both an in-depth theoretical framework and techniques useful for implementation. The information in it is pertinent to everyone from the boardroom to the individual faculty or staff member and will serve as a set of tools to improve the work of the institution. Readers who fully understand the message Miller presents and who work through the exercises as they apply to the institution or program they are assessing will have done a great service to their constituencies—to the students whom they so gratefully serve and to others, both staff and faculty, who care about the quality of their work and the important role they play in this society.

Suzanne Swope, Ed.D.
Vice President for Enrollment and Student Affairs
Emerson College, Boston

PREFACE

I wrote this book to meet the needs of two important groups associated with assessment in higher education: assessors and assessment users. The first group, assessors, consists of persons engaged in day-to-day assessment work. They are faculty, staff, and administrators with part-time or full-time, temporary or permanent responsibilities for assessment. The second group, assessment users, are persons who evaluate or judge performance results measured and conveyed by assessors. I see assessment users as the end users or customers of assessment programs.

Assessors seek avenues for measuring performance required of assessment users; assessment users seek appropriate contexts for evaluating assessment findings measured and conveyed by assessors. Often assessors and assessment users are actually the same persons. However, I choose to differentiate the roles for purposes of discussion, *assessor* referring exclusively to persons exploring matters of measurement, and *assessment user* referring exclusively to persons engaged in evaluation. I describe various groups of external and internal assessment users and explain how each group uses assessment findings to support a wide range of decisions that have a potential impact on an organization's capacity to perform.

My purpose in writing this book is to strengthen the knowledge, skills, and abilities of assessors and assessment users in higher education whether they are novices or experts. I define assessment as the measurement of organizational performance that assessment users evaluate in relation to reference points for the purpose of supporting their requirements and expectations.

The premise of this book is that assessors in higher education must go beyond assessment of student learning outcomes and institutional effectiveness and into assessment of performance of whole organizations, programs, and processes. This raises two questions: why? and how?

Why assess performance at the organization, program, and process levels? For a variety of reasons:

- Colleges and universities are open, interdependent systems in which the performance of one organization depends on and affects the performance of other organizations.

- Colleges and universities account for performance at the organizational level to many powerful external assessment users, including governing boards, governmental agencies, and organizations that affirm accreditation, rank, and classification.

- All aspects of performance should be assessed within the context of an organization's mission, goals, and requirements and the expectations of the people it serves.

- Performance at the organization, program, and process levels is complex and requires a holistic view of how one area of performance affects another area of performance within the same unit of analysis.

How is performance assessed at the organizational level?

- Performance is assessed for a designated unit of analysis whose boundaries, mission, and goals are clearly defined. For example, a unit of analysis can be the institution as a whole, a college such as the College of Arts and Sciences, a school such as the Law School or Medical School, a department such as the Chemistry Department, a program such as General Education or Writing Across the Curriculum, or an administrative office such as the Admissions Office, Development Office, or Registrar's Office. A unit of analysis can also be a key work process (such as teaching or research) or a cross-functional process (such as payroll).

- Performance is measured through performance indicators in seven interrelated areas of organizational performance, each of which is linked to specific organizational elements. The seven areas of organizational performance are effectiveness, productivity, quality (including quality of leadership systems, of inputs, of key work processes, of programs and services, and of worklife), customer and stakeholder satisfaction, efficiency, innovation, and financial durability.

- Performance is measured in selected areas of performance deemed critical to the unit's performance success.

- Performance is evaluated within the context of the unit's mission and goals.

- Performance is evaluated against specific performance requirements and expectations of the organization's powerful external and internal assessment users, other important stakeholders, and the people the unit serves.

The book's focus on performance at the organization, program, and process levels complements and advances the many published works available today on assessment of student learning outcomes and institutional effectiveness. This focus helps readers understand the interdependence of organizations in higher education and complexities inherent in organizational performance. I believe that this understanding is fundamental to the practice and scholarship of assessment.

For assessors, the book offers a conceptual framework to guide the measurement of organizational performance in all seven areas of organizational performance. The conceptual framework applies to both academic and administrative units of analysis at any level within the hierarchical structure of educational institutions; it also applies to important programs and key work processes that operate within single organizations or across several organizations or functions within an institution.

What is most exciting about this book is its examination of assessment in several new and different areas of organizational performance—areas that include but go beyond institutional effectiveness, student learning outcomes, and input quality. The following are some of the new areas of performance that assessors can measure:

- Quality of an organization's leadership system as a measure of quality of direction and support it provides to the unit under review

- Quality of organizational structure as a measure of how organizational design and governance hinders or enhances organizational performance

- Quality assurance of partnerships with important upstream systems that supply, constrain, and serve the units under review

- Quality of worklife as a measure of employee attitudes and perceptions about the quality of their work experiences and workplace

- Quality of key work processes as a measure of cycle time, cost, rework, waste, and scrap that characterize key work processes

- Organizational innovation as a measure of an organization's learning culture and a measure of creative changes put in place to improve organizational performance

- Efficiency as a measure of how well organizations use their scarce and critical resources, as well as a measure of the costs and benefits of quality management

- Customer and stakeholder satisfaction as a measure of the extent to which organizations meet the needs of the people they serve

- Financial durability as a measure of the financial health and well-being of the units under review.

For external assessment users such as governing boards, governmental agencies, and organizations that affirm accreditation, classification, rank, and eligibility, the book is designed to expand knowledge of the nature and complexity of organizational performance in higher education—knowledge that will, ideally, enhance the ability to frame appropriate accountability questions of educational leaders.

For internal assessment users, such as senior leaders, administrators, and faculty and staff, the book is designed to expand knowledge of the internal workings and interdependence of organizations both inside and outside the institution, complexities inherent in organizational performance, and important links among organizational system elements, areas of organizational performance, and assessment. This knowledge will enhance their ability, as assessment users, to frame better performance questions that lead to better assessments of organizational performance.

Finally, the book offers educational leaders specific recommendations on how to build, deploy, and evaluate assessment programs in ways that provide the right information, at the right time, in the right format to meet ever-changing needs of important external and internal assessment users. The book presents many examples and worksheets to help assessors describe their unit's organizational system elements and measure complex and interdependent areas of organizational performance using performance indicators and reference points appropriate to the organization's mission, vision, strategic goals, and critical success factors.

Organization of the Book

The book is organized into six chapters. Chapter One describes external and internal assessment user groups in higher education. It explains what types of organizational performance results assessment users want to know, how they typically use assessment findings in their decision-making processes, and what is at stake for organizations whose performance is under review. A worksheet is provided to help assessors identify assessment information required of important external and internal assessment users groups.

Chapter Two introduces systems thinking and explains the benefits of viewing organizations as open, living, unique systems with a purpose. It begins with a discussion of interdependent system elements that make up organizations, programs, and processes in higher education and explains how each system element presents opportunities for assessment. Chapter Two describes five internal system elements: leadership systems, inputs, key work processes, outputs, and outcomes. Many examples are provided for academic and administrative organizations. Worksheets are also provided to help assessors identify and describe internal system elements of units whose performance they intend to measure.

Chapter Three continues the discussion of system elements and their link to assessment. It describes three external system elements: upstream systems, customers, and stakeholders. Again, many examples are provided for academic and administrative organizations. Worksheets are also provided to help assessors identify and describe external system elements of units whose performance they intend to measure.

Chapter Four is a discussion of how to assess organizational performance. It summarizes assessment methods and terminology. The chapter begins by differentiating the work of measurement from evaluation in assessment. It explains how to clarify units of analysis and the proper ways to use time frames, critical success factors, performance indicators, and reference points. It describes methods for collecting assessment data and disseminating performance results. Worksheets are provided to help assessors identify critical success factors and build an assessment report schedule for units whose performance they intend to measure.

Chapter Five is a discussion of what to assess in organizational performance. It covers the seven operational definitions of organizational performance noted earlier in this Preface: effectiveness, productivity, quality, customer and stakeholder satisfaction, efficiency, innovation, and financial durability. Many examples of performance indicators in each area are provided for academic and administrative organizations. Worksheets are provided to help assessors identify and describe performance indicators and reference points in all seven areas (including critical success factors) and link performance areas to specific assessment user needs and preferences.

Finally, Chapter Six is about how to build, deploy, and assess new or more formalized campuswide assessment programs. It offers suggestions about the importance of clarifying purpose, identifying important assessment user groups, and ensuring two-way, ongoing communication about assessment. It explains how to create and sustain a supportive organizational culture for assessment and how to build a leadership structure that ensures program success. It describes direct and indirect costs of assessment. It presents external and internal system elements of an assessment program as well as examples of indicators for measuring performance in areas deemed critical to program success. A worksheet is provided to help assessment leaders build an assessment communication plan.

Acknowledgments

This book reflects many years of work with friends and colleagues who helped me frame and apply this conceptual model for assessing performance of organizations in higher education. In particular, I would like to thank my husband and longtime friend and colleague, Louie Miller III, who not only served as my sounding board throughout the development of this book but also provided patient guidance and expertise resulting from his long and successful professional career as a tenured professor in sociology and senior executive in information services. I would also like to thank my friend and colleague Suzanne Swope, currently vice president for enrollment and student affairs at Emerson College, for her advice and collaboration over the many years we worked together at George Mason University. I would also like to thank my longtime friend Sandra Everett at Lorain County Community College for sharing her expertise in the area of quality management and helping me understand and apply those principles in the context of organizations in higher education. Finally, I would like to thank Scott Sink, Tom Tuttle, and Carl Thor, whose early works inspired the formation of this conceptual framework for assessing performance of organizations in higher education.

Greencastle, Indiana   Barbara A. Miller
June 2006

ABOUT THE AUTHOR

Barbara A. Miller (formerly Lembcke) is an experienced administrator in higher education and has served as a director of institutional planning and research, a senior planning and policy analyst, and an internal management consultant specializing in organizational development, and continuous quality improvement. She is also an experienced faculty member who has taught courses in management, leadership theory, organizational development, and communication. Her expertise in assessment results from thirty years of experience in large public research institutions, large and medium-sized two-year comprehensive community colleges, and small liberal arts institutions. She served for two years as an examiner for the Malcolm Baldrige National Quality Award Program and one year as an evaluator in the Baldrige pilot program in education, where documentation of performance results is critical.

Miller earned her bachelor of arts degree in sociology at the University of California, Berkeley; her master of arts degree in higher education and student personnel administration at Syracuse University; and her doctorate in higher education administration at the University of Florida in Gainesville. She has also taken M.B.A. courses at the University of North Florida, Jacksonville.

Miller lives in Greencastle, Indiana, where she serves as guest scholar at DePauw University and coordinates her consulting service.

CHAPTER 1

Purpose of Assessment

Assessment in higher education has a long history in the United States. According to Victor Borden and Karen Bottrill (1994), college reputational ranking studies began in 1910, followed by peer comparisons of faculty workload and salary guidelines. Resource allocation measures emerged in the 1960s, and activity-based costing methods for generating financial performance information and benchmarking projects began in the 1990s. Finally, student outcomes assessment and process reengineering surfaced in the late 1980s and 1990s.

This book extends higher education's experience with assessment into the arena of performance of whole organizations, programs, and processes within the framework of systems thinking. For the purpose of this book, assessment of organizational performance is defined as the measurement of organizational performance that assessment users evaluate in relation to reference points for the purpose of supporting their requirements and expectations.

The discussion begins with an explanation of assessment's purpose as seen through the lens of those who use assessment results. It explores how groups inside and outside the institution use assessment, what assessment information they seek, and the potential impact they have on an organization's capacity to perform. Since assessment users are the "end users" of the assessment program, they represent the program's "customers." Indeed, it is their needs, preferences, and requirements that drive the development, deployment, and evaluation of assessment programs.

Assessment User Groups _____

Anthropology Department at a Large
State-Supported Research University

The call came early one morning, just before class. He remembers it well because it upset him so much that he had difficulty preparing for class. He had been chair of the Cultural Anthropology Department for nearly three years and was finally getting to understand, or so he thought, the politics of this large, state-supported institution. To be honest, he never really thought it was possible that the dean would seriously consider dropping the department. After all, who ever heard of a high-quality university without a cultural anthropology department?

It all began about ten years earlier when PBS filmed a program on DNA in the new DNA lab. Everyone considered DNA the answer to many of life's baffling questions. The lab catapulted the discipline of physical anthropology to the top of the dean's "list of favorites." Unlike cultural anthropology, which has been around since the beginning of time (or so it seemed), physical anthropology was a growing discipline (thanks to DNA) replete with its own professional association and refereed journals.

At this institution, national ranking was everything. Unfortunately, the Cultural Anthropology Department was ranked unacceptably low. The chair defended his department to the dean by explaining that it was extremely difficult to get published in the refereed journals because there were so many distinguished scholars in the field. He also explained that their salaries were below those in other disciplines, which made recruitment nearly impossible. And because so many positions remained unfilled, he was forced to use adjunct faculty, which, of course, contributed to a lower ranking.

This vignette exemplifies the power that external assessment users—in this case, organizations that rank academic programs—have over organizations in higher education. Their decisions have a staggering impact on an organization's capacity to perform. It is therefore very important for educational leaders to clarify for assessors (1) who their important external assessment users are, (2) the types of assessment information they need, (3) the types of decisions they make based on assessment results, and (4) the potential impact those decisions have on the organization's capacity to perform. High-quality assessment programs are robust and capable of providing the right information at the right time in the right format to meet ever-changing needs of all the organization's important assessment user groups.

There are two types of groups who use assessment results in higher education: external and internal. External user groups are governing boards; governmental agencies; potential students, donors, employees, and contractors; organizations that affirm; and external academic peers. Based on their evaluation of assessment findings, these groups make important decisions that greatly affect the following organizational aspects:

- Operating and capital resources
- Research grants and contracts
- Program mix and pricing structures
- Student financial aid
- Sanctions for noncompliance
- Accreditation
- Rank
- Eligibility
- Censure
- Future enrollments
- Future workforce
- Donations and gifts
- Access to contractors
- Workforce strikes and slowdowns

Internal user groups exist inside the institution. There are three types of internal user groups: senior leaders, administrators and managers, and faculty and staff. Internal user groups use assessment for the following purposes:

- To account to others
- To manage strategy
- To allocate resources
- To manage and control quality of processes and organizational culture
- To improve programs and services
- To support personnel decisions
- To advocate causes

This chapter explores external and internal user groups typical in higher education. It is intended that this discussion will help assessors widen their own analysis of important assessment user groups to their organizations.

External Assessment User Groups

External user groups, by definition, reside outside the institution. Each group has a unique interest in assessment based on its function and relationship with the organization. As noted earlier, the major external assessment user groups in higher education discussed in this chapter are governing boards; governmental agencies; potential students, donors, employees, and contractors; organizations that affirm; and external academic peers.

Governing Boards

For assessment purposes, governing boards are defined as bodies that govern, coordinate, and advise institutions and programs at the local and state levels. Using this definition, local governing boards and statewide boards of regents are all considered governing boards because they use assessment for similar purposes. The discussion begins with local governing boards.

Local Governing Boards

Local governing boards typically use assessment results to hold senior leaders accountable for the overall performance of the institution or program. They seek assessment findings that answer the following accountability questions, among others:

> Is the organization clear in its purpose and do members of the organizational community share a vision of excellence?
>
> Is the institution achieving its mission (outcomes performance)?
>
> To what extent do members of the organizational community practice the organization's values and beliefs?
>
> Does the organization offer high-quality programs and services? How does the organization assess its academic programs and services, and how does it use assessment findings for improvement?
>
> What is the role of sponsored and unsponsored research as defined by the institution's mission and strategic plans? What types of research are taking place? Who are the major sponsors?
>
> What are the funding patterns, overhead rates, budgetary consequences, and other financial considerations, both now and in the future?
>
> Does the organization have clear policies regarding intellectual property rights and publication of results of research sponsored by corporations?
>
> Who are the faculty, and what do they do?
>
> To what extent are students, alumni, faculty, staff, and other partners satisfied?
>
> Who graduates, and what do they end up doing?
>
> Is the organization efficiently using its critical resources?

Does the organization have adequate and reliable revenues and expenditures that ensure financial durability?

Does the organization's costs and service quality compare favorably with comparable institutions?

What is the organization's overall return on investment?

Statewide Governing Boards

Statewide governing boards seek answers to the same accountability questions as local boards, as well as additional questions pertaining to specific issues important to the state. For example, in 2005, the State Council of Higher Education for Virginia (SCHEV) established performance standards to "certify" state-supported four-year public research institutions and two- and four-year public nonresearch institutions (see State Council, 2005). For certification, SCHEV seeks answers to the following accountability questions:

Access

Does the institution provide access to higher education for all citizens throughout the state, including underrepresented populations?

Does the institution meet its enrollment projections?

Does the institution meet its degree estimates?

Affordability

Does the institution ensure that higher education remains affordable, regardless of individual or family income? What are the costs, and are they reasonable?

Does the institution conduct periodic assessment of the likely impact of tuition and fee levels net of financial aid on applications, enrollment, and student indebtedness?

Academic Offerings

Does the institution offer a broad range of undergraduate and (where appropriate) graduate programs?

Does the institution regularly assess the extent to which the institution's curricula and degree programs address the state's need for sufficient graduates in particular shortage areas as determined by the state?

Academic Standards

Does the institution maintain high academic standards by undertaking continual review and improvement of academic programs?

Is the institution decreasing the number of lower-division students denied enrollment in introductory courses?

Is the institution maintaining or increasing the ratio of degrees conferred per FTE faculty member?

Student Progress and Success

Is the institution improving its student retention and progression rates?

Is the ratio of degrees awarded increasing as the number of degree-seeking undergraduates increases?

Articulation

Does the institution develop articulation agreements that have uniform application to all state colleges?

Does the institution provide additional opportunities for associate degree graduates to be admitted and enrolled?

Does the institution offer dual enrollment programs in cooperation with high schools?

Economic Development

Does the institution actively contribute to efforts that stimulate the economic development of the state, and if so, in what ways?

Research

Has the institution increased its level of externally funded research conducted at the institution?

How does the institution facilitate the transfer of technology from university research centers to private sector companies?

K–12 Enhancement

Does the institution enhance K–12 student achievement, upgrade teachers' knowledge and skills, and strengthen leadership skills of school administrators? If so, in what ways?

All Governing Boards

Governing boards also often seek answers to a variety of accountability questions pertaining to the institution's past performance problems, hot political and economic issues, and important local, statewide, and national strategic initiatives. Governing boards typically prefer assessment findings presented within the context of past performance or comparable institutions through benchmarking (or both). Governing boards that operate under so-called sunshine laws are restricted in their use of assessment findings. Governing boards, like other important assessment user groups, make many important decisions in a scheduled and somewhat predictable time frame based on annual academic and fiscal cycles. The assessment program should be able to predict and therefore provide reports in a timely manner.

Based on their evaluation of assessment findings, governing boards make many important policy decisions that influence an institution's mission, financial resources, physical plant expansion and renovation, program mix, and pricing structures. They also make personnel decisions about the institution's leadership system.

Governmental Agencies

For assessment purposes, governmental agencies are defined as federal, state, and local governmental and quasi-governmental organizations, commissions, task forces, and legislative delegations. For discussion purposes, this definition excludes state governing and coordinating boards defined earlier as governing boards.

Governmental agencies, like governing boards, use assessment results to hold organizational leaders accountable for some or all of an organization's performance results. In addition, they use assessment to determine the extent to which institutions and programs help the government achieve its goals and objectives such as workforce development and creation and transfer of knowledge and technology. They use assessment to determine institutional eligibility for grants, contracts, and student financial aid. Finally, state and federal auditors and inspectors use assessment to ensure compliance with tax codes, labor and civil rights laws, disability laws, safety (fire) and security standards, standards for the use of human subjects and animals in research, environmental regulations, accounting standards, civil rights, affirmative action, Title IX, health and food services standards, and so forth.

In general, governmental agencies seek answers to the following questions:

Does the organization offer high-quality programs and services in areas important to the government? How do these programs and services compare with those offered by other organizations?

Does the organization have adequate and reliable revenues and expenditures that ensure financial durability?

Does the organization comply with laws, regulations, and research guidelines?

Does the organization use its critical resources efficiently?

Does the organization meet eligibility requirements to receive grants, contracts, and student financial aid?

Based on their evaluation of assessment findings, governmental agencies make important decisions that greatly affect an organization's capacity to perform. For example, they use assessment to support decisions to award grants, contracts, and student financial aid. They also use assessment to support decisions to impose sanctions and penalties for noncompliance.

An important federal agency that collects institutional data often used in assessment for comparisons and benchmarks is the National Center for Educational Statistics (NCEA), part of the U.S. Department of Education and the Institute of Education Sciences. NCEA is the primary federal entity for collecting and analyzing data related to education. The center collects data related to higher education through its program called Integrated Postsecondary Education Data System (IPEDS). IPEDS is a system of survey components designed to collect data from postsecondary educational institutions that receive federal dollars through aid, grants, and contracts (see National Center, 2005).

IPEDS collects and reports data on institutional characteristics, completions, enrollment, graduation rates, student financial aid, employees by assigned position, fall staff, salaries, and finance. An important mission of NCEA is to make statistics collected through IPEDS available to the public. NCEA disseminates IPEDS data in several formats, including peer analyses, data sets, predetermined data tables, and a searchable Web site providing current statistics on a broad range of topics.

Potential Students (Including Parents), Donors (Including Alumni), Employees, and Contractors

A third type of external assessment user group represents potential students and their parents, potential donors including alumni, potential employees, and potential contractors. This group uses assessment to support "choice" decisions.

According to Daniel Seymour (1993), potential students and their parents consider an organization's academic quality an important factor in making choice decisions. He recommends that academic leaders use assessment to "tell the quality story" to these important stakeholders. However, for leaders to use assessment findings effectively in marketing materials, they must first understand what quality means to the market and match market needs with organizational resources, vision, and competitive position to determine and communicate its competitive advantage.

To support their choice decisions, these assessment users seek answers to the following questions pertaining to academic quality:

What is this institution's quality of programs and services? What is the quality of housing and athletic facilities? How does this compare with the quality at other comparable organizations?

How satisfied are students, faculty, and staff? What percentage of students complete their educational goals (retention, transfer admission, graduation, placement, graduate school admission)?

What is the cost of attending this institution in relation to the quality of its educational offerings? How does it compare with the cost at other comparable organizations?

Does the organization have adequate resources to maintain quality in its programs and services?

What reputation, national ranking, and accreditation status does this institution and its programs have?

Potential employees seek answers to the same quality questions, however, they are also concerned with the quality of faculty and staff, quality of teaching and research facilities, and competitiveness of compensation and benefits. Potential contractors are concerned with reliability of organizational revenues that ensure financial durability and the organization's track record for making promised payments in a timely manner.

Based on their evaluation of organizational performance, this group of assessment users makes important choice decisions that greatly affect an institution's future enrollment, donations, gifts, workforce, and the willingness of qualified service providers to bid for and contract with the institution.

Organizations That Affirm

This category of external assessment users represents a variety of organizations that rule on accreditation, censure, classification, rank, and eligibility; it also includes organizations that bargain with the institution. This group uses assessment to determine how well organizations meet and comply with their specific requirements so that they can determine an organization's accreditation status, classification, rank, and eligibility. Educational leaders pay a great deal of attention to this group of assessment users because it can potentially affect many aspects of an institution's capacity to perform.

Organizations That Accredit
Accreditation is a process of external review conducted by private, nonprofit accrediting organizations. According to Judith Eaton (1999), president of the Council for Higher Education Accreditation (CHEA), there are three types of accrediting organizations: regional accreditors

that accredit public and private nonprofit and for-profit two- and four-year institutions; national accreditors that accredit public and private nonprofit and for-profit single-purpose institutions, including distance-learning colleges and universities, private career institutions, and faith-based colleges and universities; and specialized and professional accreditors that accredit specific programs or schools such as law schools, medical schools, engineering schools and programs, and health profession programs.

According to Eaton (1999), organizations in higher education seek accreditation to ensure quality for their students and the public, gain access to federal funds such as student aid and other national programs, and ease transfer of courses and programs among colleges, universities, and programs. Organizations also seek accreditation to engender employer confidence in their evaluation of job applicant credentials and decisions to provide tuition support for current employees seeking additional education. There are five key features of accreditation: self-study, peer review, site visit, action (judgment by accrediting organization), and ongoing external review.

Every accrediting agency has a unique set of standards and criteria against which it evaluates performance of an institution or program. For example, the Southern Association of Colleges and Schools Commission on Colleges (SACSCC), a regional accreditor, requires institutions and programs to provide answers to the following questions (2004):

> Does the organization have a purpose appropriate to higher education?
>
> Does the organization have resources, programs, and services sufficient to accomplish and sustain that purpose?
>
> Does the organization maintain clearly specified educational outcomes that are consistent with its mission and appropriate to the degrees it offers?
>
> Does the organization assess achievement of its intended outcomes, and does it make improvements based on assessment results?

ABET Engineering Accreditation Commission (2006) accredits four engineering programs: applied science, computing, engineering, and technology. ABET was established in 1932 and is now a federation of twenty-eight professional and technical societies representing the four engineering programs. In 2006, ABET accredited 2,700 programs at over 550 colleges and universities nationwide.

To be accredited by ABET, institutions must demonstrate that their engineering programs meet eight basic and two engineering-specific criteria. Basic criteria pertain to students, program educational objectives, program outcomes and assessment, professional component, faculty, facilities, institutional support, and financial resources. Program-specific criteria pertain to curriculum and faculty.

Prior to the 1980s, most institutional and program-specific accreditation standards focused on the quality of resources such as faculty competence, financial stability, adequacy of technology, and library resources. Today, accreditation standards focus not only on the quality of resources, processes, programs, and services but also on the achievement of educational outcomes. Accreditors have moved from an input-driven model of accreditation to a goal-based model. In fact, some standards expect institutions to address "institutional effectiveness," a standard that requires them not only to identify expected outcomes for their educational programs and administrative and educational support services but also to assess achievement of those outcomes and provide evidence of improvement based on analysis of those results.

After evaluating assessment findings, accreditors make decisions to affirm or deny accreditation for new institutions and programs and to reaffirm or deny accreditation for ongoing institutions and programs.

Organizations That Censure

The primary organization in this category is the American Association of University Professors (AAUP), a professional association with a current membership of forty-five thousand, with more than five hundred local campus chapters and thirty-nine state organizations. AAUP's mission is to "advance academic freedom and shared governance, to define fundamental professional values and standards for higher education, and to ensure higher education's contribution to the common good" (2005a, p. 1). AAUP sees its role as protecting individual rights and advancing "principles and standards of sound academic practice governing the relationship between faculty and their institutions" (2005b, p. 1.) AAUP encourages institutions to use its principles and standards as guidelines for framing faculty regulations and handbooks.

AAUP uses assessment to censure administrations of institutions that fail to adhere to principles and standards of academic governance it believes ensures academic freedom and tenure. In 1938, AAUP began censuring administrations after determining conditions for academic freedom and tenure at the institution were unsatisfactory (2005b). In its document titled "1940 Statement of Principles on Academic Freedom and Tenure" (2004), AAUP clarifies specific standards it believes protect academic freedom and academic tenure. These principles address the two issues because AAUP considers both essential to teaching and research.

AAUP investigates particular cases brought to its attention by its members on campuses throughout the United States (2005b).

When the group determines that a situation on a campus represents a major departure from its principles and the situation remains unresolved, it initiates a review process that may result in censure of the institution's administration. In January 2006, the administrations of forty-seven institutions were on AAUP's published censure list.

AAUP publishes its censure list in every issue of its publication *Academe* and highlights censured institutions in job notices published by the *Chronicle of Higher Education* and in numerous disciplinary societies such as the American Historical Association, the American Psychological Association, and the College Art Association. The group asks its members to refrain from accepting appointment to an institution so long as the institution remains on the censure list (Knight, 2003).

In addition to censuring administrations, AAUP publishes a national salary report of faculty salaries and benefits that assessors use for comparisons and benchmarks (2005a).

Organizations That Classify

This group of assessment users classifies institutions and programs based on assessment findings. This group is important because much can be at stake based on an institution's classification.

One of the leading groups that classifies higher educational institutions is the Carnegie Foundation for the Advancement of Teaching, a private foundation. According to the Carnegie Foundation (2005), the typology, first published in 1973, was called the "Carnegie Classification of Institutions of Higher Education." The foundation updated the typology in 1976, 1987, 1994, and 2000, with another review launched in 2005.

The Carnegie Foundation classifies only degree-granting American colleges and universities that are accredited by an agency recognized by the U.S. Secretary of Education. The foundation originally created the typology to ensure a representative selection of participating individuals and institutions in its higher education projects. Today, many organizations use the Carnegie classification for different purposes. One use is to qualify institutions for federal research funds; another is to organize institutions into groups for ranking and benchmarking purposes.

The Carnegie Foundation classification (2005) requires answers to two assessment questions:

> How many and what types of programs does the organization offer at the undergraduate and graduate level?

> How many and what types of degrees does the organization award?

After evaluating assessment results, the Carnegie Foundation matches the institution with one of the following classifications:

Doctorate-granting institutions

> Doctoral or research universities—extensive
>
> Doctoral or research universities—intensive

Master's colleges and universities

> Master's colleges and universities I
>
> Master's colleges and universities II

Baccalaureate colleges

> Baccalaureate colleges—liberal arts
>
> Baccalaureate colleges—general
>
> Baccalaureate or associate's colleges

Associate's colleges (community colleges)

Specialized institutions

> Theological seminaries and other specialized faith-related institutions
>
> Medical schools and medical centers
>
> Other separate health profession schools (nursing, pharmacy, and so forth)
>
> Schools of engineering and technology
>
> Schools of business and management
>
> Schools of art, music, and design
>
> Schools of law
>
> Teachers colleges
>
> Other specialized institutions (military institutes, maritime academies, and so forth)

Tribal colleges and universities

Organizations That Rank

This group of assessment users uses assessment to rank institutions and programs based on "academic quality." Organizations that rank are important external assessment users because much can be at stake based on an institution or program's ranking. As demonstrated in the vignette about the Cultural Anthropology Department at a large research institution, some academic departments live or die based on their national ranking.

The reason most organizations rank institutions or programs is to help potential students and research sponsors make informed choice decisions. Most organizations that rank institutions and programs compare organizational performance using weighted indicators. They collect data from national and local databases and surveys sent to institutions and peers.

U.S. News and World Report (2006) is one organization that annually ranks over fourteen hundred accredited schools. It divides institutions and programs into categories based on the 2000 Carnegie Classifications of Institutions of Higher Education and then ranks them based on fifteen weighted indicators in seven categories:

1. Peer assessment (25 percent), a rating of academic programs on a scale from 1 to 5 as determined by surveyed presidents, provosts, and deans of admissions

2. Retention (20 percent)

   Average freshman retention rate

   Average graduation rate

3. Faculty resources (20 percent)

   Class size, 1–19 students

   Class size, 50+ students

   Faculty compensation

   Faculty with Ph.D.s or top terminal degrees

   Proportion of full-time faculty

   Student-faculty ratio

4. Student selectivity (15 percent)

   High school class standing in top 10 percent

   SAT and ACT scores

   Acceptance rate

5. Financial resources (expenditures per student, 10 percent)

6. Graduation rate performance (5 percent), the difference between the actual six-year graduation rate for students entering in the fall of one year and the predicted graduation rate

7. Alumni giving (5 percent)

U. S. News and World Report (2005) also ranks institutions based on "best value." This score is a composite of three variables: ratio of quality to price, percentage of undergraduates receiving scholarships or grants meeting financial need, and average discount, defined as the percentage of a school's total costs covered by the average need-based scholarship or grant to undergraduates.

The National Research Council (NRC) is another organization that ranks research doctorate programs in higher education. NRC was chartered in 1916 as one of the four National Academies (2006) created to further knowledge and advise the federal government. (The others are the National Academy of Sciences, the National Academy of Engineering, and the Institute of Medicine.) All four are private, nonprofit institutions that provide science, technology, and health policy advice under a congressional charter.

In 1983 and again in 1995, NRC studied and ranked research doctorate programs with the aim of helping institutions improve the quality of their programs through benchmarking; providing potential students and the public with accessible, readily available information on doctoral programs nationwide; and enhancing the nation's overall research capacity (Ostriker and Kuh, 2003). It is currently conducting a new assessment of doctorate programs, to be completed in late 2007. Unlike previous studies, the current study will gather quantitative data on doctoral programs using online questionnaires covering the following areas:

- Scholarly productivity and impact of program faculty
- Effectiveness of doctoral education
- Research resources
- Demographic characteristics of students and faculty
- Resources available to doctoral students
- Characteristics of each doctoral program

The *Princeton Review* (2006) is another organization that ranks institutions. It bases its rankings on data gathered through student surveys and national and local databases. The *Princeton Review* publishes its findings annually in a book called *The Best 361 Colleges*. In 2004–2005, the *Princeton Review* interviewed 110,000 students at over 2,000 schools, an average of more than 300 students per school. Using a seventy-item survey, the *Princeton Review* asks students to tell about themselves, their school's academics and administration, campus life at their college, and their fellow students' attitudes and opinions. Based on student responses and institutional data, the *Princeton Review* identifies the 362 top-rated schools and ranks the top 20 of them in sixty-two areas organized into eight categories: academics, demographics, parties, schools by type, politics, quality of life, extracurricular activities, and social life. *The Princeton Review* claims that its rankings reflect a consensus of the colleges' surveyed students rather its own opinions.

Organizations That Determine Eligibility

This group uses assessment to determine eligibility of institutions and students based on specific requirements. For example, the National Collegiate Athletic Association (NCAA) uses assessment results to certify athletic programs and player eligibility (2006b). NCAA began certifying Division I institutions in 1993 after piloting the program for four years. A second cycle of certification began in 1999 and continues today.

According to NCAA (2006b), the purpose of athletics certification is to ensure integrity in institutional athletics programs and to help institutions improve their athletics departments. Certification achieves this by opening affairs of athletics to the university community and the public, by setting standards for the operation of athletics programs, and by putting tough sanctions in place for institutions that fail to conduct a comprehensive self-study or to correct problems.

According to NCAA (2006a), the core of certification is the institution's self-study and annual certification of eligibility, which is designed to benefit institutions. NCAA claims that self-studies (program reviews conducted by an institution's faculty and staff as opposed to a site-visit team made up of colleagues from peer institutions) and certification increase self-awareness, affirmation, and opportunities for improvement. NCAA seeks information in four basic areas: governance and commitment to rule compliance; academic integrity; financial integrity; and equity, welfare, and sportsmanship.

NCAA decides if an institution is "fully certified," which signifies that its athletics department is in substantial conformity with NCAA operating principles; "certified with conditions," which signifies that its athletics department is in substantial conformity with operating principles but problems identified during the self-study and a peer-review team evaluation must be corrected before full certification is issued; or "not certified" (2005b). NCAA sanctions for nonconformance include suspension, probation, and termination of membership; limitations on postseason play, recruitment, and television coverage; imposition of fines; reduction of financial aid awards; and termination or suspension of coaching staff (2005b).

In 2003, NCAA created a new academic measure, known as the academic progress rate (APR), as part of a new academic reform program (2005a). APR is based on academic eligibility, retention, and graduation of scholarship student-athletes. APR is a real-time assessment of a team's academic performance that awards two points each term to scholarship student-athletes who meet academic eligibility standards and who remain with the institution. A team's APR is determined by adding total points earned at a given time divided by total points possible. NCAA will soon introduce a new academic measure, called the graduation success rate (GSR).

Organizations That Bargain with Institutions

Not all institutions have formalized unions; however, many have internal organizations that bargain and negotiate like formalized unions. Unions are important external assessment users because they influence an organization's capacity to perform through threats of strikes and actual strikes and slowdowns.

The purpose of most unions is to advance causes and further the interests of their members. Unions such as the National Education Association (2006) also impose codes of ethics on their members and serve as lobbyists. Unions use assessment for several purposes but primarily to support a bargaining position, advocate for their causes, and ensure compliance with collective bargaining agreements.

Unions in higher education typically seek answers to the following questions:

What is the organization's current and projected workforce?

What are the organization's overall current and projected resources?

What percentage of resources has been and will be devoted to employee compensation and benefits?

What is the quality of worklife for employees?

What is the quality of the workplace (safety, security)?

How many jobs have been and will be eliminated, maintained, expanded, or outsourced?

How many grievances have been submitted and processed each year or bargaining cycle? What are the nature and scope of those grievances, and what actions typically result from them?

External Academic Peers

This last group is not an assessment user group in the same sense as the others because academic peers do not use assessment findings derived from an organization's assessment program. However, academic peers serve similar purposes as other assessment user groups in making decisions about the quality of performance (in this case, research) that have the potential of greatly influencing the reputation and future research opportunities and resources of academic organizations.

External academic peers are scholars who assess the quality and effectiveness of research submitted for publication in refereed journals. Refereed journals are published by professional associations, institutions, and other independent entities. Academic peers also assess the quality and effectiveness of published research and express their opinions through written rebuttals, formal reviews, citations, and use in follow-up studies.

As evaluators, external academic peers judge the quality of research (methodology, scope, relevance, findings) based on criteria, standards, and guidelines established by professional associations, editorial boards, institutions, and other external entities. This process of evaluation, known as peer review, has a long history in higher education and performs an important and significant role in the assessment of research.

Internal Assessment User Groups

Internal assessment user groups operate inside the institution. As noted earlier, there are three types of internal assessment users, defined by position and job responsibilities: senior leaders, administrators and managers, and faculty and staff. These groups use assessment to account to others, manage strategy, build learning organizations that strengthen innovation, allocate resources, control quality, improve programs and services, and support personnel decisions.

Senior Leaders
For purposes of assessment, senior leaders are defined as people responsible for providing the organization with direction and support. Senior leaders are presidents, vice presidents, chancellors, vice chancellors, and deans. Senior leaders operate at the institutional level; however, in some large institutions, senior leaders also operate at the college or school level.

For assessment purposes, senior leaders are distinguished from administrators and managers. In truth, many senior leaders perform management functions and many administrators and managers perform leadership functions. The important point is that people engaged in leadership activities use assessment differently than people engaged in management activities.

Because of their wide range of responsibilities, senior leaders need a variety of assessment information. Their individual information preferences vary according to their leadership and decision-making styles; however, most senior leaders, at one point or another, seek answers to some or all of the following questions:

> Are we clear in our purpose, and do we share a vision of excellence?
>
> Are we structured so as to maximize our resources and achieve our strategic goals?
>
> Are our guiding principles clear, and to what extent are we practicing them? Does our organizational culture optimize organizational performance?
>
> Do we value our public responsibilities, and do we set high standards as an organizational citizen?
>
> Are we offering the right programs and services?
>
> Are we achieving what we intended to achieve in terms of teaching, research, and service?

Are we making progress on our strategic goals?

Are we as productive as we should be?

Are we more productive than we were in the past? What organizational operations have recently increased productivity?

Are we using our resources efficiently? What human, financial, technological, and facilities resources do we waste, and how do we waste them? Are we using our resources as we expected?

What does it cost to manage quality in our programs and services in relation to benefits from those costs?

Are we as innovative as we should be? What creative changes have we implemented over the past three years? What parts of our operations have not undergone creative changes in the past three years and why? In what ways have our creative changes improved performance results?

Have we established partnerships with the right partners and suppliers? To what extent do our partnerships achieve their objectives?

What is the quality of our faculty and staff? What are their strengths and weaknesses? How prepared is our workforce to meet future requirements of our organization? Do our high-performing employees leave our organization, and if so, why do they leave? Is the departure rate better than last year?

How many worker-hours are lost to illness and injury?

Are our employees satisfied with their compensation and benefits? How do we compare with other institutions that share our mission?

What is the quality of our leadership system and organizational structure? How effectively do these systems shape and lead us toward a shared vision of excellence?

What is the quality of our infrastructure in terms of technology, buildings, and grounds? Do our level and use of technology enable us to be competitive? Does our technology encourage or impede innovation and change?

Does our location provide easy access to the people we serve and that serve us?

Do we protect our environment as much as we should and could?

How satisfied are the people we serve? How satisfied are our important stakeholders?

How effectively do we design our products and services to meet the future needs of the people we serve (students, research sponsors)?

How flexible are our key work processes, and how do we use that flexibility to meet our current and future requirements?

How much troubleshooting do we do, and how much does it cost to do it?

How many students leave before they complete their academic goals? Why do they leave? What percentage of students graduate? How long, on the average, does it take for students to graduate?

How do students pay for their education? Is this satisfactory? How much debt do they incur? What are the consequences for our institution's financial durability?

How much external funding do we receive in relation to need? What are the implications for our institution's financial durability?

How do our costs and service quality compare with those at comparable institutions? What would be gained by outsourcing some of our operations? Do our overall costs outweigh overall benefits received by the people we serve and our stakeholders?

Senior leaders use assessment for many purposes but mainly to account to important external stakeholders, manage strategy, support resource allocation decisions, and manage organizational culture. Each is discussed in turn.

Accountability

External assessment users, such as governing boards, government agencies, and major donors, hold senior leaders accountable for the performance of their organizations. Senior leaders use assessment to account to these important stakeholders in terms of mission achievement (performance outcomes), progress toward strategic goals, efficient use of resources, quality of institutional resources, programs and services, accreditation, ranking, compliance, and so forth.

Internal auditors assess performance on behalf of senior leaders. They evaluate performance against internal policies and procedures and sometimes against external laws, rules, standards, and criteria. Internal auditors report assessment findings to senior leaders through audit reports.

It is the responsibility of senior leaders to identify and clarify all the unique needs of the organization's important external assessment users. It is the responsibility of assessment leaders to build a robust assessment program that enables senior leaders to fulfill their accountability responsibilities.

Managing Strategy

Senior leaders use assessment results to manage strategy in specific ways, namely, to frame strategy; to clarify, operationalize, and align strategy; and to monitor strategy achievement.

Framing Strategy. Senior leaders use strategic planning processes to frame strategies that determine an organization's competitive advantage and place in the environment. Barbara Taylor and William Massey (1996) argue that strategic thinking requires objectivity and an honest assessment of how an institution is doing and where it is heading. Educational leaders must not only know what the organization is setting out to do but also when it has succeeded or failed.

Carter McNamara (1999b) explains that leaders use a variety of strategic planning models, including goals-based, issues-based, organic, or scenario-building models, to frame strategies. Leaders select the model best suited for their "organization's leadership, culture of the organization, complexity of the organization's environment, size of the organization, expertise of planners," and other factors (p. 1).

Strategic planning typically starts with an analysis of an organization's external and internal environment—a process known as a SWOT analysis (SWOT is an acronym for "strengths, weaknesses, opportunities, and threats.") External environmental factors, such as pending legislation, emerging health issues, demographic trends, and emerging social, economic, technology, and financial issues, present opportunities and threats to organizations in higher education that senior leaders consider when framing strategy.

Assessment is also helpful in exposing institutional strengths and weaknesses. Through assessment, senior leaders can discover a great many things, including these:

- Nature and scope of student learning
- Quality of research
- Quality of programs and services
- Levels of satisfaction of employees, students, and important stakeholders
- Quality of partnerships with important suppliers and service partners
- Quality of critical resources
- Quality of work processes
- Current levels of productivity and efficiency
- Scope of innovation
- Financial health and well-being of the institution

Institutional strengths and weaknesses, combined with external opportunities and threats, help senior leaders frame strategies to bring their institutions closer to their vision of performance excellence.

Clarifying, Operationalizing, and Aligning Strategy.   One of the important functions of assessment, according to Robert Kaplan and David Norton (1996), is to help senior leaders add meaning and clarity to strategies. Organizations that "can translate their strategy into their measurement system are far better able to execute their strategy because they can communicate their objectives and their targets" (p. 147).

One way in which assessment helps leaders clarify strategic goals is by clarifying performance expectations through performance indicators and reference points. Take, for example, the strategy to increase enrollment. Exhibit 1.1 illustrates how assessment helps leaders clarify performance expectations of this strategic goal through performance indicators and reference points.

Kaplan and Norton (1996) claim that assessment also helps leaders put strategy into action—in other words, operationalize strategy. Assessment does this by clarifying how strategy affects specific entities in the organization. For example, take the strategy "increase enrollment" and its performance indicator of "undergraduate student FTE in chemistry, physics, and engineering" and reference point of "increase by an average of 3 percent over the next five years." This performance indicator and reference point send a loud signal to the Chemistry, Physics, and Engineering Departments and their supporting organizations. The strategy, as clarified, does not explain what actions need to be taken, nor does it guarantee additional resources, but it clearly indicates which organizations need to act.

Sometimes lofty strategies need to be operationalized through subgoals more conducive to action and assessment. For example, leaders could operationalize the same strategy "increase enrollment" by creating several subgoals, one of which could be "increase retention." Leaders can measure actual performance of this strategic subgoal (depending on institutional circumstances) through performance indicators and reference points such as those listed in Exhibit 1.2.

According to Kaplan and Norton (1996), leaders also use assessment to link important strategic objectives together and to align local efforts with institutional efforts. Strategic alignment is critical to performance success and requires linkages between strategic goals, lower-level organizational goals, functional goals, personal goals, and assessment. Without alignment, "individuals and departments can optimize their local performance [and still] not contribute to achieving strategic objectives" (p. 148). Strategic alignment also requires linkages between goals and recognition, promotion, and compensation programs.

Exhibit 1.1

Performance Indicators and Reference Points
for the Strategic Goal "Increase Enrollment"

Performance Indicators	Reference Points
First-year student headcount	Increase by an average of 3 percent over the next three years
New transfer student FTE	Increase by an average of 4 percent over the next three years
Undergraduate student FTE in chemistry, physics, and engineering	Increase by an average of 3 percent over the next five years

Exhibit 1.2

Performance Indicators and Reference Points
for the Strategic Subgoal "Increase Retention"

Performance Indicators	Reference Points
Retention rate of minority student headcount	Increase by an average of 3 percent over the next five years
Retention rate of upper division transfer student headcount	Increase by an average of 3 percent over the next five years
Retention rate of entering first-year student headcount	Increase by an average of 3 percent over the next five years

Monitoring Strategy.   According to Kaplan and Norton (1996), leaders use assessment to learn when and if strategic goals are achieved. When formulating strategy, leaders create measures not only to clarify, operationalize, and align strategy but also to measure its achievement as part of their accountability and improvement responsibilities.

Mark Huselid, Brian Becker, and Richard Beatty (2005) claim that it is easier to craft a strategy than to deliver one. For this reason, leaders should build a "workforce scorecard" that identifies and monitors workforce success in relation to strategic execution. To maximize workforce potential, leaders should view human capital in terms of contribution to strategy execution rather than just cost and productivity. The authors claim that it is not the activity that counts but the impact of the activity on organizational outcomes. Leaders should recognize and accept that some positions and roles in an organization—positions that may have nothing to do with hierarchy—have a more important influence on execution and achievement of strategy than others. Leaders should differentiate those positions and label them as "A" positions. Furthermore, they should allocate a disproportionate amount of resources to them and more closely monitor their success and contributions to strategy execution.

Using Huselid and colleagues' arguments, leaders assessing the "increase enrollment" strategy should differentiate (and classify as "A") positions in the organization that have the most impact on increasing enrollment, such as recruiting positions and positions that affect retention of high-risk students. Leaders should also allocate a disproportionate amount of resources to these positions and more closely monitor their success and contributions to strategy execution.

It remains unresolved whether senior leaders, in addition to administrators and managers, should use assessment to monitor or drive strategy. Some experts believe that assessment should be used only to monitor strategy achievement and not to drive it. Others argue that assessment should make visible specific performance weaknesses that can only be addressed through strategic initiatives that take advantage of emerging opportunities. Assessment, they argue, should be used to uncover and drive strategy.

No doubt both propositions are true because senior leaders use assessment to learn when and where improvement is needed but also to compare levels of performance against strategic goals. In both uses, however, senior leaders must link assessment to performance associated with strategies derived from strategic planning processes. Without links to strategy, assessment becomes the driver of change. And when assessment becomes the driver of change, people cannot understand where the organization is going and how they fit in. Instead, they perceive assessment as a personal report card, with consequences for their job security or compensation (or both). When assessment becomes the driver of change, people are more likely to believe that they are victims of assessment and may then feel compelled to fake or sabotage data or to focus on short-term fixes rather than on long-term improvements, thereby limiting the organization's improvement potential. When people see strategies derived from strategic planning processes as the drivers of change, rather than assessment, they are more likely to support changes leading to strategic execution if they were involved in the strategic planning process; focus on long-term, systemic improvements rather than short-term fixes; and are supportive of assessment because of its focus on organizational rather than personal performance results. Finally, assessment taken out of its strategic context prevents leaders from gaining assessment's added benefit of helping them clarify, operationalize, and align strategic, organizational, lower-level, and personal goals and assessment.

Supporting Resource Allocation Decisions

Senior leaders also use assessment to support resource allocation decisions. Good decision making is usually supported by reliable and valid decision support data, much of which comes from assessment. Senior leaders face many challenging, sometimes unpopular, decisions to ensure the future success of their organizations. For example, senior leaders frequently face decisions to sustain, eliminate, reorganize, downsize, expand, outsource, or privatize all or some of the institution's operations. Senior leaders need timely and accurate assessment results about a unit's costs and benefits to support these difficult decisions.

In institutions using incentive-based, responsibility-based, and program-based budgeting processes, senior leaders use assessment to support resource allocation decisions. In institutions using formalized performance management systems, senior leaders use assessment to support high-level personnel decisions that frame employee compensation and benefits. Senior leaders also use assessment to improve organizational structure and infrastructure (buildings, grounds, technology) in an effort to optimize the institution's critical resources.

Managing Organizational Culture

Edgar Schein (1992) claims that organizational leaders have a responsibility for creating and monitoring an organization's culture. It is "the unique function of leadership to perceive the functional and dysfunctional elements of the existing culture and to manage cultural evolution and change in such a way that the group can survive in a changing environment" (p. 15).

More and more, senior leaders use assessment to ensure that organizational culture is supportive to organizational learning and innovation. Fred Kofman and Peter Senge (1993) define learning organizations as organizations that continuously adapt to changing and interdependent environments. Learning organizations are systemic, cooperative, and creative compared to traditional organizations, which are fragmented, competitive, and reactive. Richard Karash (2001) defines learning organizations as organizations in which people at all levels, individually and collectively, increase their capacity to produce results they really care about.

In 1998, Peter Drucker described ingredients for what he calls the discipline of innovation: know the organization's purpose (mission), define significant results (vision), abandon programs where they don't get results, and "reassess, reassess, and reassess." That same year, Peter Senge (1998) expanded on Drucker's discipline of innovation by adding the ingredient of working together and learning from one another's efforts. Without a culture of organizational learning, organizations stifle their innovativeness. Assessment is the core research initiative for all learning organizations. And for purposes of innovation, assessment for learning is much more powerful than assessment for evaluation, according to Senge.

Senior leaders recognize that for an organization to "learn," all members of the organizational community must understand where the organization is headed and how much progress is being achieved. The organizational community needs regular, accurate, and timely feedback on progress toward strategic goals. In a true learning organization, members use assessment to answer the performance question "How are we doing in relation to our performance goals?" Senior leaders, as well as administrators and managers, use assessment to enable the organization to learn from its past performance within the context of its desired future.

Administrators and Managers

For purposes of assessment, administrators and managers are defined as all individuals who manage the operations of an organization or a "unit of analysis" whose performance is under review. In higher education, administrators and managers generally include assistant vice presidents, assistant deans, directors, coordinators, and department chairpersons. As mentioned before, many administrators and managers perform leadership functions, and many senior leaders perform management functions. The important point is that people engaged in management activities use assessment somewhat differently than when they are engaged in leadership activities.

The expression "unit of analysis" is used in assessment to define an organization, program, or process whose performance is under review. A unit of analysis can be an entire institution, a college such as the College of Arts and Sciences, a school such as a law school or medical school, an academic department such as the Chemistry Department, an administrative office such as Admissions or Information Services, a program such as General Education or Writing Across the Curriculum, or a cross-functional process such as payroll. When properly used in assessment, a unit of analysis whose performance is under review has very clear boundaries. Boundaries can be delineated through traditional administrative and budgeting structures or other boundary-defining entities. When a unit of analysis is a cross-functional process such as payroll, the unit requires a clear beginning and ending and clear lines of responsibility and ownership.

Administrators and managers seek answers to many of the same assessment questions as senior leaders do:

Are we offering the right programs and services?

How effective are we at achieving our intended outcomes?

What is the quality of our programs and services?

What is the quality of our resources?

How productive, efficient, and innovative are we?

What is the quality of our organizational culture, and how satisfied is our workforce?

How satisfied are the people we serve?

Like senior leaders, administrators and managers use assessment to account to important stakeholders for their unit's overall performance, manage goals and objectives, support resource allocation decisions, and strengthen organizational culture to encourage innovation. However, in their managerial role, they also use assessment to monitor and control operations; improve programs, services, and processes; and support personnel decisions.

Monitoring and Controlling Operations

Many administrators and managers use assessment to monitor and control people and processes. Administrators and managers use assessment at the operational level to signal when people and processes are getting "out of control" and short-term adjustments are needed. They also use assessment to become aware of problems so that they can put a stop to "business as usual." This form of "quality control" does not necessarily improve performance—it just lets administrators and managers know that performance is not within the normal or intended range.

Administrators in higher education have always used assessment to monitor and control financial aspects of organizational performance. Whether watching for cost overruns on a construction project or overspending in a specific budget line item, administrators and managers use monthly financial reports to monitor budget-to-actual spending to learn when spending is getting out of control.

Increasingly, administrators and managers use specialized software to monitor and control other aspects of organizational performance. For example, they use technology to track technical computer problems, requests for service, computer and network usage and outages, equipment reliability, breaches of security, donor activities, and admissions inquiries, admits, and yield rates. Libraries use technology to monitor usage and track circulation of holdings. Academic advisers use technology to review student progress toward stated goals.

Administrators and managers also use assessment to make sure that resource deployment is aligned with approved plans and institutional strategic initiatives and that operations are in compliance with laws, regulations, accreditation standards, ranking criteria, funding criteria, eligibility standards, and the like. In academic organizations, responsibility for compliance is shared with the faculty. In administrative organizations, responsibility for compliance is shared with employees, but it depends on the degree of employee empowerment existing in the organization under review.

Improving Programs, Services, and Processes

One of the most important uses of assessment is to improve programs, services, and processes. In most organizations, improvement is a shared responsibility.

Administrators, managers, faculty, and staff pursue program, service, and process improvements using a variety of systematic and nonsystematic approaches. Those who use a nonsystematic and more intuitive approach base improvement actions on exposure and experience rather than on performance findings derived from an assessment program. They need and use assessment findings less because they believe that they have a full understanding of the problem, available resources, and levels of support in the political environment. An intuitive approach, which is generally less collaborative than a team-based, systematic approach, usually garners less support among the parties affected by changes that they had no part in generating.

For administrators and managers who use a more systematic approach to program, service, and process improvement, "In God we trust; all others bring data" is a familiar admonition. Systematic approaches generally start with the formation of improvement teams who use assessment every step of the way. For example, teams engaged in process reengineering, benchmarking, Six Sigma, and other traditional improvement approaches use assessment to answer some of the following questions:

How does current performance compare to a desired state? How does it compare to that of other organizations?

What would the costs to our unit and the institution be if performance is not improved now or in the future?

What are the nature and scope of performance problems?

What are the nature and scope of causes of poor performance?

In what ways can processes be improved? Will our improvements affect the performance of other institutional operations? Which improvements will optimize performance the most? Which improvements will optimize use of critical resources the most?

How will we know when performance has improved?

How much will improvements cost?

To what extent has performance changed as a result of implemented improvements, and how much has it actually cost? Have changes improved performance? Have changes affected other organizations?

How does improved performance compare to a desired state? What else needs improvement? How much will it cost?

Finally, many administrators and managers who operate within the context of program-based, incentive-based, or responsibility-based budgeting processes use assessment to support budget requests for feasibility studies and other resources required to implement programs and service improvements.

Supporting Personnel Decisions

Administrators and managers also use assessment to support personnel decisions. They use assessment to determine the relative importance of a particular position to the organization, comparable salaries for that position currently offered by competitors in the marketplace, results from a 360-degree feedback system about the individual's past performance, and some aspect of the individual's unit overall performance results. After evaluating a person's past performance in relation to stated goals and clear expectations, supervisors determine appropriate rewards or sanctions.

Administrators and managers who use organizational performance results in the appraisal of lower-level personnel must do so cautiously. Rewarding or punishing lower-level staff on the basis of results of a process in which they have less than full control is a misguided use of assessment data. For example, it is wrong for administrators and managers to hold an employee accountable for customer complaints, slow response times, or mistakes inherent in a process over which the employee has little or no control or responsibility. It is fair, however, to hold all employees accountable for identifying and solving process problems and for advocating and initiating improvements to programs, services, and work processes if supervisors have clarified these expectations early in the performance management process.

Some academic administrators use assessment to support faculty personnel decisions. However, most faculty personnel decisions, such as promotion, tenure, and salary decisions, are made or recommended by faculty committees that may or may not use assessment to support their decisions.

Faculty and Staff

Except when negotiating and bargaining as a union (described earlier as an external user group), most faculty and staff are generally interested in assessment findings pertaining to their own units or a universal topic or issue about which they are studying or making recommendations through committees and task forces.

It should be noted that faculty and staff are not only internal assessment users but also assessors who collect, analyze, and disseminate assessment results for other assessment users. Furthermore, they can also represent owners of the assessment program.

As an internal assessment user group, faculty and staff, like senior leaders, administrators, and managers, use assessment results for accountability, decision support, and improvement. However, they also use assessment results to support the work of committees and task forces conducting self-studies for accreditation and institutional program reviews, faculty personnel decisions, and other important universitywide functions.

Traditional higher educational institutions operate within the context of collegiality, a governance structure that generates many important ad hoc and standing committees and task forces. Major committees or task forces are given specific charges that determine the boundaries of their work. Those charged with the responsibility of solving particular problems or improving selected programs, services, and work processes use either a systematic or nonsystematic approach to their work. Those who use a systematic approach to improvement make copious use of assessment results, as described earlier. Committees and task forces, depending on their purpose, use assessment to understand the nature of emerging issues or problems, inform the group's decisions, support their causes, and justify their recommendations to others.

Faculty committees and task forces charged with the responsibility of conducting self-studies for accreditation and program review use assessment for two purposes: accountability and improvement, according to Catherine Palomba and Trudy Banta (1999). These committees use assessment results during the life of a program as formative assessment to modify, shape, and improve a program's performance. They use assessment after a program has been in operation for a while for accountability and to make summative judgments about its quality or worth compared to previously defined standards for performance.

Faculty skepticism and resistance to some forms of assessment is well documented. However, David Tritelli (2002) claims that even assessment's strongest critiques have "come to be overwhelmed by a sense of inevitability" (p. 3). The threshold question is not whether to assess but what and how to assess. In his historical review of the assessment of student outcomes, Peter Ewell (2002) tracks the development of faculty support for and use of assessment. He recalls an early faculty debate called the "ineffability debate." In this debate, faculty felt that initial attempts to assess student outcomes directly were both demeaning and doomed to failure. The faculty's reservations were founded on methodological, philosophical, and political concerns. Faculty eventually adopted assessment as a survival strategy, improved the assessment methods, and ultimately became comfortably rooted in a peer-based community of judgment.

Ewell (2002) also describes what he calls the "value-added debate." This revolves around whether assessment should focus on absolute levels of student achievement or institutional contributions to developing student abilities. The classic approach to assessing learning gains through pretesting and posttesting, according to this debate, poses perplexing conceptual issues and formidable methodological problems. For example, pretests may not work because students have not yet been exposed to subjects on which they will be posttested. This debate, according to Ewell, helped "forge a growing consensus that paths of student development should not be seen as linear and additive but rather as organic and transformational" (p. 18). As a result, longitudinal studies were developed that were capable of capturing large numbers of variables about both outcomes and experiences using multivariate statistics.

Ewell (2002) claims that faculty on most campuses now use assessment results one way or another; however, "fundamental transformations in instruction that might have resulted from examining systemic evidence of student learning have mostly not happened" (p. 23). Instead, faculty regard assessment of student learning outcomes as an "add-on, done principally at the behest of the administration and sustained as a superstructure outside the traditional array of academic activities and rewards" (p. 23).

Most faculty tenure and promotion requests are decided by faculty peers serving on promotion and tenure committees, many of whom use assessment to support their decisions. Most committees use assessment results focused on productivity and quality of research and service; few use assessment results focused on quality of an individual's teaching effectiveness as measured by achievement of intended student learning outcomes. According to Roger Benjamin and Richard Hersh (2002), academic cultures do not necessarily value systemic cumulative assessment of undergraduate learning to support faculty requests for promotion, tenure, and merit raises. "The metric most commonly used . . . is a system of qualitative and quantitative measures that emphasize research productivity" (p. 10).

Debate continues as to whether the results of assessments related to student learning conducted at the course and departmental levels should be used to support faculty personnel decisions. Palomba and Banta (1999) argue that assessment results should be used for the evaluation of programs, not faculty members. They explain that the "essential factor in making assessment work is building trust among faculty that the information collected through assessment activities will not be used for inappropriate purposes." Furthermore, "faculty should be rewarded for the time and energy they invest in assessment-related activities. Institutions should encourage the recognition of assessment activities in faculty review processes" (p. 70).

Barbara Walvoord (2004) takes a different view. She argues "a wise institution keeps the focus [of assessment] on collective action, not on individual blame. However, if students are learning well in a class, a faculty member may find that information highly useful at renewal, promotion, or tenure time" (p. 9). For example, evidence of learning can balance low student evaluations. But, she argues, the opposite is also true. "Evidence of inadequate student learning in one's class ought to galvanize the teacher and the department for appropriate action. That action must be collegial and supportive, just as it optimally is when a faculty member is not producing sufficient research. The truth is that assessment brings to teaching a level of accountability that was not always present before and that can be used to benefit the students, faculty, and the institution" (p. 9).

To summarize, faculty who have access to assessment findings related to the effectiveness of their teaching, research, and service may or may not use those findings to support tenure, promotion, and salary requests. It is important to note that during the initial years of higher education in the United States, faculty assessed student learning primarily for the purpose of determining teacher effectiveness. Today, faculty use assessment to measure levels of mastery, provide feedback to students, account to important stakeholders, and improve programs and services. They may or may not use assessment of student learning as a measure of their individual teacher effectiveness.

The degree to which employees at all levels use assessment meaningfully as members of a learning organization depends on several important factors, according to Margaret Wheatley (2005). Employees use assessment in meaningful ways only when they can determine what and how to measure performance. Furthermore, employees must believe assessment is a function of internal and not external forces, adaptive and evolving rather than static, and a form of feedback that increases their own capacity to grow and develop and helps the organization grow in the right direction.

Worksheet 1.1 is designed to help assessors identify their unit's important external and internal assessment user groups. Examples are provided for a fictitious Chemistry Department.

Summary

This chapter explored two types of assessment user groups: external and internal. Each group requires different types of assessment information and uses assessment for different purposes. Assessment user groups in higher education were defined as the "end users" of assessment and therefore represent the "customers" of the assessment program. External user groups are governing boards; governmental agencies; potential students (and parents), potential donors (including alumni), potential employees, and potential contractors; organizations that affirm; and external academic peers. External user groups use assessment to hold organizations accountable; support policy and resource allocation decisions; impose sanctions for noncompliance; support choice decisions; affirm accreditation status, rank, classification, administration censure, athletic eligibility, and bargaining position; and validate research quality. Internal user groups are senior leaders, administrators and managers, and faculty and staff. Internal user groups use assessment to account to others, manage strategy, manage organizational culture, allocate resources, control quality, improve programs and services, support personnel decisions, and advocate causes.

Worksheet 1.1
   Assessment User Group Analysis

Unit of Analysis: _____ (*Example: Chemistry Department*)

Today's Date: _____

Use this worksheet to analyze the unit's major assessment user groups. In column A, list all of the unit's important internal and external assessment user groups. Check column B or C to indicate whether the user group is external or internal to the institution. In column D, describe important decisions this user group makes, based on assessment results that affect the unit. Finally, in column E, using a scale of 1 (least important) to 5 (most important), rate the overall importance of each assessment user group to the unit.

Assessment User Groups (A)	External (B)	Internal (C)	Important Decisions This Group Makes Based on Assessment Findings (D)	Rating of Overall Importance to Unit (E)

Example: SACSCC Regional Accrediting Site Visiting Team	*Example:* ✔	*Example:*	*Example:*
			• Reaffirm institutional accreditation that determines
			  ◦ Eligibility for federal, state, and local funding
			  ◦ Eligibility for NCAA sports
			  ◦ Level of competitiveness with similar institutions for quality students, faculty, and staff
				Example: 5

CHAPTER 2

Organizations as Systems

Internal Elements

This chapter begins a discussion of organizations as open, interdependent, customized systems with a purpose. It describes elements of organizational systems that play important roles in the definition, assessment, and improvement of organizational performance in higher education. Internal system elements, discussed in this chapter, are leadership systems, inputs, key work processes, outputs, and outcomes. External system elements, discussed in Chapter Three, are upstream systems, customers, and stakeholders.

Systems Thinking

Payroll Department at a Large State-Supported Research University

Here he was again, a busy, highly paid assistant vice president driving throughout the metropolitan area in a panic, picking up and delivering paychecks to angry faculty and staff located on two branch campuses. He vowed never to let this happen again; surely heads would roll after this—and hopefully not his. He reminded himself to renew his request for mandatory direct deposit at the next meeting of the president's cabinet.

Early the next morning, he called all involved department heads (including those who didn't report directly to him) into his office, one at a time. He demonstrated remarkable calm, he thought, as he patiently listened to each person's interpretation of why this latest payroll crisis had happened. He knew that his own boss would be calling soon, requesting an explanation of how it happened and demanding assurances that it would never happen again. Right now, he couldn't respond on either matter—he was becoming very, very nervous.

As it turned out, the human resource staff changed a single code (locally known as the distribution code) in the new HR system. They changed it to expedite publication of an updated campus telephone directory, not realizing that the code also determined where employee paychecks were delivered. Apparently, employees who worked at several locations within the institution were asked to select where they wanted their paychecks or paystubs to be delivered.

As so often happens, the root cause of this particular payroll problem was a lack of communication and coordination between two administrative offices that report to two different vice presidents but use the same integrated administrative system. It was becoming increasingly clear that the pace of system integration was far exceeding the pace of work integration among different administrative offices. Perhaps it was time to reorganize again!

The payroll vignette reveals how truly interdependent organizations in colleges and universities are—no one operation stands alone. The performance of one organization greatly affects performance of another organization in the same system. This chapter introduces systems thinking as a tool for assessors to explore complex organizational relationships both inside and outside the institution and how these relationships affect organizational performance.

When asked to describe organizations, most educational leaders produce organizational charts that clarify hierarchical structure, staffing tables, span of control, chain of command, and formal communication and promotion channels. Unfortunately, traditional organizational charts do not clarify why an organization exists, how it operates, who it serves, or how other organizations influence its performance. Describing organizations using systems thinking expands leaders' understanding of their organizations' purpose, internal operations, interdependencies, and performance.

According to Daniel Aronson (1996), Jay Forrester, an MIT professor of engineering, invented systems thinking in 1956. Forrester was working in the field of systems dynamics when he created systems thinking as a better way to analyze and test new ideas about social systems such as organizations. Carter McNamara (1999c) explains that analysts use systems thinking as a tool of systems analysis rooted in systems theory.

W. Edwards Deming (1993) describes systems thinking as a way for leaders to understand organizations as a network of interdependent components that work together to accomplish a common purpose. This interdependence requires communication and cooperation in order for the organization to succeed. The payroll vignette illustrates how interdependently organizational systems may operate and describes what can happen when interdependent organizations fail to communicate and cooperate.

Systems thinking encourages leaders to view organizations as open rather than closed systems. Open systems continually receive input (or feedback) from their environments in order to succeed and prosper. Open systems use environmental feedback to adjust to economic, social, political, technological, and global forces that have the potential of affecting the system's capacity to perform. Closed systems, in contrast, restrict interaction and communication with their environments, causing entropy, the tendency for systems to decay over time. According to Clay Carr (1991), all open systems exist as part of larger systems in which they interact. Therefore, a change anywhere in the overall system causes significant and often unanticipated changes in other parts of the system.

Compared to traditional views of organizations, systems thinking provides several benefits to educational leaders engaged in assessment. First, systems thinking enables leaders to make better sense of the internal workings of the organization—an understanding essential for assessment. For example, systems thinking encourages leaders to recognize their organization's purpose and direction, interrelated parts, interdependence on other organizations, needs and requirements of external and internal customers and stakeholders, resources required to perform work, and products and services created for specific intended outcomes.

Second, systems thinking encourages leaders to recognize and build partnerships with systems upstream that greatly affect the organization's capacity to perform.

Third, systems thinking encourages leaders to approach problem solving by examining system-related problems rather than focusing solely on people problems. It encourages a view of problems not as isolated or random events but as sets of antecedent conditions that can be predicted and controlled. According to McNamara (1999c), systems thinking enables leaders to look at organizations from a broad perspective from which they can recognize patterns and events. In traditional analyses, leaders tend to focus assessment on just one part of an organization and neglect to examine the extent to which that one part integrates with and affects other parts.

Finally, and most important, systems thinking provides a conceptual framework from which leaders can define and assess organizational performance. In this conceptual framework, organizations are considered open, interdependent systems that use inputs from the environment to create outputs that go back into the environment. Furthermore, organizational systems are made up of two types of system elements, internal and external, each of which plays an important role in the operation, performance, and assessment of the system. As noted, internal system elements are inputs, key work processes, outputs, outcomes, and a leadership system; external system elements are upstream systems, customers, and stakeholders.

Clarifying an organization's internal and external system elements is the first step in defining and assessing organizational performance. Figure 2.1 illustrates how internal and external system elements relate to one another. Figure 5.1 illustrates how these system elements provide opportunities to measure organizational performance in the seven essential areas of effectiveness, productivity, quality, customer and stakeholder satisfaction, efficiency, innovation, and financial durability.

Internal System Elements

Organizational systems are made up of external and internal system elements, each of which presents opportunities for measuring organizational performance. There are five internal system elements: leadership systems, inputs, key work processes, outputs, and outcomes. The leadership system provides overall direction and support to the organization. Inputs come from upstream systems in the environment and represent resources the system requires to carry its out work. Key work processes are tasks and activities that transform input into outputs. Outputs are products and services received or experienced by the system's customers. Outcomes are the intended results the organization seeks when customers experience or receive outputs. Figure 2.2 illustrates the relationships among these five internal system elements.

Each internal element will be described, with an explanation of how it relates to other internal and external elements and how it informs assessment. Specific examples are provided for a typical academic department and an administrative office called Information Services. At the end of each discussion, worksheets are provided to help assessors describe internal system elements of units whose performance they wish to measure. The discussion begins with an exploration of the purpose of leadership systems and their contributions to the performance success of organizations they lead.

Leadership Systems

In assessment, a leadership system is defined as the system within an organization that provides direction and support. All organizations have a leadership system, even if actual players operate at higher levels than the unit (such as vice presidents) or are shared with other units (such as deans). Figure 2.3 illustrates that the leadership system directs an organization through mission, vision, guiding principles, strategic goals, and organizational structure. It also illustrates that the leadership system influences all other elements in the organizational system.

Figure 2.1
The Organization as a System

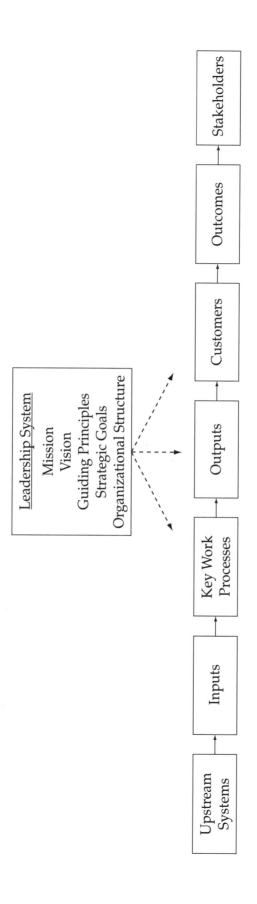

Source: Adapted from Sink and Tuttle, 1989.

Figure 2.2

Internal Elements of an Organizational System

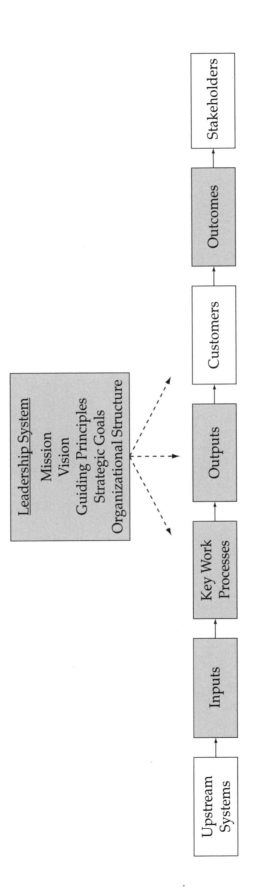

Source: Adapted from Sink and Tuttle, 1989.

Figure 2.3
Leadership Systems

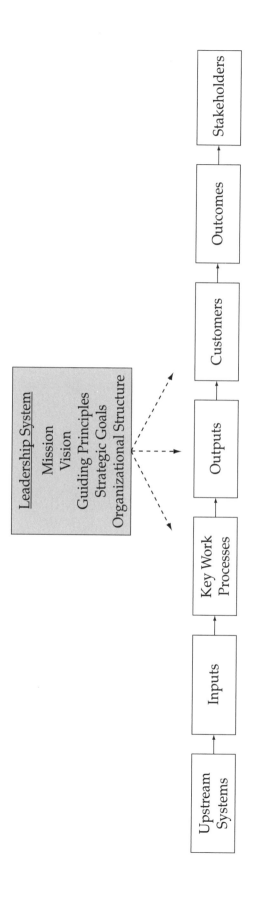

Source: Adapted from Sink and Tuttle, 1989.

Following is a discussion of how leadership systems affect organizational performance, beginning with an explanation of their external and internal responsibilities of particular importance to assessment.

External Responsibilities

Leadership systems provide one of the main pathways for organizations to send and receive feedback to and from their external environments. Leadership systems are responsible for building and maintaining positive external relations with people and organizations in their external environments. More specifically, leadership systems have the following external responsibilities:

- Building and maintaining strong partnerships with important upstream systems such as governing and advisory boards, governmental agencies, and major suppliers
- Creating positive images of the organization to targeted groups such as potential students, alumni, employees, and other external benefactors
- Identifying and serving the needs, expectations, and requirements of major external assessment users (described in Chapter One)

Assessors measure the quality of a unit's leadership system by determining the extent to which it fulfills these external responsibilities. For example, assessors measure the strength of important partnerships the leadership system creates, the quality of public images and local institutional reputation, and the satisfaction levels of external assessment users. Chapter Five provides more discussion of how assessors measure the quality of services provided by leadership systems in relation to these external responsibilities.

Internal Responsibilities

Leadership systems are also responsible for providing direction and support to their organizations. These internal responsibilities include the following:

- Clarifying and gaining support for the organization's mission
- Clarifying and gaining support for the organization's vision of performance excellence
- Clarifying guiding principles and building and sustaining an organizational culture reflecting those principles that maximize organizational performance
- Establishing and gaining support for strategic goals that help the organization find its competitive advantage and place in the environment

- Creating organizational structures (design and governance) that maximize performance
- Acquiring and allocating necessary resources to achieve mission, vision, strategic goals, and intended outcomes

We next discuss each responsibility and how it informs assessment.

Mission.   According to systems thinking, all organizational systems are open, customized systems created for a purpose. The role of a leadership system is to clarify a unit's purpose through its mission statement. Mission statements enable organizations in higher education to distinguish themselves from one another. They clarify what an organization is as well as what it is not. Mission statements answer purpose-related questions of who, how, and why. Whom does the unit serve? How does it serve them? Why does it provide this service—what results does it seek as a result of providing service to this group? Mission statements also clarify important boundaries that limit or extend an organization's service area, customers, products and services, and so forth.

Deming (1993) argues that high-performing organizations are clear and constant in their mission. Peter Senge (1998) adds that mission is the foundation of innovation. Leaders who master the discipline of innovation not only know the organization's purpose but also are truly mission-based. That is, they constantly weigh key decisions against the organization's mission.

Mission statements not only distinguish institutions but also provide direction for assessment. More specifically, missions inform assessors about whom and what to measure and provide a context for evaluating performance results. Take the mission of a two-year comprehensive community college. Part of its mission is to serve the needs of the institution's local community—a purpose not necessarily shared by a large research institution or a small, private liberal arts university. This part of the mission not only distinguishes the college from other institutions but also suggests which aspect of organizational performance is important to measure—in this case, community satisfaction with the programs and services provided by the college. Assessors can measure community satisfaction in several ways. They can measure public image and local reputation of the college through surveys, interviews, and focus groups; they can also observe the behavior of community members through attendance patterns, donations, passage rates of local levies, and so forth. Another part of the mission of a two-year comprehensive community college is to prepare students for entry into the workforce and for transfer to four-year schools. This part of the mission informs assessment by suggesting that assessors measure job placement rates of two-year terminal programs and track the performance success (admission, GPA, retention, and graduation rates) of students transferring to four-year institutions.

Not only does a mission statement inform measurement and provide a context for evaluating performance, but it also provides an avenue for evaluating the quality of the leadership system itself. As noted earlier, one of the most important internal responsibilities of a leadership system is to clarify and build consensus and support around the organization's mission. Assessors measure the quality of a leadership system by determining the degree to which organizational constituents understand and support the unit's mission, the quality of the mission statement itself, and the effectiveness of the mission statement in serving its purpose. (Measuring the quality of services provided by an organization's leadership system in relation to mission is discussed in greater detail in Chapter Five.)

Worksheet 2.1 will help assessors identify their unit's mission. Exhibits 2.1 and 2.2 offer excerpts from a mission statement for an academic department and Information Services.

Vision.   Leadership systems are also responsible for providing organizations with a clear and shared vision of performance excellence.

E-Learning Initiative at a Small Liberal Arts College

The president called a special meeting of her cabinet to make the announcement. Most members knew of the grant proposal submitted over a year ago, but few understood how significantly it would eventually affect day-to-day operations at this respected, tradition-bound liberal arts institution. The meeting was short. The president stood up and faced the small group of men and women representing the institution's senior leadership team. With a grin on her face and excitement in her tone, she announced, "I have just received notification that the college will be receiving $10 million from the Stuart Foundation to transform the way we use technology in teaching and learning. After the press conference this afternoon, I want to reconvene everyone and discuss how we can move forward from here. By the way, I think our new provost here needs to head up this effort since it was his idea from the start." The president turned toward the man sitting next to her and gently placed her hand on his broad shoulder. "I think we are about to make history in the coming years by setting new standards for what it means to bring excellence to a liberal arts education. Let's go tell the world about it, shall we?"

The new provost was an energetic, middle-aged scholar who loved new challenges. This grant had indeed been his idea from the start. The goal was simple in concept but complex in execution: to successfully marry digital fluency with the classical critical thinking, speaking, and writing strengths of a liberal arts education. He had argued in the grant proposal, apparently with success, that because we live, learn, and work in a digital world, the college needed to change. The question was how. The first challenge, of course, would be to help the faculty, staff, and alumni see the need. Then he would help them determine the path ahead. He knew that $10 million was not enough, but at least it was a good start.

The vignette tells of one leadership team's vision of the future. Visions are important forces that can propel organizations to higher levels of performance. They can also help leaders frame strategic goals and inform resource allocation decisions. When visions are shared, they can also coalesce support for strategic goals that leaders believe will help the organization find its competitive advantage and place in its external environment.

A vision of performance excellence, commonly expressed through a vision statement, is a mental model of what an organization wishes to become. It is a picture of a "desired state" that should inspire and motivate. An organization's vision should be strategic and lofty while presenting a clear and exciting picture of what the unit seeks to become. Typically, a vision statement answers the following questions:

What kind of organization do we want to become?

What do we want people to say about us as a result of what we do?

What is most important to us?

Where are we going?

Senge (1990) claims that members of organizations who enjoy a shared vision of excellence have a common identity and sense of destiny. He describes a shared vision as "a force in people's hearts, a force of impressive power." When visions are shared, he argues, people are "connected and bound together by a common aspiration." A shared vision is also vital to a learning organization, he claims, because "it provides the focus and energy for learning" (p. 206). Shared visions that are extrinsic focus on achieving something relative to an outsider, such as becoming ranked number one among peer institutions. Shared visions that are intrinsic are intended to lift people's aspirations, such as offering innovative learning opportunities. All shared visions are results-oriented and focused on the long term.

The vignette featuring a liberal arts institution receiving a grant to marry digital fluency with the classical strengths of a liberal arts education reflects the vision and desired state of the president and her senior leadership team for the tradition-bound institution. And quite appropriately, she recognized the need to begin the transformation by establishing a shared vision among the institution's faculty, staff, and alumni.

To summarize, leaders use vision statements for several purposes:

- To instill a common identity and sense of destiny for employees
- To build consensus and support for the organization's future desired state in relation to performance excellence
- To inspire and motivate employees
- To influence major decisions regarding strategic goals and allocation of resources

Vision statements are essential to assessment, because, like mission, vision provides a context against which assessment users evaluate performance results. Through vision, organizational constituents learn what excellence means. Without a clear and shared definition of performance excellence, assessors can measure performance, but assessment users cannot evaluate its worth in relation to excellence.

Finally, vision statements provide another vehicle for evaluating the quality of the leadership system itself. As noted, the leadership system is responsible for clarifying and building consensus and support for an organization's vision. Therefore, assessors can measure performance of the leadership system by determining the degree to which constituents understand, share, embrace, and are motivated and inspired by the organization's vision; the quality of the vision statement itself; and the effectiveness of the vision statement in serving its purpose. (Measuring the quality of services provided by an organization's leadership system in relation to vision is discussed in greater detail in Chapter Five.)

Worksheet 2.2 will help assessors identify their unit's vision. Exhibits 2.1 and 2.2 offer excerpts from a vision statement for an academic department and Information Services.

Guiding Principles.   Leadership systems are also responsible for providing a set of guiding principles that lay the foundation for vision and mission. Guiding principles, like mission and vision, inform assessment about what to measure and provide a context for evaluating organizational performance, particularly in terms of organizational culture. As discussed in Chapter One, Edgar Schein (1992) claims that organizational leaders have a responsibility for creating and monitoring an organization's culture. Furthermore, they must "manage cultural evolution and change in such a way that the group can survive in a changing environment" (p. 15).

Leadership systems use guiding principles to articulate desired cultural beliefs, values, and norms they believe will help the organization achieve its mission and vision of excellence. The *American Heritage Dictionary* defines a belief as "mental acceptance or conviction in the truth or actuality of something." Lewis, Goodman, and Fandt (1995) define values in organizational culture as "relatively permanent and deeply held preferences upon which individuals form attitudes and personal choices" (p. G-9); they define norms as "unwritten and often informal rules and shared beliefs about what behavior is appropriate and expected of group members" (p. G-6). Values and beliefs shared by members of the organization produce norms shaping behavior.

Guiding principles represent the basic truths and practices that guide how people behave, work, and relate to those they serve and to one another. They shape the personality or "climate" of an organization. Guiding principles also provide structural stability to organizational systems by guiding everyday decisions and choices, including the selection of strategic goals.

Some guiding principles emanate from laws, legal codes, government regulations, and institutional policies and procedures, while others emanate from formal ethical codes of conduct and generally accepted behavior rooted in organizational traditions, values, and beliefs. Formal codes of ethics in higher education are created by many groups, including professional associations, unions, institutions, student organizations, and governmental agencies. Generally, there are different codes of conduct for faculty, staff, and students. Senior leaders use assessment of guiding principles as a form of cultural quality control, according to Schein (1992).

Wheatley (2005) defines guiding principles as standards to which members of the organization hold themselves accountable. The most effective guiding principles, she argues, do not provide details about how things should be done but invite creativity and never restrict it.

Robert Newton (1992) describes two often conflicting cultural communities within higher educational institutions: the corporate and the scholarly. He explains that people in the corporate community view the institution as a business organization because of its capital assets, huge operating budgets, and differentiated workforce. Typically, these people are engaged in everything but teaching, learning, and research.

People in the scholarly community, according to Newton (1992), view the institution as a "near-sacred institution with a special and indispensable mission . . . more similar to medicine and religion than to that of industry and commercial services" (p. 10). For professionals in this culture, "teaching is not just a job but an integral component of a vocation that passes on the best of civilization's accomplishments" (p. 10). People immersed in this culture see students not as "customers" but as "neophyte members of a select intellectual community devoted to exploring the perennial questions of humankind and the best new ideas and methods of inquiry of the scholarly disciplines" (p. 10).

According to Newton (1992), these two coexisting cultural communities complicate strategic planning, assessment, and institutional innovation. In the corporate community, for example, strategic planning is seen as necessary for defining the future. Leaders build strategic goals from systematic processes that place considerable reliance on assessment data. They articulate decision criteria, timetables, and measurable results. They view assessment as difficult but necessary and reasonable. They believe that institutional innovation is derived from and coordinated with strategic goals.

For members of the community of scholars, Newton (1992) explains, planning is mostly intuitive, piecemeal, and decentralized. Assessment is seen as a "simplism concocted by persons who are ignorant about the purposes and achievement of higher learning" (p. 11). Change is generally reactive, department-based, and viewed as useful so long as it furthers the discovery and dissemination of knowledge.

Newton (1992) argues that the two cultures, corporate and scholarly, are indispensable to organizational success in higher education even though "tension between the two campus cultures is ineradicable and perennial" (p. 12). He suggests that leaders bring people of both cultures together by explaining their complementary roles to increase appreciation of one another, clarifying and adhering to each culture's decision-making spheres, and combining cultures only when needed, as in strategic planning and assessment.

One of the greatest challenges for leaders is to create and instill a shared set of guiding principles that form the most desirable organizational culture and produce the highest levels of quality of worklife for members of both the corporate and scholarly communities. Another challenge is to devise fair and just oversight processes that ensure that behavior conforms to standards established by guiding principles.

Guiding principles inform assessment in several ways. First, they suggest what to measure in organizational culture. For example, if an organization's guiding principles embrace a value for collegiality and shared decision making, assessors measure the scope of collegiality and shared decision making present in the organization's governance structures.

Second, guiding principles provide a reference for evaluating everyday behaviors—how people behave, work, and relate to those they serve and to one another. For example, if guiding principles express norms embodied in specific codes of ethics, assessors look for ways to measure the scope and frequency of unethical conduct.

Third, guiding principles provide a context against which assessment users evaluate the alignment of strategic goals and organizational structure, as well as the quality of worklife as perceived by employees.

Finally, like mission and vision, guiding principles provide a vehicle for measuring the quality of the leadership system itself. The leadership system is responsible for clarifying and building consensus and support among organizational constituents about guiding principles. Therefore, assessors measure quality of the leadership system by determining the degree to which constituents understand, share, embrace, and demonstrate the organization's guiding principles; the quality of the guiding principles themselves; and the effectiveness of guiding principles in serving their purpose. (Measuring the quality of services provided by leadership systems in relation to guiding principles is discussed in greater detail in Chapter Five.)

Exhibits 2.1 and 2.2 offer excerpts from guiding principles for an academic department and Information Services. Worksheet 2.3 will help assessors identify their unit's guiding principles.

Strategic Goals.   Another important internal responsibility of leadership systems is to set direction through strategic goals that leaders believe will help the organization find its competitive advantage and place in the environment. Through strategic goals, the leadership system sets high performance expectations that balance often conflicting needs of organizational stakeholders, customers, faculty, and staff. Through strategic goals, leaders help the organization find its competitive advantage and place in its external environment; prioritize strategic initiatives through timetables, performance measures, and reference points for each goal; clarify who is responsible and accountable for performance results; and support action with adequate resources.

Derived from the organization's strategic planning process (described in Chapter One), strategic goals help the leadership system determine direction that will lead the organization to its vision of performance excellence. Strategic goals also provide structural stability to organizational systems because they encourage organizational constituencies to participate in and work together toward accomplishing common goals.

McNamara (1999b) suggests that the process of framing strategic goals through collaborative strategic planning processes helps leadership systems achieve all of the following goals:

- Clarifying organizational purpose
- Communicating and building consensus around the organization's future
- Establishing realistic goals and objectives consistent with the mission in a defined time frame within the organization's capacity for implementation
- Developing a sense of ownership of strategic goals
- Ensuring efficient and focused use of critical resources
- Providing a base against which progress can be measured

Strategic goals at the institutional level also help leaders integrate operational plans at the functional level. Such goals integrate the following:

- Master plans for campus facilities
- Academic plans for degree and nondegree programs
- Financial plans for operational and capital funds
- Human resource plans for recruiting, hiring, and training of faculty and staff

- Information technology plans
- Library resource plans
- Plans for managing external affairs (governmental agencies, foundations, alumni relations, and community relations)
- Plans for recruiting, admitting, and retaining students, academic support, and athletics

Like mission, vision, and guiding principles, strategic goals not only inform assessment about what to measure and how to evaluate performance but also provide a vehicle for measuring quality of the leadership system itself. The leadership system is responsible for clarifying and building consensus and support among organizational constituents about the organization's strategic plans and performance expectations. Therefore, assessors measure the quality of the leadership system by determining the degree to which constituents understand and exhibit ownership of strategic goals and performance expectations, the quality of strategic goals themselves, and the effectiveness of strategic goals in serving their purpose. (Measuring the quality of services provided by an organization's leadership system in relation to strategic goals is discussed in greater detail in Chapter Five.)

Exhibits 2.1 and 2.2 offer excerpts from strategic goals for an academic department and Information Services. Worksheet 2.4 will help assessors identify their unit's strategic goals.

Organizational Structure. Another responsibility of the leadership system is to create a structure for the organizational system. In assessment, the quality of an organization's structure is measured along two dimensions: design and governance. The leadership system can specifically and intentionally design an organization's structure to optimize resources and improve organizational performance or, in the case of many small organizations, let it evolve as needs arise.

Design. Roy Autry (1998) explains that structural design represents the formal relationships among people in terms of roles and responsibilities. Organizational design represents the integration of people, information, and technology. The purpose of organizational design is to direct or pattern activities of people toward achievement of organizational purpose, goals, and vision.

Margaret Davis and David Weckler (1996) claim that organizational design can hinder or enhance organizational performance. Even though unique personalities of individuals influence everything that goes on, structural design affects employee attitudes, behaviors, opportunities, and performance. Therefore, leaders should design and redesign organizations on the basis of specific performance strategies.

Davis and Weckler (1996) define structural design as the way people and activities are clustered and related to one another. Structural design represents the division of work into functional units such as departments or divisions. Design also defines levels of hierarchy, spans of control, and centralization or decentralization of decision making. There are many bases for designing an organization, including function, product or service, customer, or geographical area. Each type of design has its strengths and weaknesses in its effects on organizational performance.

Davis and Weckler (1996) claim that an organizational design based on function reduces duplication of activities and encourages technical expertise. However, functional design also creates narrow perspectives, requires more than one department to complete a job, limits manager decision-making authority, and makes it more difficult to change and attribute accountability.

Administrative organizations in universities and colleges are usually designed on a functional basis. They are organized around functions of admissions, financial aid, counseling, physical plant, registration, facilities, security, and so forth. As a result of a functional design, students deal with a variety of organizations to be admitted, advised, registered, housed, fed, and so forth.

According to Davis and Weckler (1996), the product- or service-based design increases the quality of outputs, enhances a group's team spirit, expands the candidate pool for top management, and enables managers to respond more quickly because they have more decision-making authority. This design, however, limits resource sharing across divisions, restricts career opportunities, requires customers to deal with more than one department, and slows the organization's ability to respond quickly to changes in the product line.

Academic departments are organized around disciplines representing a product- or service-based design. Students take most of their courses in their major departments, but they also take outside courses to satisfy general education and other degree requirements. Staff in functionally designed administrative organizations are often organized on a product or service basis. For example, staff in financial aid offices, who are organized by types of aid programs such as grants, loans, scholarships, and college-work study, reflect a product- or service-based design. Such a design enables staff to remain current on continually changing program rules and regulations. In light of the fact that most students receive financial aid from multiple aid programs, however, this design requires that students meet with a variety of staff to finalize aid packages. Staff in accounting offices, who are organized by type of account, such as accounts payable or accounts receivable, reflect a product- or service-based design. This design requires that employees seeking assistance contact specific staff members, depending on the type of account in question.

Davis and Weckler (1996) suggest that a customer-based or geographical area-based design better serves the unique needs of each customer or market type, increases the organization's focus on changing customer needs, and increases the organization's probability of dropping unprofitable product lines. The downside of this design is that it reduces sharing of resources across divisional boundaries, increases duplicated efforts, and makes it more difficult for managing the overall organization.

Institutions with campuses located away from the main campus are organized on a geographical area basis. Organizations that provide a variety of services to special student groups, such as athletes, underprepared entering students, or international students, are organized on a customer basis. Staff in financial aid offices, who are organized into teams that serve the same students throughout their stay at the institution, are organized on a customer basis. Staff in payroll offices, who are organized to serve employees based on classification (classified staff, administrators, faculty), are organized on a customer basis. Recruiters in admissions offices, who are organized by type of new student they are recruiting (such as freshman, transfer, and graduate student) or by recruiting geographical region are organized on this basis. Organizational leaders use a combined customer-geographical design to respond to the needs of specific groups of customers at different geographical locations.

According to McNamara (1999a), several factors suggest when leaders should consider redesigning the organizational structure. One factor is a new strategic initiative, suggesting that a new design is needed for goal achievement. Another factor is the abundance of employee complaints about such things as too much or too little work, activity overlap, reporting to more than one boss, high employee turnover, or recurring problems in a major function or department.

Assessment of the quality of organizational design is directed toward the impact that design has on organizational performance, either intentionally or unintentionally. For example, assessors in organizations redesigned for the purpose of increasing efficiency and improving quality of worklife compare levels of organizational efficiency and quality of worklife before and after redesign. Assessors in organizations redesigned for purposes of improving quality of service and increasing customer satisfaction compare service quality and customer satisfaction before and after redesign. (The assessment of leadership systems in relation to organizational design is discussed in greater detail in Chapter Five.)

Governance.   An organization's leadership system is also responsible for creating the organization's governance structure, represented by its decision-making processes and practices. Decision-making processes and practices vary among and within organizations in higher education, depending on their mission, size, history, culture, traditions, and guiding principles. Governance structures can be systematic or ad hoc, centralized or decentralized, top-down or bottom-up, or some combination. However, most leaders in higher education strive for some level of collegiality in their governance structures; they believe that collegiality increases employee involvement through participation in ad hoc and standing committees, task forces, and improvement teams. They also believe that collegiality increases employee support for proposals and recommendations for change. The challenge for any leadership system is to design a governance structure that helps the organization achieve its mission, strategic goals, and vision of performance excellence; is consistent with the organization's guiding principles; and is suitable to a corporate or scholarly culture.

Two basic assessment questions need to be asked regarding the leadership system and governance structures: What is the quality of major decision-making processes and practices? And what is the quality of major decisions derived from those processes and practices? To measure the quality of major decision-making processes and practices, assessors compare actual practices against alignment with mission, vision, strategic goals, and guiding principles. For example, if an organization's guiding principles call for shared decision making through high levels of collegiality, assessors analyze committee and task force structures to determine the scope of employee involvement and survey employees to determine their perceptions of involvement in organizational decision making. Assessors measure the quality of decision-making processes by examining the cycle time and costs involved in major decision making by committees and individuals.

Assessors measure the quality of major decisions derived from those processes by examining the degree to which decisions reflect guiding principles and the extent to which they help the organization achieve its mission, strategic goals, and vision of performance excellence. (Measuring the quality of services provided by an organization's leadership system in relation to organizational structure is discussed in greater detail in Chapter Five.)

Exhibits 2.1 and 2.2 offer excerpts from organizational structures for an academic department and Information Services. Worksheets 2.5 and 2.6 will help assessors identify their unit's organizational design and governance structures.

Resources.   The last internal responsibility of an organization's leadership system that is important to assessment is the acquisition and allocation of resources necessary for the organization to achieve performance success as defined by its mission and vision. Using systems thinking, open social systems, such as organizations, require a variety of resources (called inputs) to perform work and create products and services (called outputs) for customers so that they can achieve their goals (called intended outcomes). These inputs include human resources, financial resources, equipment, supplies, physical space, energy, and information.

Assessors measure the quality of a leadership system in part by measuring the quality of the organization's resources. They examine quality in terms of qualifications, quantity, appropriateness, timeliness, reliability, accuracy, safety, compliance, and cost-benefit relationship. They also measure the effectiveness and quality of resource allocation processes. (Measuring the quality of services provided by the leadership system in relation to quality of resources is discussed in greater detail in Chapter Five.)

Exhibit 2.1

Excerpts from the Mission Statement, Vision Statement, Guiding Principles, Strategic Goals, and Organizational Structure for an Academic Department

Mission	Provide undergraduate, graduate, and continuing education learning opportunities that increase students' knowledge of subject matter, strengthen their critical thinking and writing skills, and prepare them to be good citizens, skilled and knowledgeable employees, and academically prepared graduate students
	Conduct sponsored and unsponsored research that advances and applies knowledge in the discipline.
	Provide services to colleagues in the discipline; members of the university community; local, state, and national governments; businesses; and educational organizations that transfer knowledge to address societal needs; better educate the state, national, and international communities; and advance local, state, and national economic development.
Vision	We strive to be recognized as the best department in the United States due to our exemplary teaching practices, innovative learning opportunities, vast resources, cutting-edge facilities that are well equipped for modern research, and outstanding faculty. We strive to be recognized worldwide for our diverse, dynamic, and innovative research program and creative and successful education of students in our discipline. We also strive to create a collaborative departmental culture supportive of the success of students, faculty, staff, and research and outreach partners.

Guiding Principles

Beliefs
- We believe that collaboration with other institutions and businesses and industries advances the discipline through research and outreach programs.
- We believe that research enhances learning at the undergraduate and graduate levels.

Values
- We cherish the free exchange of ideas inherent in academic freedom.
- We value shared decision-making practices exemplified in high levels of collegiality and strive to optimize employee involvement in all major decisions affecting the department.
- We value a sense of community among us as colleagues.

- We value the talents and diversity of one another and of the people we serve.
- We value excellence in our teaching, research, and service.

Norms

- We will honor and recognize accomplishments of one another and of the people we serve.
- We will be professional in our teaching, research, and service as explained in the institution's code of ethics and that of our discipline.
- We will treat one another and the people we serve with respect and dignity at all times.

Strategic Goals

To improve the quality of teaching and learning through technology

- Upgrade technology equipment in classrooms and teaching and research labs.
- Expand support for professional development and staff in the use of technology in teaching and research.

To improve the quality of research facilities

- Increase sponsored research dollars at the state and federal levels.
- Increase collaborative research projects with local universities and businesses and industries.

Organizational Structure

Design

The department employs scholars in our discipline. Faculty are loosely organized on the bases of majors and specialties within our discipline. The department's faculty vote to determine who will serve as department chairperson. Rotating chairpersons are usually tenured, senior members of the department's faculty who serve three-year terms. The chairperson serves as the department's official spokesperson to the university community and meets regularly with and reports directly to the dean. The department also employs graduate and undergraduate students who serve as teaching, research, and lab assistants for individual faculty members. Some assistants report directly to faculty who hire them; others report to the chairperson. The department secretary reports to the chairperson but serves individual faculty members, as assigned.

The department is affiliated with a new interdisciplinary research center that conducts research and provides contracted services. The research center is funded primarily by external research sponsors and employs faculty and graduate students from our department and others. The director of the center reports directly to the provost.

Governance

The department uses standing faculty committees to review and recommend departmental changes to curricula, tenure and promotion, teaching effectiveness, and professional development. The department also uses ad hoc committees to search for new faculty, develop new programs, and conduct self-studies. Departmental faculty approve committee recommendations before they are forwarded by the chairperson to the dean of the college for approval, who forwards them to the provost and president for final approval. Most matters pertaining to the research center go directly to the provost or vice president for research. Members of the department's nonteaching staff are represented by departmental representatives who serve on all major universitywide committees.

Exhibit 2.2
Excerpts from the Mission Statement, Vision Statement,
Guiding Principles, Strategic Goals, and Organizational
Structure for Information Services

Mission   To provide hardware, software, networks, training, and consulting services related to technology to university faculty, staff, and students that improves their individual and collective performance.

Vision   We strive to achieve excellence in the technology and service we provide to faculty, staff, and students; to maximize university resources through cost-effective procurement and efficient use of computing equipment and personnel; to anticipate end user needs and trends in a rapidly changing environment; and to encourage end user growth and development so that end users can become self-sufficient.

Guiding   *Beliefs*
Principles

- We believe that the university community depends on technology to achieve its goals and objectives and therefore it is important that we do everything we can to provide the best equipment and services possible.
- We believe that technology changes at a rapid pace and therefore we must constantly update our knowledge, skills, and abilities.
- We believe that we should service our equipment at times most convenient to our end users.

Values

- We value shared decision-making practices exemplified in high levels of collegiality and strive to optimize employee involvement in all major decisions affecting the department.
- We value a sense of community among us as colleagues.
- We value our role of helping others accomplish their goals through use of technology.
- We are committed to ensuring confidentiality and security of sensitive institutional data to which we have access.
- We value excellence in our service to others.

Norms

- We will honor and recognize the accomplishments of one another and of the people we serve.
- We will be professional in our work as explained in the institution's code of ethics.
- We will treat one another and the people we serve with respect and dignity at all times.
- We will respect the talents and diversity of one another and the people we serve.
- We prefer to agree on decision criteria before making difficult decisions about equipment and personnel.

Strategic   *To achieve ubiquitous computing for all members of the university community*
Goals

- Make computerized resources accessible to authorized end users from home, in the office, and in transit.

- Complete installation of a wireless network.
- Expand capacity for Web-based access to computerized resources.

To improve overall service quality

- Increase standardization of machines and software.
- Increase quality of service to end users through an expanded help desk.
- Strengthen technicians' technical and communication skills.

Organizational Structure

Design

The department is led by a director who reports directly to the provost. The director serves as the department's official spokesperson to the university community. The department is organized according to function: networking; training; desktop hardware and software purchasing, installation, and repair; academic computing; and administrative computing. Staff in each functional area report to a team leader, who reports directly to the director. A department secretary, who supervises office support staff, reports directly to the director.

Governance

The department uses a standing committee for professional development and ad hoc committees for staff searches and cross-functional issues such as self-studies, strategic planning, and budget development. Committees forward recommendations to the director for approval. Departmental personnel serve as advisers and consultants to many end user committees. The director makes all personnel and purchasing decisions based on items approved in the budget. The provost and president make all other major decisions with input from the director.

Inputs

In systems thinking, organizations require a variety of resources called inputs to perform work in order to create products and services for their customers. As stated earlier, the organization's leadership system is responsible for acquiring and allocating organizational resources. Figure 2.4 illustrates that upstream systems housed outside the system provide inputs to the organization and that inputs provide necessary resources for the organization to perform work and produce outputs for customers.

Disaster Recovery of a Small College Located Near the Gulf of Mexico

The storm came from the warm waters of the Gulf of Mexico six months ago. It was the first of two major storms to directly hit the region that hurricane season. Although everyone was evacuated and no one was hurt or killed, the campus was in ruins. The only physical thing kept from total destruction was the institution's databases, which were stored off campus on computers not affected by

Figure 2.4
Inputs

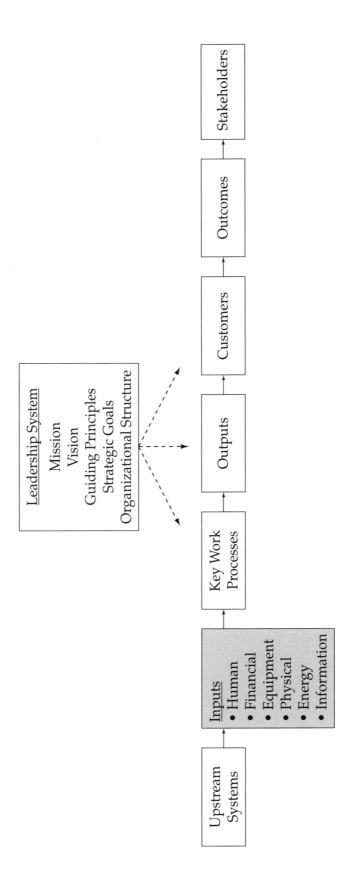

Source: Adapted from Sink and Tuttle, 1989.

the storm's devastation. After forty years as a senior administrator in higher education, the last five as the college's sixth president, the president hardly knew where to begin. He was sure, however, that he would not rebuild in the coastal region—perhaps farther north in the foothills. He took out his trusty legal pad and began listing all the critical resources he would need to rebuild his institution from scratch.

This vignette presents a picture of a president facing the daunting challenge of identifying and acquiring all the critical resources required to reconstruct his institution. The following is a discussion of important organizational resources that the president must acquire and that assessors should measure as part of the organization's quality. Organizations in higher education require six basic types of inputs: human resources, financial resources, equipment and supplies, physical space, energy, and information. Each is discussed in turn.

Human Resources

The people who perform the work of the organization constitute its human resources. Human resources are the full-time and part-time, permanent and temporary, paid and voluntary personnel who make up the institution's faculty, teaching and research assistants, administrators, professionals, technical staff, clerical support staff, student volunteers, alumni, and students. Students are important "inputs" because of their critical role in teaching and learning and because their quality has a major impact on the quality of teaching and learning. (Chapter Three explains how current students also represent an organization's "internal customers" and how former students, including alumni, represent an organization's "stakeholders.")

Because higher education as a whole is a labor-intensive service organization, many academic leaders consider faculty, staff, and students to be their most critical resource. They expect the assessment program to monitor and inform them about the quality of the workforce (new and continuing), quality of entering students, satisfaction of students and the workforce, and success of the workforce, particularly in relation to strategic execution.

As mentioned in Chapter One, Huselid, Becker, and Beatty (2005) argue that leaders should recognize and accept that some positions and roles in the organization have more influence on the execution of strategy than others. They argue that leaders should identify the positions that have more impact on strategy execution and classify them as "A" positions. They should also allocate a disproportionate amount of resources to them and more closely monitor their success in relation to strategy execution. Assessment questions related to human resources focus on levels of preparedness and qualifications, cost, and quantity; assessors also measure the success of human resources in relation to strategy execution.

Financial Resources

Adequate funding is another critical resource for organizational performance success. Financial resources in higher education may be restricted or unrestricted. They come from a variety of sources, including tuition, fees (such as lab fees, technology fees, application fees, transcript fees, testing fees, and athletic fees), state appropriations, local appropriations, financial aid, gifts, endowments, royalties, material transfer fees, and other revenues derived from commercial uses of intellectual property. Assessment questions related to financial resources focus on quantity, stability, and quality of the overall revenue structure.

Equipment and Supplies

High-quality equipment and supplies are also essential to performance success in higher education. Computers, copiers, phones, and fax machines are important in today's offices. State-of-the-art instructional and research equipment and supplies are important in classrooms, labs, distance education, and research facilities. Learning resources and library holdings are important for libraries and tutoring labs. The physical plant uses a variety of maintenance equipment, campus vehicles, and yard and construction equipment. Other equipment includes mobile display units, food preparation equipment, housing furniture, and athletic equipment. Assessment questions related to equipment and supplies focus on quality, quantity, currency, reliability, safety, and suitability.

Physical Space

Organizations in higher education require a variety of physical space (buildings and grounds) to achieve their missions. They require buildings for such amenities as offices, lounges, reception areas, conference rooms, storage, treatment rooms, workrooms for equipment (copiers, printers) and mailboxes, classrooms, teaching and research labs, libraries, parking, residence halls, cafeterias, and athletic facilities. They require grounds for gardens, horticulture and livestock, recreation and athletic facilities, and parking. Assessment questions related to physical space focus on quantity, currency, healthiness, safety, and accessibility.

Energy

As the cost of gas, oil, and electricity increases, leaders monitor the reliability, cost, and use of energy, always seeking ways to minimize energy use and costs. Assessment questions related to energy focus on cost, quantity, quality, reliability, and efficient use of energy.

Information

Information is another critical resource for organizations in higher education. To ensure performance excellence, organizations require high-quality information at the right time. For example, they need information about changing needs and requirements of the people they serve and the strategic directions the institution is taking. They also require information specific to their mission. For example, academic organizations need current information about their discipline, students, and academic policies and regulations. They need databases for research, requests for proposals from research sponsors, and institutional and program accreditation standards. Administrative offices need information about changing student markets and enrollment targets; institutional accreditation standards; federal, state, and local laws, regulations, and deadlines; emerging equipment and services; and trends in energy costs. Assessment questions related to information focus on quality, quantity, accuracy, timeliness, and efficient use of information.

Assessment of organizational performance in terms of the quality of its inputs is not new to higher education. For years, accrediting agencies have accredited and ranked institutions, programs, and libraries on the quality of their inputs. Many institutions promote their "quality" by announcing test scores, GPAs and high school class ranking of entering students, percentage of full-time versus part-time faculty, and percentage of faculty with terminal degrees.

In general, high-performing organizations seek to use the fewest inputs of the highest quality and the lowest cost to support key work processes that create and deliver outputs in order to achieve desired results. (Measuring the quality of inputs is discussed in greater detail in Chapter Five.)

Exhibits 2.3 and 2.4 offer examples of inputs for an academic department and for Information Services, respectively.

Worksheet 2.7 will help assessors identify their unit's inputs.

Key Work Processes

The third internal organizational element essential to assessment of organizational performance is key work processes. A key work process describes how work is performed in an organization. People and machines perform tasks and activities called "work" to create products, services, and information. Work in most organizations is organized into four to eight major processes central to the organization's mission. These important work processes are called key work processes. Tasks and activities that make up key work processes transform inputs into outputs so that the organization can achieve its purpose. Figure 2.5 illustrates that key work processes receive inputs in order to produce outputs received or experienced by customers.

On process maps and flowcharts, assessors and process improvement teams diagram tasks and activities to illustrate the sequence of work in hopes of discovering and eliminating wasteful tasks and ac-

Exhibit 2.3

Examples of Inputs for an Academic Department

Human Resources

- Full-time and adjunct faculty, scientists, and engineers
- Teaching and research assistants and lab technicians
- Administrative and professional staff
- Clerical support staff
- Tutors
- Student and alumni volunteers
- Enrolled students

Financial Resources (Restricted and Unrestricted Funds from a Variety of Sources Such as the Following)

- Tuition and fees
- State subsidies
- Gifts
- Financial aid
- Sponsored research grants
- Contracts
- Royalties, material transfer fees, and other revenues from commercial uses of intellectual property

Equipment and Supplies

- Office equipment such as computers, copiers, phones, and fax machines
- Instructional equipment for classrooms, labs, and distance education
- Research equipment and supplies for research facilities
- Departmental library holdings
- Campus vehicles
- Equipment and supplies used to feed and maintain horticulture and livestock

Physical Space

- Offices
- Conference rooms
- Storage space
- Workrooms for copiers, printers, and mailboxes
- Faculty and staff lounges
- Lockers
- Classrooms and instructional labs
- Auditoriums and lecture halls
- Other research labs, pastures, barns, and so forth

Energy

- Electricity for heating, cooling, lighting, and office equipment
- Gas and other fuels for operating equipment and vehicles

Information

- Institutional and external policies, procedures, and regulations
- Institutional databases
- Research databases
- Requests for proposals from research sponsors and contractors
- Institutional strategic initiatives

Exhibit 2.4

Examples of Inputs for Information Services

Human Resources

- Full- and part-time administrative, professional, technical, and clerical support staff
- Students
- Interns
- Consultants

Financial Resources

- General operating funds
- Technology fees
- Grants
- Equipment donations

Equipment and Supplies

- Hardware, software, and supplies for end users and academic computer labs
- Network machines, software, switches, cables, and other supplies
- Server machine and software
- Uninterrupted power supplies and generators
- Backup tapes and disks and other supplies
- Campus vehicles
- Office equipment such as computer hardware, software, and supplies as well as copiers, phones, and fax machines
- Training classroom instructional equipment and supplies

Physical Space

- Controlled, secured, fireproof spaces for operating equipment and backup tapes and disks
- Staff offices
- Secure, fireproof storage areas
- Loading docks
- Repair shops and other workrooms
- Training classrooms and labs
- Instructional labs
- Open reception areas
- Staff lounges
- Lockers

Energy

- Electricity for heating, cooling, lighting, and office equipment
- Gas and other fuels for operating equipment and vehicles

Information

- Institutional and external policies, procedures, and regulations
- Current information about emerging technology and technical standards, equipment costs, customer needs, and institutional strategic initiatives

Figure 2.5
Key Work Processes

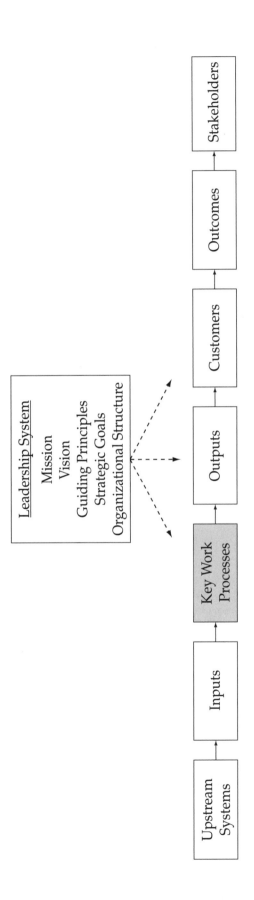

Source: Adapted from Sink and Tuttle, 1989.

tivities that add no value. A thorough knowledge of the design and performance of work enables organizational leaders to make informed decisions about future process improvements intended to streamline operations, reduce costs, reduce nonconformance to standards, and increase customer satisfaction. High-performing organizations typically enjoy key work processes that are robust, responsive, cost-efficient, and in total compliance with laws, standards, policies, and procedures. (Measuring the quality of key work processes is discussed in greater detail in Chapter Five.)

Academic Organizations

Work in academic organizations can be organized in a number of ways. Most academic organizations organize work into four key work processes: teaching, research, service (also called outreach or engagement), and management. Specific tasks assigned to each key work process can also vary. The following discussion represents one way to organize tasks and activities of a typical academic department whose mission includes teaching, research, and service.

Teaching.   Tasks and activities in the teaching process include all the activities associated with planning and evaluating curriculum; planning, delivering, and evaluating instruction; preparing for and managing classroom activities; assessing student learning outcomes; and advising students and cocurricular activities.

Research.   Tasks and activities in the research process encompass all the activities associated with proposal development, project management, research work itself, and knowledge transfer. These activities and tasks can be directed toward fundamental or basic research designed to create new knowledge or toward applied research in which knowledge is applied in clinical trials or in activities intended to solve certain problems or to invent new materials, methods, machines, and so forth.

Service.   Tasks and activities in the service process vary considerably in academic organizations. One way to organize service-related tasks and activities is by beneficiary. For example, faculty service on departmental committees benefits the department. Faculty service on institutional boards benefits the institution. Faculty service editing journals, reviewing articles, and holding office in professional associations benefits the discipline. And faculty service through outreach programs and contracted services benefits external entities such as local, state, national, and international businesses, governments, and schools.

Management.   Tasks and activities in the management key work process are activities required to run a smooth department. These activities include planning and budgeting, searching for and orienting new faculty, hiring and training professional and student staff, writing reports, and scheduling classes. Management activities might also include processing student appeals and imposing and monitoring disciplinary sanctions. Exhibit 2.5 offers more examples of tasks and activities in these four key work processes of an academic department.

Administrative Organizations

Key work processes of administrative organizations are mission-specific. There are usually four to eight key work processes in most major administrative departments. For example, some of the key work processes of an admissions office are recruitment, application processing, market research, and transcript evaluation. Examples of key work processes of a purchasing office are requisition processing (into purchase orders with or without bids), contract processing, and vendor management. Examples of key work processes of a registrar's office are registration, records processing, and course scheduling. All work must be performed in total compliance with laws, standards, policies, and procedures. Exhibit 2.6 identifies examples of key work processes in Information Services—desktop and laptop computer support; network services; server administration; application support; training, consulting, and problem solving; and management.

Worksheet 2.8 will help assessors identify their unit's key work processes.

Outputs

Another internal system element essential to assessment of organizational performance is outputs. Figure 2.6 illustrates how outputs in the form of products, services, and information are created through tasks and activities embedded in key work processes and received or experienced by customers. Outputs are designed and delivered specifically for the purpose of meeting or exceeding the needs and requirements of customers, stakeholders, faculty, and staff.

It is important in assessment to distinguish outputs from outcomes. Outputs are created by work. For example, outputs from teaching are learning opportunities embedded in credit and noncredit courses, seminars, workshops, field trips, internships, and student research projects. Outcomes are intended results the organization seeks as a result of customers' receiving or experiencing outputs. To return to our example, teaching creates outputs (courses) that lead to intended outcomes (student learning) as a result of customers' (students') engaging in or receiving outputs (courses). The distinction between outputs and outcomes is important in assessment because it allows assessors to measure both the quality of outputs (such as

Exhibit 2.5
Examples of Key Work Processes for an Academic Department

Key Work Process	Tasks and Activities
Teaching	▪ Planning, changing, and evaluating curriculum and instruction at the program and course levels
	▪ Specifying student learning outcomes at the course and program levels
	▪ Preparing and delivering lecture materials
	▪ Designing and facilitating classroom activities
	▪ Preparing, grading, and giving feedback on homework assignments, exams, independent studies, and student research activities
	▪ Serving on graduate student thesis or dissertation committees
	▪ Creating class databases and other record management systems
	▪ Ordering books
	▪ Advising students
	▪ Creating and advising student exchange programs, clubs, organizations, and other cocurricular activities
	▪ Setting up internships and cooperative programs
Research	*Managing research projects*
	▪ Developing grant proposals (nature and scope of research, intellectual property rights, budget, personnel)
	▪ Planning and scheduling events and activities
	▪ Hiring, training, and supervising research personnel
	▪ Purchasing and maintaining research facilities, equipment, and supplies
	▪ Accounting
	Conducting research
	▪ Conducting experiments
	▪ Conducting fieldwork (surveys, interviews, observations, document analysis)
	▪ Analyzing data
	Disseminating research findings
	▪ Writing and submitting articles for publication
	▪ Giving speeches and interviews
Service	*Benefits to the department*
	▪ Observing teaching of colleagues
	▪ Serving on and chairing departmental committees such as self-study and program review committees
	▪ Coordinating visiting scholar programs
	▪ Coordinating professional development activities
	▪ Mentoring young faculty members
	▪ Recruiting students
	▪ Meeting with potential employers of new departmental graduates
	Benefits to the institution
	▪ Serving on and chairing institutional committees such as tenure and promotion committees and curriculum committees

(continued on the next page)

Exhibit 2.5, *continued*
Examples of Key Work Processes for an Academic Department

- Serving on institutional governing and program advisory boards
- Building and participating in outreach programs that form partnerships with local, state, national, and international businesses, governments, and schools

Benefits to the discipline

- Editing journals
- Reviewing articles and proposals submitted for publication
- Holding office and serving on committees of professional associations

Benefits to external entities

- Developing contract proposals
- Performing and evaluating contracted services
- Evaluating other institutions as experts in ranking surveys
- Serving on accreditation site visit teams
- Building and participating in outreach programs that form partnerships with local, state, national, and international organizations, governments, and schools
- Serving on other organizations' governing and advisory boards
- Giving speeches and interviews

Management

- Planning, searching, and orienting new teaching and research faculty
- Selecting new graduate students
- Scheduling sabbaticals
- Hiring and training professional and student support staff
- Developing class schedules
- Writing reports
- Coordinating assessment activities
- Providing committee support
- Tracking program, equipment, facility, and staffing proposals framed by departmental committees
- Coordinating student appeals and disciplinary sanctions
- Developing budget requests
- Managing departmental budgets
- Purchasing and maintaining equipment and supplies
- Developing records management systems
- Serving as departmental liaison with other academic and administrative departments and senior leaders

alignment of courses to program objectives) and achievement of intended outcomes (such as achievement of student learning).

Assessment of the quality of an organization's outputs is an essential component in any assessment program. Poor-quality outputs can be fatal to an institution or program by causing it to lose accreditation, national ranking, future funding for research and contracted services, enrollment, and jobs. Quality of outputs in higher education

Exhibit 2.6

Examples of Key Work Processes for Information Services

Key Work Process	**Tasks and Activities**
Desktop and Laptop Computer Support	▪ Specifying, purchasing, installing, maintaining, repairing, and updating machines and software
Network Services	▪ Specifying, purchasing, installing, maintaining, repairing, securing, and updating machines, switches, cables, and software
Server Administration	▪ Specifying, purchasing, installing, maintaining, repairing, securing, and updating machines and software for both academic and administrative end users; backing up system files
Application Support	▪ Specifying, purchasing, installing, maintaining, securing, and updating both administrative and academic programs and systems ▪ Advising academic and administrative offices of future technological innovations
Training, Consulting, and Problem Solving	▪ Developing, scheduling, implementing, and assessing technical training programs, learning outcomes, and learning resource materials ▪ Providing one-on-one consultation and training ▪ Developing and maintaining Web-based knowledge databases ▪ Advising departments on future technological innovations
Management	▪ Developing strategic plans and disaster recovery plans ▪ Helping departments and offices develop business continuity plans in case of emergency shutdowns ▪ Searching, hiring, and training new staff ▪ Coordinating self-studies ▪ Developing program, facilities, and staffing proposals ▪ Developing budget requests ▪ Managing departmental budgets ▪ Writing reports ▪ Building vendor partnerships ▪ Purchasing equipment and supplies ▪ Developing records management systems ▪ Serving as departmental liaison with other academic and administrative departments and senior leaders

Figure 2.6
Outputs

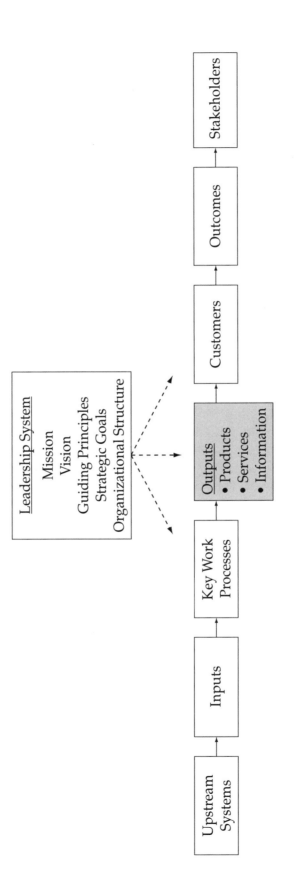

Source: Adapted from Sink and Tuttle, 1989.

is generally measured in terms of completeness, timeliness, price, accuracy, convenience, academic rigor, and appropriateness.

It is important that an organization's assessment program measure the quality of its outputs from the perspective of the people it serves. High-performing organizations use assessment to monitor changing requirements of the people they serve and scrutinize the extent to which their outputs meet or exceed those requirements.

Academic Organizations

Academic organizations produce outputs from each of the four key work processes listed in Exhibit 2.5.

Teaching.   The process of teaching produces learning opportunities embedded in credit and noncredit courses, seminars, workshops, field trips, research activities, exchange programs, cocurricular activities, and so forth. (Measuring the quality of outputs is discussed in greater detail in Chapter Five.)

Research.   The process of research produces intellectual property. Basic research produces new knowledge that advances the discipline; applied research produces specific deliverables such as new materials, procedures, products, and technology or solutions to specified problems. New knowledge created from basic and applied research is generally transferred through articles, books and other publications, presentations, interviews, speeches, news releases, contracted services, collaborative partnership programs between universities and businesses, and other types of outreach programs.

Service.   The process of service produces many types of outputs, depending on the beneficiary. For the institution and department, service produces committee membership and committee reports and recommendations; for the discipline, service produces reviewed articles and officers in professional associations; for external entities, service produces contracted and outreach services and members and reports of site visit teams.

Management.   The process of management produces new and oriented faculty, trained staff, new and repaired equipment, course schedules, budget proposals, annual reports, and so forth.

Administrative Organizations

Outputs of administrative organizations are mission-specific and result directly from each key work process. For example, an admissions office's key work process of "application processing" produces admission decisions spelled out in decision letters sent to applicants. A registrar's office's process of "records processing" produces transcripts and grade reports; the process of "course scheduling" produces a schedule of classes. A purchasing office's process of "requisition processing" produces purchase orders, and the process of "contract processing" produces contracts.

Outputs of Information Services are produced from each of the key work processes listed in Exhibit 2.6. For example, the process of desktop and laptop computer support produces new and restored desktop and laptop computers and software end users use to receive, transmit, and process data; the network services process produces routers, switches, bridges, and repeaters that provide internal and external connections to end users; server administration produces functioning servers that receive, transmit, and process data; application support produces software that end users use to enter, access, and process data; training produces learning opportunities such as workshops and consulting; and management produces reports, plans, and so forth. Exhibits 2.7 and 2.8 offer more examples of outputs of an academic department and Information Services, respectively, for each key work process listed in Exhibits 2.5 and 2.6.

Worksheet 2.8 can also be used by assessors to help them identify their unit's outputs for each of its key work processes.

Outcomes

The final internal system element essential to assessment of organizational performance is outcomes. Figure 2.7 illustrates that outcomes are achieved through customer interactions with the system's outputs.

Outcomes, as noted earlier, are distinguished from outputs. Whereas outputs are created by tasks and activities in key work processes, outcomes are the intended or desired results an organization seeks to achieve as a consequence of customers' receiving or experiencing its outputs. Outcomes are mission-specific, and their achievement is critical to organizational survival.

There are a variety of outcomes in higher education. There are planned or intended outcomes, unintended outcomes, and actual outcomes that are either intended or unintended. There are short-term outcomes such as entry-level employability and long-term outcomes such as becoming an accomplished nurse, educator, or community leader. There are outcomes that benefit the customer, such as student learning; outcomes that benefit the organization, such as a high national ranking; and outcomes that benefit stakeholders and the larger society, such as an educated public and a skilled workforce essential to economic development. There are leading outcomes, such as high-quality faculty, and lagging outcomes, such as student learning. Because intended outcomes are mission-specific, they vary significantly between and among academic organizations and administrative organizations in higher education.

Exhibit 2.7

Examples of Outputs for an Academic Department

Teaching

- Learning opportunities embedded in credit and noncredit courses, seminars, workshops, field trips, student research projects, internships, cooperative work programs
- Lectures, classroom activities, homework assignments, exams, reading lists
- Class databases
- Student exchange programs
- Clubs, organizations, and other cocurricular activities
- Academic advice and counsel

Research

- Research proposals
- Basic research: new knowledge creating intellectual property
- Applied research: project-specific deliverables such as new materials, procedures, products, technology, and solutions to specific problems
- Articles submitted for publication
- Presentations and interviews
- Patent applications

Service

- Committee reports
- Peer evaluations and site visit team reports
- Visiting scholars and other academic programs
- Business-university partnerships
- Outreach programs
- Professional development programs
- Edited journals
- Reviewed articles and proposals
- Papers, presentations, speeches, interviews

Management

- Strategic and operational plans
- Annual and monthly reports
- Budget, capital equipment, and personnel requests
- Course schedules for each semester or year
- Calendar and schedule of events
- Faculty committee assignments
- New, oriented faculty and trained staff
- New and repaired equipment
- Assessment reports

Exhibit 2.8

Examples of Outputs for Information Services

Desktop and Laptop Computer Support

- New or restored desktop and laptop computers and software in offices, classrooms, labs, and research facilities

Network Services

- Routers, switches, bridges, and repeaters that provide internal and external connections to end users
- Network ports for end user machines
- Network accounts for end users

Server Administration

- Functioning and server and multiuse software
- Upgraded databases
- Backup tapes

Application Support

- Programs and databases used by end users: software documentation, calendaring, Internet and Web, e-mail, registration and class scheduling, enrollment management, human resources, financial accounting, billing, payroll, development, server-based operating systems, e-services (class enrollment, grade posting, class management such as Blackboard, and so forth)

Training, Consulting, and Problem Solving

- Workshops, seminars, and Web-based knowledge databases
- Training materials
- Advice and consultation
- Software documentation

Management

- Vendor partnerships
- Strategic and operational plans
- Annual and monthly reports
- Assessment reports
- Operating and capital equipment requests
- Project and work schedules
- Committee assignments
- Calendar and schedule of events
- New, oriented, and trained staff

Academic Organizations

Intended outcomes of academic organizations emanate from their four key work processes of teaching, research, service, and management.

Teaching. The primary intended outcomes of teaching are student learning, personal growth and development, employability, and readiness for advanced study. Specific learning outcomes are defined at the course and program levels.

Figure 2.7
Outcomes

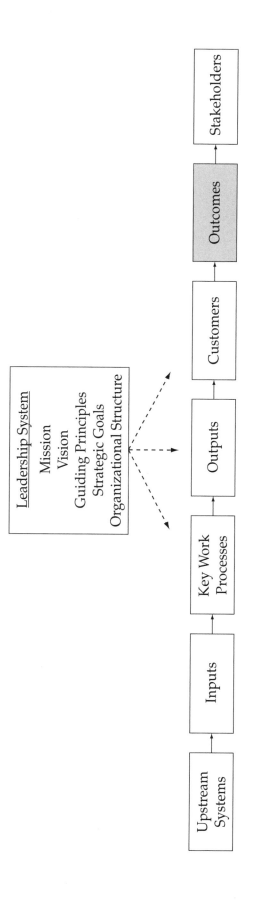

Source: Adapted from Sink and Tuttle, 1989.

Palomba and Banta (1999) explain that student learning outcomes answer the performance question—what should a graduate or program completer know, believe, value, or be able to do, and at what level? Assessors measure learning outcomes before students enter a program, while they are part of a program, at the end of a program, years after graduation, or at any combination of times.

Every academic organization has a unique set of intended student learning outcomes. Many academic departments seek student learning outcomes in both cognitive and affective areas. Dary Erwin and Steven Wise (2002) explain that cognitive learning outcomes include higher-order thinking skills, general education goals, competence in the major, and professional skills. Affective or psychosocial development outcomes are maturity, personal growth, interpersonal relationship skills, independence, identity and self-concept, and curiosity.

Peter Gray (2002) differentiates two sets of philosophical assumptions about education that determine how educators understand and express student learning outcomes: a positivist or scientific view and a subjectivist or intuitionist view. The positivist or scientific view understands learning outcomes as "knowable in advance, specifiable, measurable, and related to behaviors that can be directly observed" (p. 51). From this view, student outcomes are described in terms of student behaviors, and assessment is generally focused on general education knowledge and skills or discipline-specific facts, terms, concepts, and processes.

From a subjectivist or intuitionist view, Gray (2002) explains, some student outcomes may be quite "conceptually clear, specific, concrete, and even behavioral" (p. 52). However, many of them will be "more vague, general, abstract, and nonbehavioral" states of being. "There is no assumption that learning will ultimately be defined in terms of behaviors. Instead, there is a focus on the whole range of knowledge, skills, and values of an educated person" (p. 52).

Research.   The intended outcomes of research vary significantly even though research methods are similar and all research produces intellectual property. For example, applied research seeks to solve specific problems or invent new machines, materials, methods, and technology—outcomes specified in approved project proposals. Fundamental or basic research seeks to create new knowledge in the disciplines specified in approved proposals but discovered for no specific or known application or action. According to Michael Patton (2002), the primary outcome from basic research is to "generate or test theory and contribute to knowledge for the sake of knowledge. Such knowledge, and the theories that undergird knowledge, may subsequently inform action and evaluation, but action is not the primary purpose of fundamental research" (p. 11).

At the organizational level, academic organizations seek additional outcomes from research that go beyond outcomes embedded in specific research projects. For example, through research, organizations seek to improve their national reputations, increase student and faculty employment opportunities, and enrich graduate and undergraduate learning experiences. More recently, universities have used research to supplement institutional revenues by capitalizing on the commercial value of intellectual property—an outcome necessitated by decreasing state support for professional programs, such as medicine, according to Eric Meslin, director of Indiana University Center for Bioethics (personal communication, Mar. 9, 2002). More efforts are being made to assess and protect intellectual property rights that can eventually lead to revenues from royalties, patent fees, material transfer fees, and other commercial endeavors. Meslin suggests that institutions can no longer rely solely on philanthropy, subsidies, grants, and contracts to support research, at least in the life sciences.

Assessment of research varies with its purpose. At the organizational level, assessors measure research performance in relation to the degree to which it serves its purpose: Did research enhance student learning? Did research increase jobs and supplement salaries? Did research bring additional revenues to organizations facing decreased state support?

At the research project level, external academic peers, sponsors, contractors, and institutions who sponsor research evaluate effectiveness and quality of research by asking, Did the project achieve its intended goals? Did researchers use methods that meet acceptable standards? Did researchers efficiently use their resources? External academic peers evaluate effectiveness and quality of research described in articles submitted for publication in refereed journals based on standards and criteria established by the discipline, professional societies, editorial boards, institutions, governmental agencies, and other entities.

Service.   The primary intended outcomes from service in academic organizations vary according to the type of service performed and the beneficiary. Some services, such as those delivered through outreach programs, are designed to promote social, economic, scientific, and technological advancement of local, regional, national, and internal organizations, governments, and communities. Service such as faculty participation on departmental and universitywide committees is designed to enhance institutional and departmental communication and governance. Service such as editing journals and serving as officers in professional associations is designed to advance the discipline and the profession.

Management.   The primary intended outcome from management is a well-managed academic organization that is fully staffed, equipped, and funded and that operates in full compliance.

Administrative Organizations

Intended outcomes of administrative organizations vary with their mission. For example, an admissions office seeks to provide the university with a targeted number of highly qualified, matriculated new students; the registrar's office seeks to provide students and faculty with timely access to accurate information and to ensure that students are in compliance with academic policies; the purchasing office seeks the best buy for the dollar and informed buying. Information Services seeks to increase the productivity of end users by providing reliable and suitable equipment and networks. Exhibits 2.9 and 2.10 offer more examples of intended outcomes for an academic department and for Information Services, respectively. Worksheet 2.8 can be used by assessors to help them identify their unit's intended outcomes for each key work process. (Measuring the achievement of intended outcomes is discussed in greater detail in Chapter Five.)

Summary

This chapter explained how systems thinking can help organizational leaders view organizations as open, living systems with integrated, interdependent elements. The chapter defined five internal elements of organizational systems: leadership systems, inputs, key work processes, outputs, and outcomes. It explained how each internal system element provides potential opportunities for assessing organizational performance. Examples of system elements were described for both academic and administrative organizations. Worksheets were provided to help assessors identify internal system elements of organizations whose performance they intend to measure.

Exhibit 2.9

Examples of Intended Outcomes for an Academic Department

Teaching

- Student achievement of specific learning outcomes, by course and program
- Student growth and development (social, physical, psychological)
- Enriched student life experiences on campus through participation in activities and sports
- Employability
- Readiness for graduate studies
- Coordinated and continuous progress toward student academic goals
- Graduate students who are experienced in teaching

Research: Project Level

- Advancement of the discipline
- Advancement specific to individual research projects such as improvements in productivity, economic development, health and human services, and quality of life

Research: Organizational Level

- Increased income to the institution, department, and faculty through research grants, contracts, royalties, donations, and commercial endeavors
- Enhanced reputation of the institution, department, and discipline
- Expanded research opportunities in the future
- Enriched student learning experiences
- Increased student and faculty employment opportunities
- Revitalized and energized faculty

Service

- Advances specific to individual contracts, such as improvements in productivity, economic development, health and human services, and quality of life
- Benefits derived from outreach programs and partnerships that strengthen social, economic, scientific, and technological advancements in local, state, regional, national, and international businesses, education, and health care
- Enhancements to institutional and departmental communication and governance through committees and peer review
- Enhancements to professional associations and the discipline through participation as journal editors, committee members, office-holders, and conference presenters

Management

- A well-managed academic department that is fully staffed, equipped, and funded
- High employee satisfaction
- Total compliance with laws, regulations, policies, procedures, and codes of conduct.

Exhibit 2.10
Examples of Intended Outcomes for Information Services

Desktop and Laptop Computer Support

- Highly productive end users who are able to accomplish computing-related tasks without interference or delays due to unsuitable or malfunctioning machines and software

Network Services

- Highly productive end users who are able to accomplish computing-related tasks anywhere and anytime, without interference or delays due to network downtime or slowdown time

Server Administration

- Highly productive end users who are able to accomplish computing-related tasks without interference or delays due to server crashes or slowdowns
- End users who are confident about the security and privacy of their data housed in IS-supported computers and processed by IS-supported applications

Application Support

- Highly productive end users who are able to enter and process data using current, reliable, convenient, and secure software

Training, Consulting, and Problem Solving

- Knowledgeable and skilled end users

Management

- A well-managed department that is fully staffed, equipped, and funded
- Total compliance with laws, regulations, standards, policies, procedures, and codes of ethics

Worksheet 2.1
Mission Analysis

Unit of Analysis: _____ *(Example: Chemistry Department)*

Today's Date: _____

Use this worksheet to describe the unit's mission by answering in column B each question in column A.

(A) Question	(B) Answer
What products and services does the unit provide?	*Example:* The Chemistry Department provides undergraduate, graduate, and continuing education learning opportunities in analytical, inorganic, organic, physical, and theoretical chemistry. It also conducts research and provides contracted and other outreach services that transfer knowledge discovered in research.
To whom does the unit provide these products and services?	*Example:* The Chemistry Department primarily serves • Undergraduate and graduate students and postdoctoral fellows • Other majors who enroll in chemistry service courses • Members of the general public who attend symposia, workshops, and lectures and participate in outreach programs • Federal, state, and local governmental agencies and businesses that sponsor research • State and local businesses, industries, and nonprofits that contract for services and participate in collaborative research, entrepreneurial, and outreach programs • The university's new Biosciences Research Center, which conducts interdisciplinary research and provides contracted services
What goals does the unit seek as a result of providing these products and services to those it serves?	*Example:* The Chemistry Department seeks to • Provide educated students to become independent scientists and scientifically literate citizens • Create a community of scholars who expand fundamental, molecular-scale understandings of the chemical reactions and properties of matter and apply that understanding in innovative ways that improve the world at large • Apply chemical sciences that address societal needs; educate state, national, and international communities; and advance local, state, and national economic development
What boundaries exist in terms of whom the unit serves and what and how it serves them?	*Example:* • New chemistry majors must meet university and department-specific selection criteria. • Undergraduate student admission preference is given to state residents over out-of-state residents and foreign nationals. • Degree programs are limited to those approved by the state. • Most courses are offered on campus, except for selected graduate and noncredit courses offered off campus or online.

Worksheet 2.2

Vision Analysis

Unit of Analysis: _____ *(Example: Chemistry Department)*

Today's Date: _____

Use this worksheet to describe the unit's vision of performance excellence. If a vision statement does not currently exist, develop one using the following questions to guide discussion: What kind of organization does the unit want to become? What does the unit want people to say about it as a result of what it does? What values are most important to people in the unit? Where is the unit going?

Vision Statement

Example:

We strive to be recognized as one of the best Chemistry Departments in the United States due to our exemplary teaching practices, innovative learning opportunities, vast resources, cutting-edge facilities that are well equipped for modern chemical research, and outstanding faculty. We strive to be recognized worldwide for our diverse, dynamic, and innovative research program and innovative and successful education of students in the chemical sciences. We also strive to create a collaborative departmental culture supportive of the success of students, faculty, staff, and research and outreach partners.

Worksheet 2.3
Guiding Principles Analysis

Unit of Analysis: _____ *(Example: Chemistry Department)*

Today's Date: _____

Use this worksheet to describe the unit's guiding principles. Guiding principles articulate the unit's desired cultural beliefs (mental acceptance or conviction in the truth or actuality of something), values (relatively permanent and deeply held preferences on which individuals form attitudes and personal choices), and norms (unwritten and often informal rules and shared beliefs about what behavior is appropriate and expected of group members).

Guiding Principles

Example:

Beliefs

- We believe that collaboration with other institutions and businesses and industries advances the discipline through research and outreach programs.
- We believe that learning takes place inside the classroom, through research activities, and through cocurricular activities.
- We believe that research enhances learning at the undergraduate and graduate levels.

Values

- We cherish the free exchange of ideas inherent in academic freedom.
- We value shared decision-making practices exemplified in high levels of collegiality and strive to optimize employee involvement in all major decisions affecting the department.
- We value a sense of community among us as colleagues.
- We value excellence in our teaching, research, and service.

Norms

- We will honor and recognize the accomplishments of one another and of the people we serve.
- We will be professional in our teaching, research, and service as explained in the institution's code of ethics and that of our discipline.
- We will treat one another and the people we serve with respect and dignity at all times.
- We will respect the talents and diversity of one another and the people we serve.

Worksheet 2.4
   Strategic Goals Analysis

Unit of Analysis: _____ *(Example: Chemistry Department)*

Today's Date: _____

Use this worksheet to analyze the unit's strategic goals. In column A, list the unit's strategic goals. In column B, list performance indicators to measure goal achievement, and in column C, reference points to evaluate goal achievement. In column D, describe data sources, and in column E, describe due dates for providing assessment results.

Strategic Goals (A)	Performance Indicators (B)	Reference Points (C)	Data Sources (D)	Assessment Report Due Dates (E)
Example: Improve quality of teaching and research labs and equipment	*Example:* • Dollars spent on new equipment • Percentage of outdated equipment replaced • Percentage of labs with updated equipment	*Example:* • 20 percent more dollars spent than last year • 100 percent of outdated equipment replaced • 100 percent of labs with updated equipment	*Example:* • Budget reports • Equipment inventory	*Example:* August (annually)

Worksheet 2.5
Organizational Design Analysis

Unit of Analysis: _____ *(Example: Chemistry Department)*

Today's Date: _____

Use this worksheet to describe the unit's organizational design. In this description, explain the unit's hierarchical structure and major functional units, the chain of command and reporting relationships, and the unit's official spokespersons.

Organizational Design

Example:

Departmental faculty are organized on the basis of specific fields in the discipline of chemistry: analytical, inorganic, organic, physical, and theoretical. The Chemistry Department employs a staff of full- and part-time technicians, engineers, scientists, and clerical staff. The Chemistry Department also employs graduate and undergraduate students who serve as teaching, research, and lab assistants. Some assistants report directly to faculty, who hire them through research grants; others report to the chairperson. The chairperson serves as the department's official spokesperson to the university community and meets regularly with and reports directly to the dean of the College of Arts and Sciences. The department's secretary reports to the chairperson but serves individual faculty members, as assigned.

The Chemistry Department is affiliated with the university's new interdisciplinary Biosciences Research Center, which conducts sponsored research and provides contracted services. The new center is primarily funded by external research sponsors and employs several faculty and graduate students from the Chemistry Department and two other departments. The director of the center reports directly to the provost.

Worksheet 2.6
Organizational Governance Analysis

Unit of Analysis: _____ *(Example: Chemistry Department)*

Today's Date: _____

Use this worksheet to describe the unit's governance structure. In this description, list all major committees and task forces including their purpose, decision-making authority, and membership structure; differentiate types of major decisions made solely by unit leaders versus decisions typically made by or originating in committees; and explain how unit leaders are selected or elected and the duration of each appointment.

Organizational Governance Structure

Example:

The Chemistry Department supports three standing departmental committees: (1) the Curriculum Committee to review and recommend departmental changes in curricula, (2) the Tenure Committee to review requests for tenure and promotion, and (3) the Professional Development Committee to coordinate departmental professional development activities and develop guidelines for use of faculty development funds. The Chemistry Department uses ad hoc committees to search for faculty, conduct program reviews, and conduct studies. Departmental faculty always review and approve major committee recommendations before they are forwarded to the chairperson, who submits them to the dean of the College of Arts and Sciences for approval and then forwards them to the provost and president's cabinet for final approval. Most matters pertaining to the Biosciences Research Center go directly to the provost and vice president of research. Classified staff are represented by departmental representatives who serve on all major universitywide committees. Faculty vote determines who will serve as department chairperson. Rotating chairpersons are usually tenured, senior members of the faculty who serve three-year terms.

Worksheet 2.7
  Inputs Analysis

Unit of Analysis: _____ *(Example: Chemistry Department)*

Today's Date: _____

Use this worksheet to describe the unit's major inputs. For each type of input listed in column A, identify important inputs the unit requires to perform its work and produce outputs in column B.

Type of Input (A)	Inputs (B)
Human Resources	*Example:* Full- and part-time faculty, engineers, scientists, research and teaching assistants, lab technicians, tutors, clerical support staff, and student volunteers
Financial Resources	*Example:* University funds from tuition, fees, financial aid, and state subsidies Sponsored research dollars from local, state, and federal research sponsors Revenues generated from royalties, material transfer fees, and so forth Scholarship funds for undergraduate and graduate students
Equipment and Supplies	*Example:* Computers, specialized chemistry equipment, supplies for classrooms and distance education, teaching and research labs, offices, and storage Chemistry library holdings
Physical Space	*Example:* Offices, classrooms, lounges, lockers, teaching and research labs, specialized storage, auditoriums, workrooms Chemistry library
Energy	*Example:* Electricity and specialized fuels for teaching and research labs, equipment, vehicles, and storage
Information	*Example:* Body of knowledge in analytical, inorganic, organic, physical, and theoretical chemistry supporting teaching and research activities Requests for research proposals University academic, human resource, research, purchasing, planning, and budgeting policies and procedures Professional journal publication guidelines and schedules Announcements of ongoing and proposed research projects being conducted at similar institutions Fluency with advancements in knowledge and technology related to chemistry needed for business and industry

Worksheet 2.8
  Key Work Processes, Outputs, and Outcomes Analysis

Unit of Analysis: _____ *(Example: Chemistry Department)*

Today's Date: _____

Use this worksheet to describe the unit's key work processes, outputs, and intended outcomes. In column A, list four to eight key work processes of this unit. In column B, describe the major outputs derived from each key work process. In column C, describe intended outcomes resulting from customers receiving or interacting with outputs listed in column B.

Key Work Process (A)	Outputs (B)	Intended Outcomes (C)
Example: Teaching	*Example:* Learning opportunities embedded in credit and noncredit courses, seminars, symposia, workshops, field trips, internships, and student research projects	*Example:* Student learning, personal development, employability, and preparation for advanced study

CHAPTER 3

Organizations as System

External Elements

This chapter introduces three external system elements important to assessment: upstream systems, customers, and stakeholders. These three external elements, combined with the five internal elements described in Chapter Two, represent all of a system's elements.

External System Elements

Chemistry Department of a Medium-Sized State-Supported University

Enough is enough, he thought to himself as he wandered through campus returning to his office after class. What a disaster! How can I possibly create a positive learning environment under these conditions? Everything is a mess!

It was a disastrous day indeed for this longtime, highly respected faculty member. Just two years ago, he received the prestigious Vandermurphy Professor of the Year Award. He had always loved teaching this upper-division chemistry class—perhaps it was because most ill-prepared and unwilling students had weeded themselves out by the time they reached his level. Today was different, however. For the first time that he could remember, he no longer liked teaching. What was happening to this fine institution that made teaching so extremely difficult?

As he continued his trek across campus, he decided to make a list of all the things that had gone wrong over the last few days. First on the list was the poor condition of his classroom this semester. The few armed desk-tables that were not broken were either left-handed or too small for people taller than five foot six. The wall-mounted air conditioner's fan rattled annoyingly every time it kicked on. Two of the overhead lights were either blinking or buzzing as only fluorescent lamps can. Campus construction next door created a constant banging, forcing him to shout most of the time. The final touch, however, was the nonfunctioning ceiling-mounted projector and broken network connection, which combined to render his carefully prepared PowerPoint presentation with demonstrations of lab experiments totally useless.

Quality of his classroom was one thing, he told himself, but what really upset him was the lack of textbooks for five of his thirty students. The bookstore had really messed things up this time. After three weeks of class, five students were still borrowing books from classmates or using the one worn copy he placed on reserve in the library (which, he reminded himself, the library misplaced but fortunately found after the first week of class). The mix-up started in August when the department chair told him the other section was cancelled due to lack of funds, so he would have to increase his class enrollment by ten more students than he normally had. How could he possibly teach this upper-division chemistry course to thirty students? His student evaluations would surely be down this semester.

Then, of course, there was the mix-up with his paycheck yesterday. Maybe that was the straw that broke the camel's back! Almost every fall, he ended up with less than full pay for one or sometimes two months because his federally funded grant didn't come in until late October, after the start of the federal government's fiscal year. But why couldn't payroll come up with a better solution that didn't put such an unfair burden on the faculty? Anyway, wasn't this the grant that the dean almost didn't fund because the university cut his matching funds to hire a new administrator in the assessment office? What's a guy to do?

The vignette drives home the interdependence of organizations in higher education and the effect that organizations in a large system have on the performance of others in the same system. All faculty have encountered some of these experiences. This vignette illustrates the extent to which performance of the Chemistry Department depends on the performance of the Physical Plant Department and Information Services that maintain, furnish, and equip classrooms, the bookstore and library that supply books to students, the payroll office that distributes paychecks to employees, and the dean who allocates matching research funds and influences class size through budget constraints. Performance of the Chemistry Department also depends on external organizations, such as the federal government, that disburse grant funds on a fiscal year different from the traditional academic year.

In Chapter Two, organizations were described as open, living, unique systems with a purpose that receive and react to feedback from their environment. External system elements provide important opportunities for organizations to interact with their environments. External system elements exist either inside or outside the larger system. Each external system element serves a different function and operates in a unique relationship with internal system elements. For example, upstream systems supply and constrain inputs necessary for the organization to perform work. Customers receive or experience outputs created through work. Finally, stakeholders are downstream systems that depend on and benefit from system achievement of intended outcomes. Figure 3.1 illustrates the relationship between an organization's external and internal system elements.

Figure 3.1

External Elements of an Organizational System

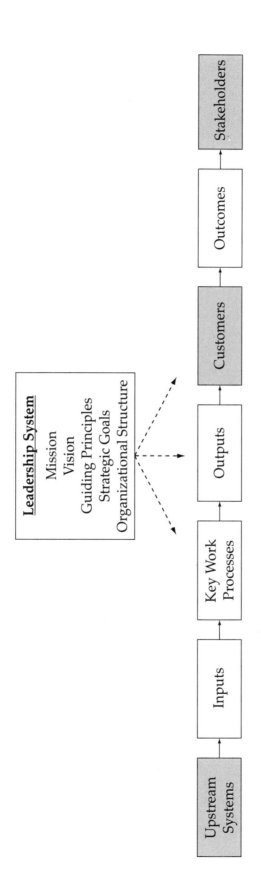

Source: Adapted from Sink and Tuttle, 1989.

External system elements have the potential of significantly affecting an organization's capacity. Therefore, like internal system elements, they present additional opportunities for measuring organizational performance. We shall examine each in turn.

Upstream Systems

There are three types of external and internal upstream systems important to assessment: suppliers, constraining systems, and service partners. Figure 3.2 illustrates that upstream systems supply, constrain, and serve their downstream systems. Supplier and constraining systems affect the quality and quantity of inputs the system requires to perform work and create outputs.

Suppliers

Upstream suppliers provide essential products, services, and information required of organizations to perform work and create outputs for customers. Graduate schools that prepare faculty and staff, businesses that supply equipment, and contractors who build buildings are examples of important external suppliers operating upstream of organizations in higher education. Academic departments are important internal suppliers of academic advising centers because they supply current program-specific rules and regulations advisers pass along to students.

To ensure quality service from suppliers, many educational leaders create partnerships that specify roles and responsibilities of both partners and ensure that both partners benefit equally from the partnership. This is more common with external suppliers than with internal suppliers. Vendor certification programs, business-education partnerships, articulation agreements, and consortiums are examples of common partnerships in higher education. As noted, successful partnerships are designed as win-win arrangements in which both partners benefit equally. For example, vendor certification programs ensure that certified vendors get their partner's future business so long as they maintain quality service and charge reasonable and fair prices. Business-education partnerships ensure that business partners receive specialized training for employees in exchange for donated equipment or jobs for program graduates.

Assessors monitor costs and benefits of these important partnerships as a form of quality control of upstream systems to make sure that partnerships continue to deliver intended benefits at reasonable costs to both partners. (Measuring the impact of supplier systems on organizational performance is discussed in greater detail in Chapter Five.) Exhibits 3.1 and 3.2 provide examples of supplier systems for an academic department and for Information Services, respectively.

Figure 3.2
Upstream Systems

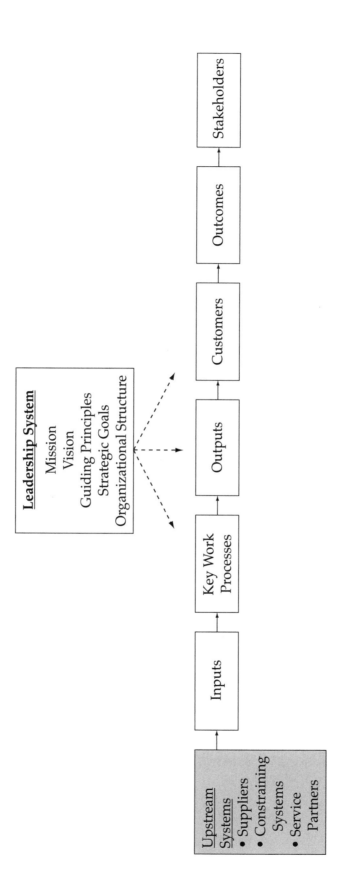

Source: Adapted from Sink and Tuttle, 1989.

Exhibit 3.1

Examples of Upstream Supplier Systems for an Academic Department

- Graduate schools providing faculty
- Graduate schools determining new graduate student entrance requirements
- Vendors delivering and servicing equipment
- Professional associations providing professional development to faculty and staff
- Physical Plant Department cleaning and maintaining academic facilities
- Information Services installing and repairing computers
- Payroll Office withholding taxes and disbursing paychecks and paystubs
- Human Resources supporting employee searches and personnel management
- Sponsored Research Office helping faculty develop grant proposals and manage grant projects and funds

Exhibit 3.2

Examples of Upstream Supplier Systems for Information Services

- Schools, colleges, universities, and other organizations educating and training technical staff
- Vendors providing hardware, software, consultation, and services
- Vendors and professional associations providing professional development to technical staff
- Energy companies providing power
- Physical Plant Department cleaning and maintaining facilities
- Payroll Office withholding taxes and disbursing paychecks and paystubs
- Human Resources supporting employee searches and personnel management

Constraining Systems

Upstream constraining systems place limits on downstream systems by establishing parameters for what they can offer, resources they can have, customers they can serve, methods they can use, prices they can charge, and so forth. Like suppliers, constraining systems exist both outside and inside the institution.

State legislatures and governing boards are examples of external constraining systems that restrict organizational operating and capital budgets and determine which programs and degrees institutions can offer. Governmental agencies are also external constraining systems because they determine who gets financial aid, grants, and contracts; they also enact laws, codes, and regulations that establish parameters of what and how work can be performed and how resources can be used. Accrediting bodies are constraining systems because they set performance standards for accreditation.

Senior leaders are internal constraining systems to lower-level organizations because they set direction, allocate resources, and create policies and procedures that establish local standards about who performs which jobs and how; they also determine compensation and benefits for employees who work in the system. (Measuring the impact of constraining systems on organizational performance is discussed in greater detail in Chapter Five.) Exhibits 3.3 and 3.4 provide examples of upstream constraining systems for an academic department and for Information Services, respectively.

Exhibit 3.3

Examples of Upstream Constraining Systems
for an Academic Department

- Accrediting organizations determining institutional and program standards and criteria
- State governing boards determining which programs and degrees can be offered at what price
- Governmental agencies setting research agendas; awarding grants, contracts, and student financial aid; and setting safety standards
- Senior leaders clarifying institutional mission, vision, guiding principles, strategic goals, and organizational structure
- Senior leaders allocating operating and capital funds, setting personnel policies, and allocating teaching positions
- Facilities Planning Office determining renovations and new construction of classrooms, labs, and research facilities

Exhibit 3.4

Examples of Upstream Constraining Systems for Information Services

- Accrediting organizations determining institutional and program standards and criteria related to technology infrastructure and service
- Vendors, professional associations, and other organizations setting national and statewide technology standards
- Senior leaders clarifying institutional mission, vision, guiding principles, strategic goals, and organizational structure
- Senior leaders allocating operating and capital funds, setting personnel policies, and allocating staff positions
- Accrediting organizations determining institutional and program standards and criteria
- Facilities Planning Office determining renovations and new construction of IS-related facilities

Service Partners

Service partners complement an organization's operations by serving its customers before or during their experience in the organizational system. Service partners are important upstream systems because they affect an organization's performance through their influence on the organization's customers. For example, high schools and community colleges are external service partners to four-year institutions because they prepare entering students. High schools and community colleges affect the four-year institution's performance by contributing to the quality of entering freshmen and transfers. They are also constraining systems when they influence student choice decisions about where to apply and which schools to attend.

Internal service partners are important to the performance success of academic organizations because they have a major influence on student learning. Internal service partners of academic departments are campus libraries, tutoring centers, academic advising centers, and other student services that directly support student learning.

Service partners for administrative offices are unique to the organization's mission. For example, an important service partner to the admissions office is the financial aid office, which determines award packages for student applicants. Important service partners for Information Services are departmental technical computing staff who train and support end users using IS technology. (Measuring the impact of service partners on organizational performance is discussed in greater detail in Chapter Five.) Exhibits 3.5 and 3.6 provide examples of upstream service partners for an academic department and for Information Services, respectively.

Because organizational capacity (and eventually performance) depends so much on the performance of upstream systems, as illustrated in the vignette about the Chemistry Department, organizations create and monitor partnerships with major upstream systems such as vendor certification programs and articulation agreements, as noted earlier. High-performing organizations are not only selective in determining which partnerships to create but also skillful at monitoring the partnership's impact on the organization's capacity to perform. For example, assessors monitor costs and benefits of important partnerships and analyze the quality and quantity of resources (and constraints) upstream partners provide to the system.

Organizations tend to create less formal partnerships with internal upstream systems; however, they are wise to foster good relations and build ongoing communication structures with upstream systems that directly affect their organization's capacity to perform. The vignette about a faculty member trying to teach an upper-division chemistry course in a classroom fraught with problems is an example

Exhibit 3.5

Examples of Upstream Service Partner Systems
for an Academic Department

- Feeder schools preparing entering freshmen, transfers, and graduate students (high schools, community colleges, undergraduate schools)
- Other academic departments providing general education and elective courses to department majors
- Centers, institutes, and governmental agencies providing research data sets
- Libraries providing study space, reference services, books, serials, and networks supporting student learning
- Information Services providing technology training to students
- Academic, personal, and career counselors advising, counseling, and placing students
- Housing office housing students
- Food service feeding students
- Bookstore providing books and supplies to students

Exhibit 3.6

Examples of Upstream Service Partner Systems
for Information Services

- Departmental computing support staff providing training and technical support to end users
- Vendors and professional associations providing technical training to end users

of how important it is for the Chemistry Department to build good relations with the Physical Plant and Information Services departments, which maintain, furnish, and equip their classrooms. Formal and informal partnerships provide many opportunities for organizational systems to interact with and influence their external environments, a factor important to the survival and success of all open systems.

Worksheet 3.1 will help assessors identify their unit's upstream systems.

Customers

Customers are the reasons why an organization exists. In assessment, customers are defined as the groups or individuals who directly receive or experience the organization's outputs. It is the customers' preferences and requirements, along with input from stakeholders and senior leaders, faculty, and staff, that define what the organization creates and how it creates and delivers its products and services. It is the response of customers as they interact with an organization's outputs that determines the degree to which organizations achieve their intended outcomes.

This definition of customers—persons and organizations who directly receive or experience an organization's products and services—is important in assessment because it identifies those preferences and perceptions that serve as reference points for evaluating output quality and customer satisfaction. Dissatisfied customers not only go elsewhere for service (when they can) but also complain loudly to stakeholders, other customers, and upstream systems that can affect an organization's future capacity to perform.

Organizations have potential and present customers; they also have external and internal customers. External customers are outside both the institution and the unit of analysis. Internal customers are inside the institution but outside the unit of analysis. Both external and internal customers have specific and changing preferences and requirements that the organization must understand and meet (or, in the case of performance excellence, exceed) through the products and services it supplies. The identification of customer preferences and perceptions and the assessment of output quality and customer satisfaction against those preferences and perceptions are very important components of an organization's assessment program. Figure 3.3 illustrates that customers receiving system outputs enable the system to achieve its intended outcomes.

External Customers

External customers are people and organizations the organization serves that reside outside the institution. External customers, by definition, are customers only when they directly receive or experience the organization's outputs. Using this definition, external customers of academic organizations are patrons attending events; the general public attending noncredit workshops and lectures; organizations sponsoring research; and governmental agencies, educational institutions, and businesses contracting for services. For purposes of assessment, currently enrolled students are defined as internal, not external, customers. Alumni are defined as stakeholders.

External customers of administrative organizations vary according to their mission. For example, the external customers of an admissions office and athletics departments are the potential students they are recruiting. External customers of the registrar's office are governmental agencies receiving enrollment statistics and alumni seeking

Figure 3.3
Customers

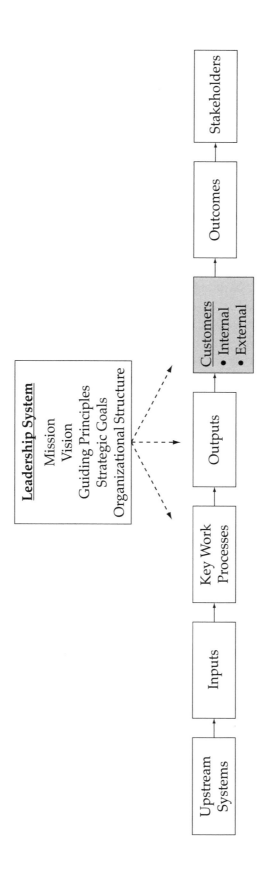

Source: Adapted from Sink and Tuttle, 1989.

transcripts after graduation. External customers of the purchasing office are vendors seeking purchase orders. External customers of the development office are potential donors. External customers of Information Services are businesses contracting for IS computing services.

Internal Customers

Internal customers, unlike external customers, are people and organizations the organization serves that reside inside the institution. Using this definition, internal customers of academic organizations are students currently enrolled in courses, colleagues and administrative staff receiving recommendations and decisions from faculty committees, and faculty and staff attending departmental events as patrons.

The primary customers of most administrative organizations are internal customers. For example, the primary customers of the registrar's office are students who register for class and who receive the schedule of classes, grade reports, and transcripts. The primary customers of the purchasing office are offices and departments seeking purchase orders. The primary customers of the academic advising center are students receiving academic advice. The primary internal customers of Information Services are faculty, staff, and student end users.

Students as Inputs, Customers, and Stakeholders

It should be noted that in assessment, potential, current, and past students represent three types of system elements: inputs, customers, and stakeholders. Figure 3.4 shows these relationships.

Students as Inputs.   Current students enrolled in classes represent inputs as described in Chapter Two for two important reasons: they play an active role in teaching and learning, and they must meet specific qualifications and readiness standards like other critical resources.

Students as Customers.   Potential students represent external customers of organizations for admissions offices and athletic departments that recruit them. Current students enrolled in courses represent internal customers of academic and administrative organizations because they are admitted and therefore part of the institution; they directly engage in program-based learning opportunities; they directly receive and experience academic and administrative support services; their preferences, expectations, and requirements (along with stakeholders and system personnel) drive design and delivery of curricula, pedagogy, and administrative support services; and their preferences, expectations, and requirements present reference points for evaluating output quality and customer satisfaction.

Figure 3.4
Students as Inputs, Customers, and Stakeholders

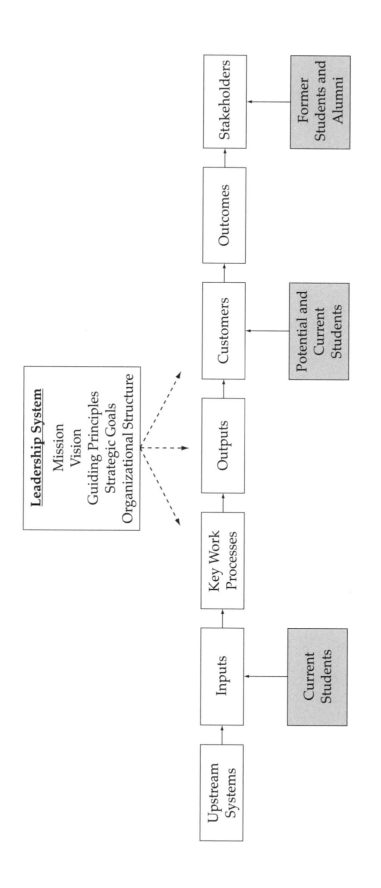

Source: Adapted from Sink and Tuttle, 1989.

Students as Stakeholders. Past students, including alumni, are external stakeholders (the reasons will be explained shortly). They are stakeholders because they have a stake in, depend on, and benefit from the continued success of the institution and its programs. Enrolled students are internal stakeholders for many administrative organizations because they benefit from organizational effectiveness.

Exhibits 3.7 and 3.8 offer examples of internal and external customers for an academic department and for Information Services, respectively. (Measuring customer satisfaction is discussed in greater detail in Chapter Five.)

Worksheet 3.2 will help assessors identify their unit's internal and external customers.

Exhibit 3.7

Examples of Internal and External Customers
for an Academic Department

External	Internal
▪ Potential students being recruited	▪ Current students registered and enrolled in credit and noncredit classes
▪ General public attending lectures and symposia	▪ Colleagues and staff receiving committee recommendations and decisions
▪ Patrons attending departmental events	▪ Faculty, staff, and students attending events as patrons
▪ Research sponsors	▪ Registrar's office receiving grades and class schedule data
▪ Individuals and organizations contracting for services	▪ Libraries receiving faculty recommendations for books
▪ Professional organizations publishing books and journals	▪ Academic advisers receiving program-specific rules and requirements

Exhibit 3.8

Examples of Internal and External Customers
for Information Services

External	Internal
▪ General public using e-mail, Web sites, and other computing services	▪ Faculty, staff, and current student end users
▪ Businesses and organizations contracting for computing services (such as bill printing)	

Stakeholders

Stakeholders are broadly defined as individuals and groups who have a stake in, depend on, and benefit from organizational effectiveness—the achievement of intended outcomes. At the institutional level, stakeholders refer to the general public and local, state, and national governments, organizations, and businesses that benefit from an educated public, skilled workforce, and creation and transfer of new knowledge. At the academic or administrative department level, stakeholders are specific groups who directly benefit from departmental outcome achievement. Stakeholders operate from a downstream position in the system, as illustrated in Figure 3.5.

Stakeholders are downstream systems that depend on upstream systems to succeed. From the perspective of stakeholders, organizations operating upstream provide important, often critical resources and services they require to succeed. For example, one stakeholder of academic departments is employers who hire department graduates. Employers are stakeholders because they depend on departments to prepare future workers so that the employers can meet business needs. In assessment, stakeholders, like employers, are not considered customers because they do not directly engage in learning. Employers are not considered upstream systems because in this context they are not supplying, constraining, or serving the department. Rather, they are depending on the organization to prepare their future workforce. Some academic departments whose funding depends on student placement rates actively seek feedback from employers not only about their satisfaction but also about their workforce needs, preferences, and expectations.

In general, academic departments have more external stakeholders than administrative organizations because intended outcomes of academic organizations are more closely aligned with institutional missions. For example, external stakeholders of academic departments are people and organizations outside the institution that benefit from an educated public, an educated workforce, and the creation and transfer of new knowledge. An example of an internal stakeholder of an academic department is another academic department that benefits from service courses provided to its majors that meet general education requirements.

Stakeholders of administrative organizations are generally quite different from stakeholders of academic organizations due to their different missions. In fact, most stakeholders of administrative organizations are customers of their internal customers. For example, stakeholders of the admissions office are academic departments that depend on admissions to attract their future customers—qualified

Figure 3.5
Stakeholders

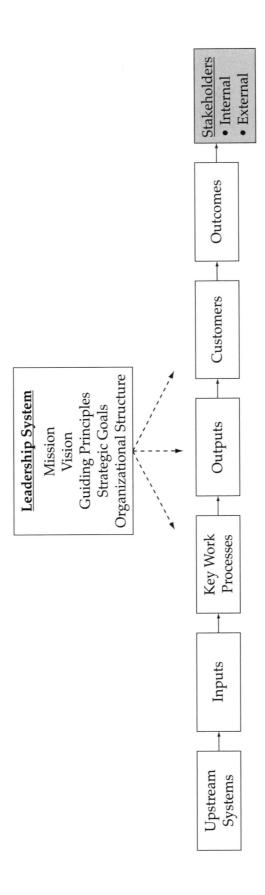

Source: Adapted from Sink and Tuttle, 1989.

students. Stakeholders of the financial aid office are academic departments who depend on that office to provide aid to their student customers. Stakeholders of Information Services are students benefiting from IS-supported technology used by the registrar's office, financial aid office, and other administrative organizations that are internal customers of Information Services. Students who benefit from faculty using IS-supported technology in teaching are also important Information Services stakeholders.

Assessors seeking to identify their organization's important stakeholders begin by asking, Who depends on this organization? Who benefits from this organization's successful achievement of intended outcomes and strategic goals? Not all stakeholders are equally important to the performance success of an organization. But the ones that are present another opportunity to assess organizational performance in terms of stakeholder satisfaction. (Measuring stakeholder satisfaction is discussed in greater detail in Chapter Five.) Exhibits 3.9 and 3.10 offer examples of important internal and external stakeholders for an academic department and for Information Services, respectively.

Worksheet 3.3 will help assessors identify their unit's internal and external stakeholders.

Exhibit 3.9

Examples of Internal and External Stakeholders
for an Academic Department

External	Internal
▪ Employers hiring department graduates	▪ Other academic departments whose majors enroll in courses to fulfill General Education requirements
▪ Four-year schools admitting department majors as transfer students	▪ Other academic and administrative organizations receiving funds and positions supported directly or indirectly through externally sponsored research in this department
▪ Graduate schools admitting department grads	
▪ Alumni and former students enrolled in graduate school or transfer institutions	
▪ Businesses directly benefiting from application of new knowledge	

Exhibit 3.10
Examples of Internal and External Stakeholders
for Information Services

External	Internal
[None]	▪ Students benefiting from academic and administrative support organizations using IS-supported technology
	▪ Employees benefiting from Human Resource and payroll departments using IS-supported technology

Summary

This chapter described three important external system elements that exist outside the unit of analysis but inside or outside the institution: upstream systems that operate as suppliers, constraining systems, and service providers; customers; and stakeholders. These system elements provide structured opportunities for the organizational system to interact with its environment, a factor critical to survival for open systems. External system elements serve important functions for a system, exist in unique relationships with the system, and potentially affect the system's capacity to perform. Examples were provided for both academic and administrative organizations. Worksheets were provided to help assessors identify external system elements of organizations whose performance they intend to measure.

Worksheet 3.1
Upstream Systems Analysis

Unit of Analysis: _____ *(Example: Chemistry Department)*

Today's Date: _____

Use this worksheet to describe the unit's major external and internal upstream systems. Describe major suppliers in column A, and describe what each supplier supplies in column B. Be sure to consider suppliers of all types of inputs listed in Worksheet 2.7. Describe major constraining systems in column C and describe what each constrains in column D. Describe major service partners in column E and describe services each partner provides to the unit's customers in column F.

Suppliers (A)	What Is Supplied? (B)	Constraining Systems (C)	What Is Constrained? (D)	Service Partners (E)	What Service Is Provided? (F)
Example: Chemistry lab equipment manufacturers	*Example:* Equipment for teaching and research labs	*Example:* State Board of Regents	*Example:* Programs and degrees the Chemistry Department can offer	*Example:* Other academic departments	*Example:* General education and elective courses for chemistry majors

Worksheet 3.2
Customers Analysis

Unit of Analysis: _____ *(Example: Chemistry Department)*

Today's Date: _____

Use this worksheet to describe the unit's major external and internal customers. In column A, list the unit's outputs described for each key work process in Worksheet 2.8. For each output, describe major customers in column B and check column C or D to indicate whether the customer is external or internal to the institution. In column E, summarize customer quality needs and expectations for each type of output. Finally, in column F, using a scale of 1 (least important) to 5 (most important), rate the overall importance of each customer to the unit.

Outputs (A)	Customer (B)	External (C)	Internal (D)	Customer Needs and Expectations of Output Quality (E)	Rating of Overall Importance to Unit (F)
Example for research: Research deliverable (new polymer for dentistry)	*Example:* NSF, the research sponsor	*Example:* ✔	*Example:*	*Example:* On-time delivery of a new polymer that meets or exceeds project specifications and requirements	*Example:* 5
Example for teaching: Upper-division chemistry courses	*Example:* Chemistry majors	*Example:*	*Example:* ✔	*Example:* ▪ Courses cover material required to pass the chemistry exit exam ▪ Faculty start and end classes on time ▪ Classrooms and labs are well equipped, comfortable, and conducive to learning ▪ Faculty are prepared for class ▪ Faculty grade exams, homework, and papers in a fair and timely manner	*Example:* 5

Worksheet 3.3
  Stakeholders Analysis

Unit of Analysis: _____ *(Example: Chemistry Department)*

Today's Date: _____

Use this worksheet to describe the unit's important external and internal stakeholders. In column A, list all of the unit's important external and internal stakeholders. Check column B or C to indicate whether the stakeholder is external and internal to the institution. In column D, describe what is at stake for each stakeholder, and in column E, describe what is at stake for the unit. Finally, in column F, on a scale of 1 (least important) to 5 (most important), rate the overall importance of each stakeholder to the unit.

Stakeholder (A)	External (B)	Internal (C)	What Is at Stake for This Stakeholder? (D)	What Is at Stake for the Unit? (E)	Rating of Overall Importance to Unit (F)
Example: Ace Chemicals, Inc., a company that regularly hires chemistry graduates	*Example:* ✔	*Example:*	*Example:* • Quality of Ace Chemicals' entry-level workforce • Company competitiveness	*Example:* Chemistry Department will not be able to place future graduates with this employer, which can diminish the reputation of the university and future departmental resources (such as donated equipment)	*Example:* 4
Example: English Department	*Example:*	*Example:* ✔	*Example:* English majors meet general education requirements	*Example:* • Enrollments supporting chemistry service courses • English majors who are scientifically literate citizens • Reciprocal English service courses that help chemistry majors meet their general education requirements	*Example:* 4

CHAPTER 4

Assessment Methods and Terminology

This chapter explores assessment methods and terminology underlying a well-conceived assessment program. It is about how to measure performance, not what to measure—that discussion is in Chapter Five. This chapter examines methods for and issues associated with measuring, evaluating, and conveying organizational performance results.

An understanding of assessment begins with a discussion of the differences between measurement and evaluation. In practice, assessment is the combined process of measuring, evaluating, and conveying performance results of a particular unit of analysis over a set period of time for a specified assessment user group. The discussion begins with measurement.

Measurement

Performance at the organizational level is operationalized through measurement. Without measurement, performance cannot be evaluated. To measure organizational performance, assessors must first clarify boundaries of the unit whose performance is to be assessed and time frames during which performance will be measured. Next, they build a family of performance indicators to measure multiple areas of organizational performance, beginning with areas deemed critical to the unit's overall performance success and survival. Finally, they collect data using a variety of methods and convey performance results within the context of reference points in reports for assessment users to evaluate.

Unit of Analysis

An organization whose performance is under review is defined as a "unit of analysis." As noted in Chapter One, a unit of analysis can be an organizational unit such as the institution as a whole, or it can be a college such as the College of Arts and Sciences, a school such as a law school or medical school, a department such as the Chemistry Department, a program such as General Education or Writing Across the Curriculum, or an administrative office such as admissions or the registrar's office.

In assessment, units of analysis must have clear boundaries. Units can be organizational units whose boundaries are delineated by budgetary and personnel structures. Or they can be programs or processes that operate within an organizational unit or across organizational units. Whether the unit is an organization, a program, or a process, assessors must always clarify boundaries and consistently apply those boundaries as they measure, evaluate, and convey performance results.

Assessors define unit boundaries in many ways, depending on the purpose of the assessment effort. Boundaries of cross-functional processes usually begin with a request for a product or service and end after products and services are received or experienced by customers. Boundaries are also defined on the following bases:

- Types of customers, stakeholders, or suppliers
- Types of programs, products, or services offered
- Definitions prescribed in accreditation standards or reporting requirement of organizations that rank, classify, and otherwise judge

Time Frame

In assessment, the time frame is the period during which performance occurs. The performance time frame can be a week, a month, a year, or several years. It is important when making comparisons to measure and evaluate performance representing the same time frame.

Performance Indicators

Assessors use performance indicators to measure organizational performance. Performance indicators can be quantitative or qualitative, direct or indirect, soft or hard, objective or subjective, and leading or lag indicators. According to Borden and Bottrill (1994), performance indicators are similar to descriptive statistics in that they lack worth when viewed by themselves. To be evaluated, performance measured through performance indicators must be compared to reference points. Also, performance indicators do not necessarily convey information about causation.

Carl Thor (1993) advocates using a family of performance indicators to form a balanced composite of an organization's overall performance picture. This balanced composite offers an effective means to articulate and communicate strategies and operational goals, convey priorities, and monitor and compare results. Kaplan and Norton (1996) argue that the most powerful performance indicators are linked to strategic goals (as discussed in Chapter Two). They also claim that the process of identifying performance indicators and reference points helps senior leaders clarify strategies and increase support from everyone involved in and affected by impending change.

When measuring student learning, Palomba and Banta (1999) distinguish direct from indirect performance indicators. Direct performance indicators are derived from student demonstrations of knowledge and skills, such as test scores and grades on presentations and classroom assignments. Indirect performance indicators are derived from students' reflections on their learning, captured through surveys and structured interviews.

Chapter Five provides many examples of indicators in the seven operational areas of organizational performance: effectiveness, productivity, quality, efficiency, customer and stakeholder satisfaction, innovation, and financial durability. Each area of organizational performance is linked to external or internal elements of the organizational system described in Chapters Two and Three. For example, productivity is defined in Chapter Five as a ratio of outputs created to inputs consumed by the system. Examples of performance indicators that measure productivity in academic departments are number of course credit or contact hours taught per teaching faculty FTE, cost to develop new courses and programs, and number of grant proposals submitted or articles submitted for publication per faculty FTE. Examples of performance indicators that measure productivity of an administrative office for Information Services include cost to repair a desktop or laptop computer and number of help desk calls received and served per help desk staff FTE. Chapter Five offers many examples of performance indicators in all seven areas of organizational performance.

Kaplan and Norton (1996) differentiate leading from lag performance indicators. Leading indicators are performance drivers that provide early indication of whether a strategy is being implemented successfully. Examples of leading performance indicators are cycle time and cost for a key work process and the qualifications of faculty or technical staff. Lag indicators, by contrast, are generic, core measures of outcome achievement. Performance indicators such as "percentage of graduates obtaining field-related jobs within the first three months after graduation" and "percentage of graduates admitted to graduate school" are lag indicators measuring goal achievement. The organization's family of performance indicators, which Kaplan and Norton call a "balanced scorecard," should be a mix of both leading and lag indicators tied to strategies.

Critical Success Factors

As mentioned earlier, a good assessment program uses a family of performance indicators to measure multiple areas of organizational performance. A family of performance indicators begins in areas deemed critical to the unit's overall performance success and survival. These areas are known as "critical success factors." Critical success factors are mission-specific and therefore unique to each unit of analysis; factors that are critical to the success of one unit may not be critical to another.

Critical success factors play an important role in the design of assessment programs. Assessors use critical success factors to inform the selection of areas of performance to measure. They also use critical success factors to prevent information overload by reminding them to focus on what is critical and not necessarily on what is easy to measure. All organizational constituents must agree on which factors are critical to the success of the organization early in the assessment process.

Critical success factors for organizations in higher education have evolved over time. Some reflect emerging environmental factors or current political "hot spots"; others reflect the unit's centrality to the institution's mission. Critical success factors in some academic departments reflect the unit's need to maintain high national ranking,

Exhibit 4.1

Examples of Critical Success Factors for an Academic Department

- Program accreditation
- High national reputation and ranking
- High student placement rates
- Highly qualified faculty and staff
- Stable or increasing student demand
- Highly qualified undergraduate and graduate students in the major
- High-quality academic and research resources (classrooms, labs, technology, and library)
- Centrality to the institution's instructional mission

Exhibit 4.2
Examples of Critical Success Factors for Information Services

- Reliable equipment and networks
- Rapid response time for service and consultation
- Highly skilled, competent, and experienced staff
- Highly satisfied customers and stakeholders
- Adequate capital funding to purchase technology
- High-quality processes for purchasing, delivering, and installing equipment

while others reflect the need to maintain high placement rates linked to funding formulas.

Critical success factors are always framed by the unit's mission-specific vision of performance excellence, its strategic goals, and its unique set of guiding principles. Exhibits 4.1 and 4.2 offer examples of critical success factors for an academic department and for Information Services, respectively.

Worksheet 4.1 will help assessors identify their unit's critical success factors.

Evaluation

Assessment, as noted earlier, is the combined process of measuring, evaluating, and conveying performance results. Assessment users evaluate organizational performance, as discussed in Chapter One. Assessors enhance their ability to evaluate performance by framing performance results within the context of reference points, sometimes as a gap analysis.

Reference Points

To enhance evaluation, assessors present performance results within a context of reference points aligned with organizational mission, vision, and strategic goals. Many educational leaders make the mistake of assuming that all members of the organizational community, including stakeholders, share a common understanding of performance expectations. Reference points clarify performance expectations and set the context for evaluating performance results.

Exhibit 4.3 offers examples of reference points for evaluating the performance of academic and administrative organizations in higher education.

Exhibit 4.3
Examples of Reference Points

- Degree of centrality to institutional and instructional mission and core competencies
- Purpose as expressed in the unit's mission
- Results articulated in the unit's vision statements
- Values, beliefs, and norms expressed in the unit's guiding principles
- Goals expressed in the unit's strategic plans (market share, increased quality and effectiveness, and so forth)
- Past performance over time
- Planned versus actual performance
- Curricula and other requirements
- Accreditation standards and criteria
- Laws, regulations, guidelines, codes, policies, procedures
- Ranking criteria
- NCAA performance standards
- Carnegie Foundation classification requirements
- Professional licensure requirements
- Faculty research protocols
- Reputation and guidelines of refereed journals
- Performance of other organizations within the institution
- Performance of competitor organizations outside the institution
- Performance (benchmarks) of best-in-class organizations
- Performance preferences and perceptions of customers, stakeholders, faculty, staff, and senior leaders

Gap Analysis

Assessors use gap analysis to enhance evaluation of performance results. One purpose of gap analysis is to clarify gaps between actual performance and one or more reference points. Gap analysis is a particularly useful method for evaluating customer satisfaction, but it requires a detailed knowledge and understanding of customer preferences and perceptions.

Table 4.1 provides an example of a gap analysis to enhance evaluation of performance in the Registrar's Office. The performance indicator used is cycle time to post student grades at the end of each semester. In this example, the Registrar's Office announced it would post grades within five working days after the last scheduled final exam. Students at this school, however, prefer that the Registrar's Office post grades the same day as the last scheduled final exam. In addition, students hold a perception that even though the Registrar's Office says it will post grades within five days, it normally takes seven days. Finally, even though the Registrar's Office hopes and plans to post grades within five days after the final scheduled exam, its long-term goal is to post grades as fast as or better than the benchmark of one day after the last scheduled exam, established through discussions with colleagues at comparable institutions.

Table 4.1 is a matrix table designed to reveal performance gaps between actual performance and one or more reference points for specific performance indicators—in this case, cycle time to post grades each term. The table reveals that the Registrar's Office outperformed its own planned and announced goal by one day (see cell A). However, it fell four days short of student preferences (see cell B) and three days short of its benchmark (see cell C). The table also shows that even though students prefer to wait zero days for grades (see cell D) and the Registrar's Office actually posted grades one day earlier than it announced (see cell A), students still perceive the Registrar's Office as taking seven days to post grades (see cell E). Furthermore, a seven-day gap (see cell E) remains between the time when students would prefer to receive their grades and the time when they perceive they will receive their grades.

The analysis in Table 4.1 illustrates the importance of evaluating organizational performance against multiple reference points, including perspectives and preferences of the people the organization serves.

Data Collection

The collection of data for assessment purposes can be challenging and requires skill and patience. Numerous data collection issues affect an assessment program's credibility.

Data Credibility

Credibility of data is a major critical success factor for any high-quality assessment program. Data credibility is imperative for assessment to be effective and achieve its purpose. Many factors determine the credibility of assessment data. Some of these are reliability, validity, proper selection of participants, and timing.

Reliability

Assessment data are reliable when the same results occur, regardless of when the assessment occurs or who does the scoring. Reliability is a necessary but not sufficient condition for validity. There are many sources of reliability errors in assessment. According to Mark Shermis and Kathryn Daniels (2002), one of the major sources of reliability error is rater bias—the tendency of raters "to rate individuals or objects in an idiosyncratic way" (p. 150). These authors suggest that rater bias can be reduced through computer data collection strategies.

Table 4.1
Gap Analysis: Cycle Time for the Registrar's Posting of End-of-Term Grades (Number of Days After Last Scheduled Final Exam)

	Actual Results: 4 days	Organization's Planned, Announced Goals: 5 days	Customer Preference: 0 days	Customer Perceptions of Actual Performance: 7 days	Benchmark or Target Goal: 1 day
Actual Results: 4 days	4 days	+1 day (A)	−4 days (B)	+3 days	−3 days (C)
Organization's Planned, Announced Goals: 5 days	+1 day	5 days	−5 days	+2 days	−4 days
Customer Preference: 0 days	−4 days	−5 days	0 days (D)	−7 days	−1 day
Customer Perceptions of Actual Performance: 7 days	+3 days	+2 days	−7 days (E)	7 days	−6 days
Benchmark or Target Goal: 1 day	−3 days	−4 days	−1 day	−6 days	1 day

Validity

Assessment data are valid when they actually measure what they intend to measure. Shermis and Daniels (2002) define validity as the extent of the relationship between a performance indicator and the construct it measures. Evidence of construct validity is important when trying to establish that a performance indicator adequately measures some hypothetical construct, such as intelligence or anxiety; these constructs become real only when they are operationalized through scores from an assessment instrument. Validity is always a concern for locally designed tests.

Selection of Participants

Measurement in several areas of organizational performance, such as achievement of student learning outcomes and customer or stakeholder satisfaction, requires careful selection of participants, raising questions of how many participants should be selected and what methods should be used to select them. Gary Pike (2002) points out that the number of participants selected, data collection methods used, and research design all depend on the purpose of the assessment activity.

Timing

The jury is still out as to when data related to goal achievement, such as student learning, should be collected. For example, should assessors collect data during or after students complete their coursework or at both times? Should they collect alumni data at two, five, ten, or fifteen years out? If they collect data through longitudinal studies, how long should the study continue? When is the best time to assess student demonstration of critical thinking and reasoning skills?

Data Collection Methods

Assessors use a variety of methods to collect performance data at the organization, program, and process levels. The data collection methods they choose are based on the sources available to them, the types of data needed, and the overall design of their research.

Sources

For all practical purposes, assessors collect assessment data about organizational performance from three main sources:

- People, either directly or indirectly through others
- Databases, internal and external to the institution
- Documents, internal and external to the institution

Types of Assessment Data

Types of assessment data vary according to source. From people, assessors collect three types of data: attitudinal (knowledge, opinions, beliefs, values, and so forth), behavioral (skills and abilities), and characteristics or traits. From internal databases, assessors collect descriptive data about institutional resources; from external databases, assessors collect comparable and benchmark data. From internal and external documents, assessors collect a wide range of performance data.

Methods

As just noted, assessors use a variety of direct and indirect methods to collect data, depending on the types of data needed, the sources available to them, and the overall research design. Direct methods require assessors to collect data directly from people whose attitudes, knowledge, characteristics, and behaviors are important to assessment; indirect methods require assessors to seek data already collected by others that may or may not have been collected for purposes of assessment.

Direct Methods.   There are several direct methods that assessors use to collect assessment data at the organizational, program, and process levels. Direct methods used by assessors collect attitudinal and behavioral data directly from people. For example, assessors gather attitudinal data from employees, students, and stakeholders using self-reporting methods, such as surveys, structured and open interviews, focus groups, and journals, in order to understand employee, student, and stakeholder needs, perceptions, and levels of satisfaction. Direct methods are also used to document student behavior through periodic and end-of-program exit and licensure examinations, presentations, demonstrations, performances, and portfolios to measure the levels of knowledge, skills, and abilities of individuals who complete various programs.

Indirect Methods.   Using indirect methods, assessors seek data already gathered by others that may or may not have been collected for purposes of assessment. The most common methods are querying databases, analyzing documents, and surveying other people who have opinions or access to performance data.

Querying Databases.   Assessors query databases housed inside and outside the institution. From institutional and departmental databases, assessors collect the following types of descriptive data about institutional resources:

- Employees (present and past)

    Qualifications and credentials

    Demographics and characteristics

    Marital and family status

    Employment history (job title and workload)

    Compensation and benefits

    Leave (sick and vacation) accrued and used
- Students (potential, current, past)

    Demographic, socioeconomic, and geographical characteristics

    Residential status (in-state or out-of-state, native or foreign, on-campus or off-campus)

    Marital and family status

    Financial aid

Previous academic work

Program of study

Current academic status (matriculated or nonmatriculated, undergraduate or graduate, upper-division or lower-division, at-risk or not)

Grades

Course load (enrolled, completed, withdrawn, incomplete)

Degrees awarded

- Donors

Demographic, socioeconomic, and geographical characteristics

Prior association with institution

Donations

- Financial assets (revenues, by type and source; expenditures, by account and line item)

- Equipment and supplies (by type, dollar value, age, and location)

- Physical plant assets (amount, usage, age, and condition)

- Energy data (amount, cost, usage)

Assessors also query external databases, such as national databases like IPEDS (described in Chapter One), state databases, regional databases, and professional association databases (such as the National Association of College and University Business Officers and AAUP). They query external databases primarily to collect comparative and benchmark data.

Analyzing Internal and External Documents.   Assessors also collect data by analyzing internal and external documents. These documents supply a rich variety of important organizational performance data, such as the following:

- Allegations and sanctions against the organization (and people in the organization) for violations of laws, regulations, and legal codes

- Allegations and sanctions against the organization (and people in the organization) for noncompliance with standards, criteria, and requirements (such as those of accreditors, AAUP, and NCAA)

- Allegations and sanctions against the organization (and people in the organization) for noncompliance with institutional and departmental policies, procedures, and codes of ethics

- Lawsuits, crimes, strikes and slowdowns, grievances, complaints, injuries, and sick leave
- Awards and recognitions to people and organizations for outstanding performance
- Recorded complaints by customers, employees, and stakeholders
- Personnel management decisions: promotions, demotions, terminations, and tenure decisions
- Reputations and rankings of people and organizations
- Participation and attendance data
- Past performance data from audits, NCAA reports, program review reports, accreditation self-studies, committee reports, and feasibility studies
- Projected performance data in plans, budgets, and proposals
- Creative changes put into place as reported in individual and collective annual reports

Surveying Others.   Finally, assessors collect data by surveying other people who have opinions or access to performance data that may or may not have been collected for purposes of assessment. For example, assessors collect data from peers to determine their perceptions of quality and from employees who interact daily with customers and stakeholders to determine employee perceptions of customer satisfaction.

Quantitative and Qualitative Methods.   The selection of data collection methods is based on whether a quantitative or qualitative design has been selected for the research. Pike (2002) explains that quantitative research uses experimental, quasi-experimental, or correlational designs. Palomba and Banta (1999) note that quantitative research yields numbers generated from statistical analysis, whereas qualitative research yields direct quotations, descriptions, and excerpts generated from fieldwork.

Erwin and Wise (2002) suggest that qualitative methods provide a valuable complement to quantitative methods. They claim that qualitative studies are ideal for discovery and provide the best information for understanding which educational interventions work best, particularly when researchers do not know enough to formulate hypotheses for quantitative studies. Pike (2002) claims that a quantitative approach is more appropriate for assessing levels of student satisfaction and amounts of change in student learning, but a qualitative approach, where leaders use participant observation, grounded theory, and critical incidents, is more appropriate for assessing the nature of students' experiences.

Patton (2002), who has written extensively on qualitative methods, explains that data for qualitative analyses typically come from fieldwork in which a researcher "spends time in the setting under study—a program, an organization, a community, or wherever situations of importance to a study can be observed, people interviewed, and documents analyzed" (p. 4). He explains that qualitative data grow out of three types of qualitative data collection methods: in-depth, open-ended interviews; direct observations; and written documents. Interviews produce direct quotations from people about experiences, opinions, feelings, and knowledge. Observations yield detailed descriptions of people's activities, behaviors, actions, and observable interpersonal interactions and organizational processes. Document analyses yield excerpts from written materials, publications, diaries, letters, artistic works, photographs, and memorabilia that record and preserve context. The validity and reliability of qualitative measures largely depend on the methodological skill, sensitivity, and integrity of the researcher. Therefore, useful and credible qualitative findings require discipline, knowledge, training, practice, creativity, and hard work.

According to Patton (2002), well-conceived qualitative methods require a strategy or overall direction that provides a framework for decision making and action. John Creswell (1998) describes five common traditions or strategic themes in qualitative research: biography, phenomenology, grounded theory, ethnography, and case studies.

Qualitative data can be presented alone or in combination with quantitative data. Many assessors combine approaches to provide a full understanding of organizational performance.

Technology in Assessment.   Technology is an important data collection tool in assessment. Commercial testing services and licensure examiners use Web-based examinations to collect and disseminate student achievement data. Shermis and Daniels (2002) suggest that a growing number of faculty are using computer-based testing through multimedia, Web-based surveys and electronic portfolios to assess student learning outcomes. Erwin and Wise (2002) believe that multimedia formats, quicker feedback, and decision rules for test item presentation (such as computerized adaptive testing) are emerging technologies offering new possibilities for faculty engaged in student assessment.

At the organization, program, and process levels, assessors use technology to collect performance data for administrators and managers who use assessment for quality control, as described in Chapter One. Administrators and managers use specialized software to monitor and control financial and nonfinancial aspects of organizational performance. They use technology to track technical computer problems, requests for service, computer and network usage and outages, equipment reliability, donor activities, payroll errors, breaches of security, admissions yield rates, and so forth. Libraries use technology to monitor usage and track location of their holdings. Academic advisers use technology to review student progress against stated goals.

Assessors also use technology to collect performance data for faculty and staff assessment users engaged in program and process improvement efforts, as described in Chapter One. For example, assessors working with program review and self-study committees use Web-based surveys to collect and process attitudinal data from students and employers, measure student outcomes achievement, and query descriptive data about organizational resources housed in institutional databases. Assessors also use technology for disseminating assessment findings, as described next.

Dissemination of Assessment Findings

Chapter One characterized external and internal assessment user groups as customers of the assessment program. Each assessment user group has a unique interest in performance results and generally uses assessment for different purposes. Each user group also has a preferred method and time frame for receiving assessment findings. A high-quality, robust assessment program delivers exactly what assessment users want and need, when they need it, and in the format they prefer. Senior leaders are responsible for identifying important assessment users and their unique needs, preferences, and expectations.

Formats and Channels

Assessors use a variety of formats and channels to convey performance results to assessment users. Some assessment users prefer personal, one-on-one informal presentations followed by written reports; others prefer formal or informal presentations with heavy documentation. Most users prefer reports that are succinctly written. Some prefer annotated results; others prefer graphics with or without data tables. Many people prefer graphic images because "a picture is worth a thousand words." Some users prefer hard copy to electronic format; others prefer information posted to the Web site or sent via e-mail. Some prefer reports framed as report cards; some prefer executive guides.

Report Cards

Report cards are like the dashboard of a car or airplane. Report cards present performance results in selected areas of organizational performance that convey a picture of the overall health and well-being of the unit for a specific time period. User groups determine what types of results they want to review in the report card, in what format, and how often. Report cards usually present performance results related to the unit's critical success factors.

Executive Guides

Executive guides represent an expansion of the report card and are often preferred by senior leaders. Executive guides typically require support from executive staff who routinely analyze issues emerging from planning and assessment activities. For example, executive guides often include analyses of strategic relationships and alternative outcomes of major issues facing the unit. They may also report sources of data and whether data are routinely reported externally and to whom. Finally, they may clarify assumptions, provide a more extensive analysis of the data, and explain related issues and possible solutions already in place.

Timeliness of Assessment Reports

High-quality assessment programs make assessment reports available to users exactly when they prefer them. This sounds almost impossible, but many assessment users make important decisions on a regular basis, providing a somewhat predictable timetable for assessors. For example, annual or biannual planning and budgeting cycles, accreditation schedules, annual publication dates, scheduled program review cycles, annual performance management cycles for personnel, and official athletic seasons offer assessors guidelines for the timing of assessment reports.

Many assessment user groups make decisions based on annual cycles. However, in higher education, annual cycles are very complex. For example, faculty generally operate on an academic year beginning in August or September and ending in June or July; however, continuing education and many technical programs operate on a twelve-month cycle, beginning and ending classes whenever it is convenient for students and employers. Official athletic seasons begin and end at specified but sometimes overlapping periods throughout the year. The fiscal year usually begins July 1 and ends June 30; however, tax schedules are based on calendar years beginning January 1 and ending December 31. The federal government's fiscal year (for grants and contracts) begins October 1 even though most faculty, who are funded in part or entirely by federal grants and contracts, typically start work a month or two earlier.

Worksheet 4.2 will help assessors schedule major assessment reports for each important assessment user group identified on Worksheet 1.1.

Confidentiality

Because assessment delves into many sensitive aspects of organizational operations, assessment results must be disseminated prudently. Like data credibility and timeliness of reports, confidentiality is a critical success factor for a high-quality assessment program. Assessors must ensure at the beginning of any new assessment initiative that everyone has a clear understanding of who gets what, when, and how. And they must honor those understandings to maintain integrity of the program and ensure its survival over the long run.

Summary

This chapter explored assessment terminology and methods. It explained how the measurement of organizational performance is operationalized through performance indicators. Assessors can use a variety of types of performance indicators so long as they form a family of indicators, beginning with those related to areas critical to the organization's success. Assessment users evaluate performance by comparing actual performance against reference points aligned with the unit's mission, vision, guiding principles, strategic plans, and specific user group requirements. Gap analyses help evaluators understand performance gaps between actual performance and one or more reference points. It is critical that assessors ensure data credibility in terms of reliability, validity, proper selection of participants, and timing. Assessors collect data through a variety of direct and indirect methods. They also convey performance results to assessment user groups through different reporting mechanisms. Timeliness and confidentiality are crucial to the integrity and long-term survival of assessment programs. Examples of reference points were provided. Worksheets were provided to help assessors identify critical success factors and schedule recurring assessment reports of organizations whose performance they intend to measure.

Worksheet 4.1
   Critical Success Factor Analysis

Unit of Analysis: _____ *(Example: Chemistry Department)*

Date: _____

Use this worksheet to identify and rank the unit's critical success factors. In descending order of importance, list major factors considered critical to the performance success of this unit.

Critical Success Factors

Example:
High national ranking
Competitive faculty salaries
High-quality teaching and research lab facilities and equipment

Worksheet 4.2
  Assessment Report Schedule

Unit of Analysis: _____ (*Example: Chemistry Department*)

Date: _____

Use this worksheet to schedule major assessment reports for important assessment users. In column A, list major assessment user groups named on Worksheet 1.1. In column B, identify routine assessment reports provided to each assessment user group. In column C, indicate the date (day and month) on which routine reports are due.

Assessment User Group (A)	Assessment Report Title (B)	Due Date (C)
Example: Dean, College of Arts and Sciences	*Example*: Student Placement Report Alumni Survey Results	*Example*: October 1 (annually) August 1 (biannually)

CHAPTER 5

Defining and Measuring Organizational Performance

As explained in Chapter One, assessment of organizational performance is defined as the measurement of organizational performance that assessment users evaluate in relation to reference points to support their needs, expectations, and requirements. Whereas previous chapters explained how to measure organizational performance, this chapter is about what to measure. It offers definitions and sample indicators for measuring organizational performance that build on the discussions of internal and external system elements in Chapters Two and Three.

As explained earlier, assessors are differentiated from assessment users for discussion purposes. Assessors are the people doing the actual day-to-day assessment work. They are usually staff and faculty with part-time or full-time, temporary or permanent responsibilities for assessment. In comparison, an assessment user group evaluates assessment findings against requirements unique to that particular group. Assessors seek avenues for measuring performance required of assessment user groups; assessment users seek appropriate contexts from which they can evaluate assessment findings measured and conveyed by assessors. Often the assessors are the assessment users. However, the roles are best separated for purposes of discussion. The term assessor refers only to a person who is exploring matters of measurement, and the term assessment user group is limited to persons engaged in evaluation—even though the same persons may actually serve in both roles.

A high-quality assessment program is capable of assessing many areas of organizational performance to meet all of the varied needs of its assessment users. One of the greatest challenges for assessors engaged in measuring performance at the organization, program, and process levels is to understand the nature and complexity of organizational performance. Organizational performance is defined and measured in multiple dimensions, each of which is linked to specific system elements. This is why assessment of organizational performance always begins with an analysis of the system's external and internal elements as described in Chapters Two and Three.

Wise assessors generally do not measure all dimensions of organizational performance all the time. They are selective, choosing the right performance areas based on specific needs and expectations of different assessment user groups, critical success factors, strategic goals, past performance issues, emerging political and social issues, and other relevant considerations.

Areas of Organizational Performance

Organizational performance can be defined operationally in many ways. In 1989, Scott Sink and Thomas Tuttle operationally defined seven areas of organizational performance. I formed them into a new combination more suited for assessment in higher education. By now you will recognize these seven areas of organizational performance as the following:

1. Effectiveness: a measure of the extent to which the unit achieves its intended outcomes

2. Productivity: a ratio of outputs created to inputs consumed

3. Quality: a complex area of performance measured in six dimensions:

   Quality of upstream systems (Q_1)

   Quality of inputs (Q_2)

   Quality of key work processes (Q_3)

   Quality of outputs (Q_4)

   Quality of leadership systems (Q_5)

   Quality of worklife (Q_6)

4. Customer and stakeholder satisfaction: a measure of the level of satisfaction of internal and external customers and stakeholders

5. Efficiency: a measure of resource utilization and the costs and benefits of quality management

6. Innovation: a measure of creative changes put into place to improve organizational performance

7. Financial durability: a measure of the organization's financial health and well-being

Figure 5.1 illustrates links between each area of organizational performance and its system elements. Each of the seven areas of performance will be discussed in detail, with examples of performance indicators and data collection methods given for both academic and administrative organizations.

Effectiveness

Communication Department at a Small Liberal Arts College

This was the third time the Communication Department's chair had called a special faculty meeting on the same topic: how to assess the Debate Club. Her frustration with the faculty's inability to complete this seemingly simple task was growing. She was concerned about the dean's persistent e-mail threats of reducing departmental funding for the debate program if the department didn't submit a proposal soon. The truth was that none of the department members, herself included, had any experience assessing anything other than classroom learning and conducting program reviews; they were stuck, and she realized that all the meetings in the world wouldn't improve their lot. As she finished sending e-mails announcing the upcoming meeting, she made a mental note to call a colleague at a nearby university before the meeting. Maybe her friend would have some ideas, given that he had made a presentation on assessment at a recent national conference.

When the faculty reconvened, the chair had a wide grin on her face. She began the meeting by summarizing the dean's e-mail threats and her recent phone conversation with her colleague—a conversation that was surprisingly brief. "The solution to our assessment problem," she explained to the beleaguered faculty, "begins at the end." She rose from her chair and headed for the blackboard on the front wall of the small conference room. Chalk in hand, she turned to the group and said, "All we have to do is clarify our goals for the debate program and then decide how we want to measure each goal." She turned to the board, lifted her hand, and said loudly, "So what do we hope will happen to students as a result of their successful participation in our debate program?"

The Communication Department faculty in the vignette is engaged in a struggle to measure effectiveness. Effectiveness is an area of organizational performance that is crucial to the overall success of all organizations. It represents a measure of the extent to which organizations, programs, and processes achieve their strategic goals and intended outcomes.

Figure 5.2 illustrates that effectiveness is linked directly to a system's outcomes and indirectly to strategic goals supplied by the leadership system. Almost all external and internal assessment users are interested in this crucial area of organizational performance. Assessors engaged in the measurement of organizational effectiveness

Figure 5.1
The Seven Areas of Organizational Performance

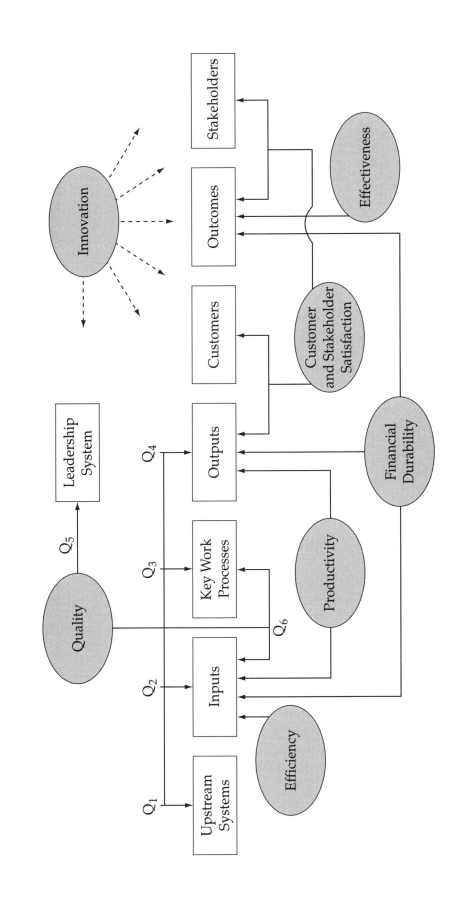

Source: Adapted from Sink and Tuttle, 1989.

Figure 5.2
Effectiveness

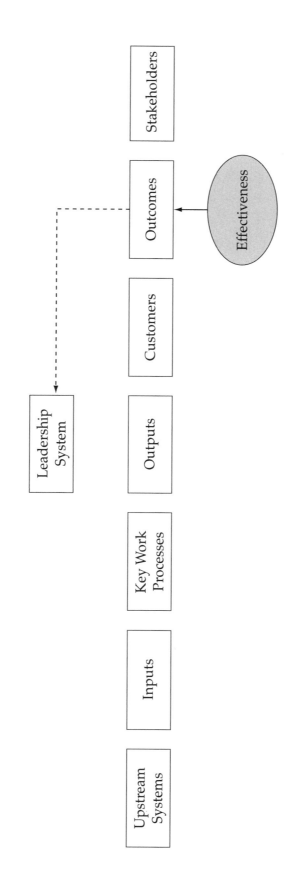

Source: Adapted from Sink and Tuttle, 1989.

face many challenges. First of all, organizations must have clearly defined strategic goals and intended outcomes; these are key to good measurement of effectiveness. The requirement of clear intended outcomes is demonstrated in the Communication Department's struggle to measure the effectiveness of the debate program, a cocurricular activity. Other challenges that assessors engaged in the measurement of effectiveness face are measuring achievement of intended outcomes while simultaneously monitoring unintended outcomes, measuring goal or outcome achievement at the right time and using valid and reliable methods, and measuring and conveying levels of goal or outcome achievement within the context of user group requirements, organizational mission, vision, guiding principles, strategic goals, and critical success factors.

Academic Organizations

Examples of strategic goals for a typical academic department were presented in Exhibit 2.1 and intended outcomes from each of the four key work processes (teaching, research, service, and management) in Exhibit 2.9. A discussion of the measurement of organizational effectiveness in relation to achievement of these strategic goals and intended outcomes is provided here.

Teaching Effectiveness

Assessors measure teaching effectiveness by examining the degree to which students achieve program-level intended learning outcomes, personal development, employability, preparation for advanced study, and so forth. When measuring achievement of student outcomes, assessors consider the most appropriate times for measuring learning outcomes; how to address the value-added dimension of learning; how to attribute learning, or lack thereof, to specific learning experiences; and how to use appropriate, credible data collection methods (discussed in Chapter Four).

Assessors use both direct and indirect methods of collecting data to measure student outcome achievement, depending on what types of data they need. For example, assessors use direct data collection methods such as periodic and end-of-program exit and licensure examinations, presentations, demonstrations, and portfolios to observe levels of mastery of knowledge, skills, and abilities of program completers. Mark Chun (2002) suggests that assessors use direct self-reporting methods (surveys, interviews, focus groups, and journals) to collect student attitudes and opinions about their collegiate experiences; levels of satisfaction; and self-assessments of improvements in their academic and personal development, and achievement of knowledge, skills, and abilities in relation to their personal, educational, and employment goals.

Assessors also use indirect methods of data collection to measure the department's overall teaching effectiveness. For example, they query databases to collect data about student grades, graduation rate, and retention rates. They survey employers and alumni to collect data about job placement rates. They analyze documents to determine how many faculty are nominated for and receive teaching awards and honors from peers, how many students receive achievement awards and scholarships, campus incidents, student participation rates in cocurricular activities, and so forth.

Finally, assessors convey measurement data within the context of intended student learning outcomes embedded in academic programs to help assessment users evaluate organizational performance in terms of teaching effectiveness. Palomba and Banta (1999), Banta (2002), and Walvoord (2004) offer extensive discussions on assessment of teaching effectiveness. Exhibit 5.1 provides examples of performance indicators that measure teaching effectiveness in relation to student outcomes reported in Exhibit 2.9 for a typical academic department.

Research Effectiveness

Assessors measure research effectiveness by examining the degree to which research (whether sponsored or not) serves its purpose and achieves its intended outcomes for the organization. For example, looking at intended outcomes of organizations actively engaged in research listed in Exhibit 2.9, assessors conduct surveys and analyze documents to determine the organization's research reputation. They survey students and faculty to determine the extent to which research enhances learning and revitalizes faculty. They query databases and analyze documents to determine how many jobs and salary dollars are supported by grants and contracts. They track total dollars received from endowment revenues, donations, grants, contracts, royalties, patent fees, material transfer fees, and other sources derived from commercial uses of intellectual property to determine the degree to which research supplements organizational revenues. They determine how many faculty are nominated for and receive research awards and honors from peers. Finally, they track articles submitted and accepted for publication in refereed journals, number of citations in other works, and patents applied for and approved.

Note that in this conceptual framework for assessing organizational performance, assessment of research methodology is an assessment of quality of research work (explained later in this chapter as Q_3: Quality of Key Work Processes) and not an assessment of research effectiveness (goal achievement). However, assessment of research always requires an assessment of effectiveness, in conjunction with an assessment of process quality, and other areas of organizational performance such as customer and stakeholder satisfaction. Examples of

Exhibit 5.1

Examples of Performance Indicators for
Effectiveness in an Academic Department

Intended Outcomes from Exhibit 2.9

Teaching: Student Learning Outcomes

- Percentage of majors reporting achievement of knowledge, skills, and abilities in relation to personal, educational, and employment goals
- Graduation rates, by program
- Student placement rates, by program
- Percentage of graduates admitted to graduate schools
- Percentage of graduates who pass licensure and certification exams the first time

Teaching: Student Personal Development Outcomes

- Percentage of majors reporting achievement of personal growth and development goals
- Percentage of majors placed on probation or suspended for inappropriate conduct
- Percentage of majors active in student activities, intramural sports, and intercollegiate sports
- Number of reported visits to campus health clinics
- Number of student leadership awards received by majors
- Number of reported drug- and alcohol-related incidents on campus involving department majors

Research-Related Outcomes

- Total dollars generated from research as a percentage of total revenues
- Number of jobs supported by external research dollars
- Departmental reputation
- Research doctorate program ranking
- Number of articles submitted and accepted for publication in refereed journals
- Percentage of students and faculty who report positive responses when asked if research enhances learning
- Number of undergraduate and graduate students engaged in research activities related to their academic fields
- Number of patent applications
- Number of faculty nominated for and receiving awards and honors from peers
- Number of citations in other works

Service Outcomes Benefiting Institution and Department

- Total dollars generated from contracted services as a percentage of total departmental revenues
- Number of jobs supported through contracted services
- Departmental reputation among the general public, peers, and K–12 educators in the discipline
- Success rate of local tax levy campaigns
- Q_5: Quality of Leadership System (see Exhibits 5.13 to 5.20)
- Q_6: Quality of Worklife (see Exhibit 5.21)

Service Outcomes: Benefiting Discipline

- Percentage of faculty holding office in professional associations
- Percentage of faculty reviewing articles submitted for publication in refereed journals

Service Outcomes: Benefiting External Organizations

- Percentage of business and education partners reporting benefits from departmental outreach programs and services
- Number of spin-off companies originated by students and faculty
- Number of new business starts attributed to partnerships and incubator programs

Management

- Number of vacant positions as a percentage of total funded positions
- Scope and nature of audit citations from internal, state, and federal audit reports
- AAUP administration censure
- Q_5: Quality of Leadership System (see Exhibits 5.13 to 5.20)
- Q_6: Quality of Worklife (see Exhibit 5.21)

Departmental Strategic Goals from Exhibit 2.1

Improve quality of teaching and learning through technology

- Number of pieces and dollar value of new equipment purchased for classrooms and teaching labs
- Faculty release time to support additional professional development in use of technology in the classroom as a percentage of total time
- Percentage of faculty using Web-based course management systems (such as Blackboard) to support part or all of their courses taught
- Number of hours faculty spent in technology-related professional development as a percentage of total hours

Improve quality of research facilities

- Number of pieces and dollar value of new lab equipment purchased for research facilities
- Number of pieces and dollar value of lab equipment renovated or repaired in research facilities
- Number of pieces and dollar value of lab equipment donated by equipment manufacturers
- Percentage of research facilities with new and renovated equipment
- Number of new collaborative research projects with local universities that have superior equipment available for use by researchers

---

performance indicators for measuring research effectiveness in relation to intended research outcomes reported in Exhibit 2.9 for a typical academic department are also provided in Exhibit 5.1.

Service Effectiveness

Assessors measure service effectiveness through various avenues. They review documents to determine how many faculty serve as journal editors, article reviewers, and officers in professional associations. They survey peers, conduct general public image studies, and monitor the rate of passage of local tax levies in support of two-year colleges to de-termine improvements in institutional and program reputations; they survey employees to determine their opinions about the quality of in-stitutional communication and governance structures (see later discus-sions about measuring Q_5: Quality of Leadership Systems and Q_6: Quality of Worklife). Finally, assessors survey businesses, industries, ed-ucators, health care providers, and others to determine the nature and scope of benefits they are acquiring from their participation in partner-ships and outreach programs. Examples of performance indicators for measuring service effectiveness in relation to outcomes reported in Ex-hibit 2.9 for a typical academic department are provided in Exhibit 5.1.

Management Effectiveness

Assessors measure effectiveness of management practices in academic departments to determine how well academic organizations are man-aged. For example, they look at results from employee satisfaction and quality-of-worklife surveys and interviews, and they analyze docu-ments to determine citations in internal, state, and federal audit reports, formal complaints, grievances, and lawsuits against the organization. They also look at documents to understand AAUP's "administration censure." (Effectiveness of an organization's leadership system is dis-cussed further in connection with Q_5: Quality of Leadership Systems.) Examples of performance indicators for measuring management effec-tiveness in relation to outcomes reported in Exhibit 2.9 for a typical academic department are also provided in Exhibit 5.1.

Strategic Goal Achievement

Organizational effectiveness is also a measure of the extent to which an organization achieves its strategic goals. Exhibit 2.1 presented two examples of strategic goals for a typical academic department: to im-prove quality of teaching and learning through technology and to improve quality of research facilities. Exhibit 5.1 presents examples of performance indicators assessors could use to measure achieve-ment of these two strategic goals.

Administrative Organizations

When measuring effectiveness of administrative organizations, as-sessors require clear and specific organizational outcomes because each outcome presents an opportunity for assessing the organization's effec-tiveness. For example, one of the primary outcomes of an admissions office is to admit a targeted number of highly qualified matriculated new students. A measure of an admissions office's effectiveness in regard to this specific outcome requires comparisons of headcount and FTE of new students against targets, the qualifications of new students against selection goals and criteria, yield rates, and the percentage of new students who matriculate. Another example is the outcome of the registrar's office, which is to provide timely access to accurate information to students and faculty. A measure of the registrar's effectiveness in terms of this specific outcome requires an examination of the accuracy of information and the extent to which students and faculty have access to it. Another example is the outcome of the purchasing office to seek the best buy for the dollar and informed buying. A measure of the purchasing office's effectiveness in terms of these specific outcomes requires an analysis of dollars spent and a survey of buyer knowledge. One of Information Services' intended outcomes is highly productive end users who are able to accomplish computing-related tasks without interference or delays due to unsuitable or malfunctioning networks, machines, or software. A measure of IS's effectiveness in relation to this outcome is the percentage of end users reporting increased productivity as a result of suitable and functioning networks, machines, and software, network and server downtime, and so forth.

Assessors measure effectiveness of managerial practices in administrative organizations the same way they measure it in academic organizations.

Exhibits 5.1 and 5.2 offer more examples of performance indicators that measure effectiveness of an academic department and for Information Services, respectively, using examples of intended outcomes from Exhibits 2.9 and 2.10 and strategic goals from Exhibits 2.1 and 2.2.

Worksheet 5.1 will help assessors assess their unit's effectiveness.

Exhibit 5.2

Examples of Performance Indicators for
Effectiveness in Information Services

Intended Outcomes from Exhibit 2.10

Desktop and Laptop Computer Support

- Percentage of end users reporting that IS-supported machines and software increased their productivity and effectiveness
- Frequency and nature of customer service requests
- Number of hours or days employees are without full use of their desktop or laptop computers or printers as a percentage of total hours or days

Network Service

- Network downtime as a percentage of total time
- Transmission time, by user and time of day
- Network traffic statistics
- Number of network-related service requests and complaints

(continued on the next page)

Exhibit 5.2, *continued*
Examples of Performance Indicators for Effectiveness in Information Services

- Network statistics indicating number of inappropriate accesses to network servers and system files by location and time of day

Server Administration
- Server downtime as a percentage of total time
- Number and type of server crashes and repairs
- Frequency and nature of requests for data stored on backup tapes
- Server statistics indicating number of inappropriate accesses to key system files, by location and time of day

Application Support
- Percentage of end users reporting improvements in their work resulting from new systems
- Transaction time, by user, time of day, and type of job
- Reliability of query results
- Number of nonprocessed queries in backlog
- Number of end user queries as a percentage of total queries

Training, Consulting, and Problem Solving
- Level of increased end user skills resulting from IS training and consultation, determined in proficiency tests and through end user surveys
- Frequency and nature of end user requests for assistance
- Frequency and nature of problems and complaints caused by deficiencies in end user knowledge, skills, and abilities

Management
- Number of vacant positions as a percentage of total funded positions
- Scope and nature of audit citations from internal, state, and federal audit reports
- Q_5: Quality of Leadership System (see Exhibits 5.13 to 5.20)
- Q_6: Quality of Worklife (see Exhibit 5.21)

IS Strategic Goals from Exhibit 2.2

Ubiquitous Computing
- Percentage of campus capable of wireless network connections
- Percentage of classrooms, theaters, labs, and offices without network connections
- Percentage of faculty, staff, and student laptop computers owned by the institution with wireless connection capability
- Scope of computerized resources accessible to authorized end users from home, from office, and in transit
- Improved overall service quality
- Percentage of help desk customers reporting positive responses to help desk service received
- Number of new services offered at the expanded help desk
- Frequency and number of end user contacts with the help desk
- Technician hours spent in technical training as a percentage of total hours

Productivity

A second area of organizational performance is productivity. Sink and Tuttle (1989) define productivity as a ratio, calculated as outputs created divided by inputs consumed. Although productivity is of interest to all assessment user groups, internal users, such as administrators and managers, are most interested in this aspect of organizational performance. Figure 5.3 illustrates that productivity is linked to a system's inputs and outputs.

Highly productive organizations seek maximum outputs through minimum consumption of inputs. Leaders must recognize, however, that highly productive organizations may or may not be highly effective. For this reason, leaders design assessment programs that measure multiple areas of performance, with an emphasis on areas critical to success and the attainment of strategic goals.

Databases that track and report output data over time provide important data. However, for assessment purposes, output data do not necessarily measure productivity until they are compared with inputs consumed. For example, data collected from institutional databases describing how many course credits an academic department offers over three years are not a measure of productivity until course credits are compared with resources used to offer those credits (such as dollars spent or teaching faculty FTE). The assessment of productivity is particularly informative when tracked over time and when compared with other organizations with similar missions, programs, and services.

Sink and Tuttle (1989) warn of several potential validity and reliability problems for assessors measuring productivity. The "intangibility of outputs" is a problem for assessors measuring the productivity of organizations with outputs that are intangible, such as advice from academic and career advisers. The "fuzzy unit of analysis" problem plagues assessors who fail to lock in on boundaries of the unit of analysis. And the "undefined scope" problem afflicts assessors who fail to use the same time frame for both outputs and inputs.

Sink and Tuttle (1989) contend that productivity can be a good diagnostic measure of organizational performance in other areas. They argue that assessors who measure productivity well "end up learning something about effectiveness, efficiency, and quality" (p. 181). They also remind process improvement teams that productivity can be increased by increasing outputs, decreasing inputs, or both.

Assessors of academic organizations measure productivity by querying databases and analyzing documents to collect data about outputs created, such as number of courses offered (as measured by course credits or contact hours), advising hours, research proposals, billable consulting hours, and publications, and comparing them to

Figure 5.3
Productivity

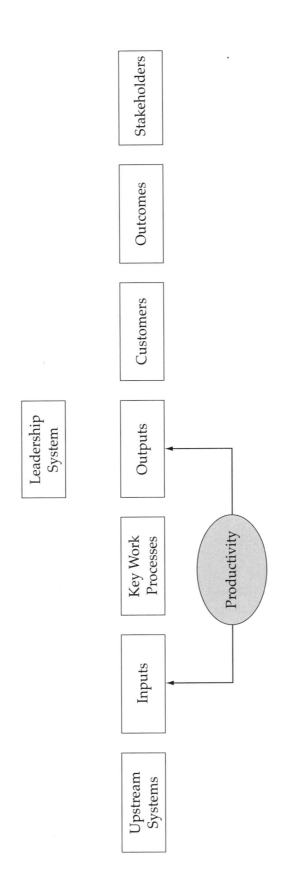

Source: Adapted from Sink and Tuttle, 1989.

indicators of inputs consumed, such as faculty and staff FTE used and dollars spent.

Assessors of administrative organizations measure productivity by querying databases and analyzing documents to collect data about outputs created, such as number of decision letters prepared, course schedules published, purchase orders processed, and contracts processed, and comparing them to indicators of inputs consumed, such as employee FTE used or dollars spent. Productivity in Information Services is measured by average cost and people-hours to repair machines, support networks, write programming code, and so forth.

Exhibits 5.3 and 5.4 provide examples of performance indicators that measure productivity of an academic department and of Information Services, respectively, using examples of outputs from Exhibits 2.7 and 2.8 and examples of inputs from Exhibits 2.3 and 2.4.

Worksheet 5.2 will help assessors assess their unit's productivity.

Quality

Quality is a complex area of performance measured in six dimensions, each coded Q. Figure 5.4 illustrates how each dimension is linked to specific system elements: Q_1 for measure of quality of

Exhibit 5.3

Examples of Performance Indicators for
Productivity in an Academic Department

Teaching

- Course credit or contact hours generated per teaching faculty FTE
- Student credit hours generated per teaching faculty FTE
- Number of sections taught per graduate teaching assistant FTE
- Average instructional cost per departmental major
- Number of students advised per teaching faculty fTE
- Average cost and hours to develop a new course or program

Research

- Number of grant proposals submitted per faculty FTE
- Number of patent applications, published articles, and presentations per research faculty FTE

Service

- Total contract service hours billed per contract faculty FTE
- Number of departmental committees served per faculty FTE
- Number of institutional committees served per faculty FTE

Management

- The ratio of administrative FTE to teaching faculty FTE and to research faculty FTE

Exhibit 5.4
Examples of Performance Indicators for
Productivity in Information Services

Desktop and Laptop Computer Support
- Average cost and hours to repair a desktop or laptop computer
- Average cost and hours to install new application software on a desktop or laptop computer
- Number of help desk calls received and served per help desk staff FTE

Network Services
- Number of servers or networks installed and maintained per network staff FTE
- Number of backups performed, network accounts supported, and network ports supported per network staff FTE

Server Administration
- Number of servers supported per server support staff FTE

Application Support
- Line of code per application support staff FTE

Training and Problem Solving
- Average cost and hours per workshop developed and workshop offered
- Number of workshops and seminars taught per training staff FTE.
- Number of consultations provided per consulting staff FTE

Management
- The ratio of administrative FTE to faculty FTE and to staff FTE

---

upstream systems, Q_2 for quality of inputs, Q_3 for quality of key work processes, Q_4 for quality of outputs, Q_5 for quality of leadership systems, and Q_6 for quality of worklife.

A number of user groups are interested in quality. At the institutional level, external assessment users and senior leaders are interested in the quality of outputs because the quality of programs and services (including research) can make the difference in achieving or maintaining accreditation, acquiring donations and gifts, increasing or maintaining program enrollments, and keeping jobs. At the department level, administrators, managers, faculty, and staff who are responsible for organizational operations are very interested in quality. Each area of quality is discussed further.

Q_1: Quality of Upstream Systems

Quality of upstream systems, according to Sink and Tuttle (1989), is a measure of "the selection and management of upstream systems" (p. 172). It reflects the strength and effectiveness of an organization's

Figure 5.4
Quality

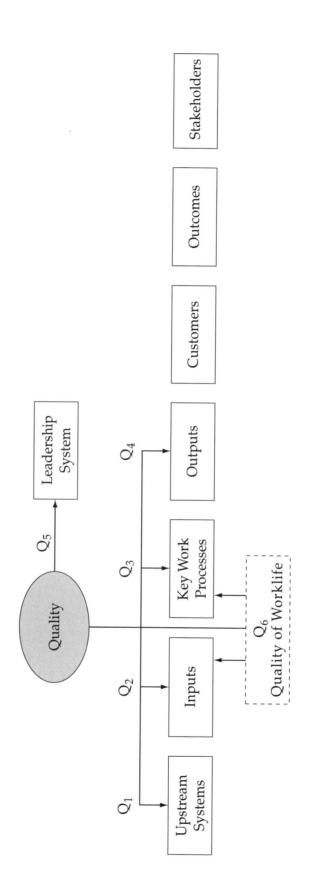

Source: Adapted from Sink and Tuttle, 1989.

partnerships with critical upstream systems outside the unit of analysis, whether inside or outside the institution. Sink and Tuttle argue that it is easier for a unit to assess quality of partnerships with external upstream systems than with internal upstream systems because internal customer-supplier roles are often unclear. "Who works for whom" is sometimes very unclear between and within administrative and academic organizations.

Assessment of an organization's performance in terms of quality of upstream systems reinforces leaders' awareness of the role their organization plays in relation to other organizations inside and outside the institution. This measure of quality helps leaders understand the dynamics and interdependencies of organizations operating in the same larger system; it also helps leaders clarify how well their unit serves others and vice versa.

As discussed in Chapter Two, wise leaders build strong partnerships with important upstream systems; however, building and sustaining these partnerships requires time and money. Therefore, leaders are not only selective in determining which partnerships to create but also skillful at monitoring the partnership's impact (costs and benefits) on the unit's capacity to perform.

Assessors measure quality of upstream systems from several directions. First, they measure the strength and success of a partnership by examining the quality and quantity of resources, constraints, and services an upstream system provides to a unit. Second, assessors measure the quality of processes used by the organization to identify and select important upstream systems for partnerships (see the discussion of Q_3: Quality of Key Work Processes). Finally, assessors measure the quality of the partnership itself to make sure that it presents and maintains equal benefits at a fair price for all partners.

Academic Organizations

Exhibits 3.1, 3.3, and 3.5 provided examples of external and internal upstream systems for a typical academic department. To measure the quality of external upstream systems, assessors of academic organizations collect data about such matters as quality of entering students from feeder schools, timeliness and scope of guidelines for requests for proposals received from important research sponsors, quality of services the bookstore provides to students, adequacy and timeliness of financial aid distributions from the federal and state governments, and quality of operating and capital financial resources from state and local governments.

To measure the quality of internal upstream systems, assessors in academic organizations collect data about such matters as qualifications of new undergraduate students recruited and admitted by the admissions office, scholarship dollars raised for students by the development office, quality and accessibility of library holdings and quality of reference services provided by the library, quality of classrooms and teaching and research labs maintained by the physical plant department, quality of technology and training provided by Information Services, quality of counseling and advice given to students by the counseling center and academic advising center, and academic, financial, and personnel policies created by senior leaders.

Administrative Organizations

Assessors in administrative organizations also measure quality of partnerships with internal and external upstream systems by measuring quality and quantity of resources each partner provides to the system. For example, assessors in the admissions office monitor the percentage of SAT and ACT test takers who send their scores and the timeliness of test scores sent by the College Board. Assessors in the financial aid office monitor federal programs for changes in program guidelines and procedures; they also monitor lists of potential new students from admissions that need financial aid assistance. Assessors in the registrar's office monitor the timeliness and accuracy of course offering information and grades provided by academic departments, as well as new academic requirements and policies created by academic leaders. Assessors in the purchasing office monitor certified vendors to make sure that they continue to meet certification requirements. Assessors in Information Services monitor partnerships with important vendors to ensure that they provide the best discount and the most current advice about rapidly changing technology.

Exhibits 5.5 and 5.6 provide examples of performance indicators that measure Q_1: Quality of Upstream Systems in a typical academic department and in Information Services, respectively, using examples of upstream systems from Exhibits 3.1 through 3.6.

Worksheet 5.3 will help assessors evaluate the quality of their unit's important upstream systems as identified on Worksheet 3.1.

Q_2: Quality of Inputs

Measurement of input quality is an important area of organizational performance for all organizational systems—as the saying goes, "garbage in, garbage out." Measurement of input quality is a familiar interpretation of assessment in higher education. For years, leaders defined institutional or program quality in terms of the credentials and qualifications of faculty and incoming students. As noted, measurement of input quality is also a form of quality assurance for upstream systems because this area of organizational performance measures the degree to which upstream systems provide quality resources to a unit. Finally, as will be described, measurement of input quality is also a

Exhibit 5.5

Examples of Performance Indicators for Q_1:
Quality of Upstream Systems in an Academic Department

Supplier Systems

- Academic and professional qualifications of new, tenure-track faculty
- Number of pieces and dollar value of equipment donated each year
- Percentage of discounts offered by vendors
- Percentage and dollar value of defective equipment and supplies returned to vendor and requiring unscheduled maintenance
- Accuracy and timeliness of paychecks (including withholdings) disbursed by the payroll office
- Percentage of offices, classrooms, labs, and research facilities lacking adequate furnishings and equipment
- Quality of services provided by Human Resources in support of employee searches and personnel management
- Reliability and overall quality of technology provided and maintained by Information Services in classrooms, labs, and offices
- Quality of services provided by Human Resources in support of faculty searches and personnel management
- Quality of support services provided to faculty by the sponsored research office

Constraining Systems

- Program accreditation status
- Scope of programs and degrees offered approved by the Board of Regents
- Clarity and timeliness of requests for proposals from governmental research sponsors
- Dollar value of departmental funding from state subsidies
- Number and dollar value of departmental facilities renovations and new construction
- Academic and demographic profile of entering first-year, transfer, and graduate students from feeder high schools (test scores, GPA, ethnicity, gender, residency, and age)
- Percentage of qualified entering students enrolled in remedial courses
- Quality of general education and other elective courses offered to majors by other departments
- Quality of services provided to majors by the library, bookstore, student health center, housing and food services, and Information Services
- Quality of IS training provided to students

---

measure of the quality of services provided by leadership systems responsible for providing and allocating resources to their organizations.

Exhibits 2.3 and 2.4 offered the following types of inputs for organizations in higher education: human resources, financial resources, equipment and supplies, energy, physical space, and information. Let's examine how assessors measure the quality of each of these inputs.

Exhibit 5.6
Examples of Performance Indicators for Q_1:
Quality of Upstream Systems in Information Services

Supplier Systems

- Quality of advice vendors provide about emerging technology
- Quality of vendor discounts
- Number and quality of bids submitted by vendors
- Academic and professional qualifications of new technical employees
- Number and length of power outages in buildings housing IS technology equipment
- Percentage and dollar value of defective equipment and supplies returned to vendor
- Quality of services provided by Human Resources in support of employee searches and personnel management
- Accuracy and timeliness of paychecks (including withholdings) disbursed by the payroll office
- Quality of furnishings and equipment in offices, labs, and classrooms maintained by the physical plant department

Constraining Systems

- Number and dollar value of IS-related facilities renovations and new construction
- Dollar value of capital budget for major IS equipment purchases
- Appropriateness of technology standards set nationally and statewide

Service Partners

- Percentage of end users responding positively to technical support and training received from computer technicians hired by other departments

---

Human Resources

Because higher education is a labor-intensive service organization, many assessors closely monitor the qualifications, value, cost, and contributions of an organization's human capital. Measurement of human resource quality examines levels of preparedness and qualifications, quantity, cost, and success of an organization's human resources. Assessors seek answers to the following performance questions about a unit's human resources:

> Does the workforce have the knowledge, skills, and abilities required to move the organization forward in terms of its vision and strategic goals? Are employees keeping their knowledge, skills, and abilities current?

> Is the organization adequately staffed?

> How well does the workforce perform, particularly in connection with strategic initiatives?

> Is the workforce compensated adequately? How does what the institution pays compare with other organizations?

How satisfied are employees with the organization's leadership and quality of worklife?

To what extent do employees exhibit behaviors aligned with the organization's guiding principles?

How productive is the workforce?

Are members of the faculty and staff recognized by peers for their outstanding performance?

As noted in Chapter One, Huselid, Becker, and Beatty (2005) recommend that assessors measure the quality of human resources in relation to their unique contribution to the unit's strategy achievement. Assessors build a "workforce scorecard" to measure performance of an organization's human capital, with special attention given to the performance of positions (classified as "A" positions) that directly contribute to execution of strategy. On the scorecard, assessors measure the quality of a unit's workforce in four categories:

1. Workforce success, or the extent to which the workforce contributes to strategy execution

2. Leadership and workforce behaviors required for workforce success and achievement of strategic objectives

3. Workforce competencies, or the knowledge, skills, abilities, and personality characteristics representing the foundation for workforce behaviors

4. Workforce mind-set and culture, or assumptions and values that drive behaviors

Assessors measure human resource input quality by examining documents and querying databases to collect data about employee credentials and qualifications and quantity and ratios of employees, broken down by category, and competitiveness of employee salaries. Academic organizations measure student quality by surveying faculty about their perceptions of student quality and by querying databases and analyzing documents to collect data about new and returning student qualifications (test scores, GPA, and other academic and demographic data). Exhibits 5.7 and 5.8 provide examples of performance indicators assessors use to measure quality of human resources in an academic department and in Information Services.

Financial Resources

Assessment questions pertaining to quality of financial resources focus on quantity, adequacy, reliability, restrictiveness, and timeliness. Assessors seek answers to the following performance questions about financial resources:

Exhibit 5.7

Examples of Performance Indicators for Q_2:
Quality of Inputs in an Academic Department

Quality of Faculty and Staff

- Percentage of faculty with terminal degrees, broken down by tenured, full-time or part-time, gender, age, and ethnicity
- Faculty salaries, by rank
- Number of faculty nominated for and receiving teaching and research awards and honors from peers

Quality of Students

- Academic and demographic profile of majors, by status (test scores, prior and current GPA, ethnicity, gender, residency, and age)
- National merit scholars as a percentage of all majors

Quality of Financial Resources

- Dollar value of departmental funding, by source
- Percentage change in departmental funding compared with previous years
- Number of endowed faculty positions
- Endowment ranking
- Dollar value of research grants and contracts

Quality of Other Resources

- Inventory of all teaching- and research-related equipment, by age, cost, and location
- Results from inspections of offices, classrooms, labs, and research facilities for size, cleanliness, and condition of furnishings
- Downtime of HVAC equipment and technology in offices, classrooms, labs, and research facilities
- Number of breakdowns of departmental vehicles
- Number of equipment-related injuries
- Quality and quantity of departmental library holdings
- Number of accidents attributed to design and maintenance of facilities
- Number of illnesses attributed to "sick buildings"
- Reliability of power in campus facilities used by the department
- Convenience and adequacy of parking, determined by results of surveys and interviews of faculty and staff who park on campus
- Timeliness, accuracy, and clarity of RFPs from important research sponsors

---

Does the organization have adequate and reliable funding for it to achieve its purpose and move forward in terms of its vision and strategic goals?

Does the organization receive state and federal funding in a timely manner?

Is funding configured so that it adequately supports specific types of costs inherent in agreed-on goals?

Exhibit 5.8

Examples of Performance Indicators for Q_2:
Quality of Inputs in Information Services

Quality of Staff

- Percentage of technical staff with terminal degrees, broken down by gender, age, and ethnicity
- Technical staff salaries, by classification
- Number of employees nominated for and receiving awards and honors

Quality of Equipment and Supplies

- Age, currency, cost, and location of IS-supported desktops and laptops and related equipment, by age, currency, cost, and location of IS-supported servers and networks
- Percentage and dollar value of equipment and supplies destroyed or stolen from the dock, storage, and other locations on campus as a result of poor security
- Percentage of desktop and laptop computers not replaced as scheduled
- Percentage of servers and network equipment not replaced as scheduled
- Dollar value of equipment and supplies destroyed or broken due to poor facilities conditions
- Inventory of all servers and operating systems, by age, cost, and location
- Currency of administrative systems
- Transmission and transaction speeds
- Number of IS-supported vehicle breakdowns
- Number of service calls to repair or replace equipment, by type of equipment
- Number of equipment-related injuries

Quality of Financial Resources

- Dollars funded for scheduled hardware, software replacement, and other new equipment as a percentage of total dollars requested
- Percentage of new equipment funded in capital projects adequately funded in terms of installation, maintenance, and replacement in IS operating budgets

Quality of Other Resources

- Quality of server rooms, wiring closets, and equipment storage areas in terms of security, fire and flood protection, electrical continuity, and air quality (temperature, humidity, contaminants)
- Reliability of power to campus facilities housing IS-supported technology (surges, brownouts, outages)
- Results from inspections of offices, workrooms, and labs with respect to size, cleanliness, and condition of furnishings
- Downtime of HVAC equipment in facilities housing IS-supported servers and network equipment
- Convenience and adequacy of parking, determined by results of surveys and interviews of employees who park on campus

At the institutional level, assessors measure quality of financial resources by examining the overall revenue structure. For example, assessors measure current fund revenues by category (tuition and fees; state and local appropriations; federal grants and contracts; private gifts, grants, and contracts; endowment support for operations; and royalties, material transfer fees, and other revenues from commercial use of intellectual property) to determine what percentage of total current fund revenues comes from each source. Exhibits 5.7 and 5.8 provide many examples of performance indicators that assessors of an academic department and Information Services use to measure quality of financial resources.

Equipment and Supplies

Assessment questions related to equipment and supplies focus on quality, replacement and maintenance costs, quantity, currency, reliability, safety, and suitability. Assessors seek answers to the following performance questions related to equipment and supplies:

> Does the organization have equipment and supplies that will help it achieve its intended outcomes and move forward in relation to its vision and strategic goals?
>
> Is the organization's equipment reliable, particularly during times of peak need?
>
> How does the organization's equipment compare to that of competitors, especially those to whom the unit's operations could be outsourced?
>
> Is the workforce fully trained in the use of all equipment, particularly new or dangerous equipment?
>
> How current is the equipment?

To measure quality of equipment and supplies, assessors query databases and analyze documents to determine frequency and number of hours of equipment downtime, number of equipment-related injuries, and annual repair costs. They also compare currency and amount of equipment with those of competitors and amount of equipment stolen or damaged.

Physical Space

Assessment questions pertaining to physical space focus on quality, quantity, currency, healthiness, safety, maintenance costs, and accessibility of buildings and grounds. Assessors seek answers to the following performance questions pertaining to physical space:

> Does the organization have facilities that are appropriate for its mission?

Are the facilities adequate for the organization to achieve its intended outcomes and move forward in relation to its vision and strategic goals?

How do the organization's facilities compare to those of its competitors, especially competitors to whom the organization's operations could be outsourced?

How healthy and safe is the environment inside and outside the buildings in which employees and students spend their time?

Are offices and buildings in compliance with all health and safety codes?

Do all buildings permit unimpeded access for all employees and customers?

How convenient and safe is campus parking?

To measure quality of physical space, assessors survey faculty, staff, and students to determine their opinions about the quality, comfort, and convenience of departmental offices, lounges, reception areas, storage, parking areas, and other facilities such as theaters and lecture halls. Assessors also collect data on age of facilities, major unscheduled maintenance and renovations, number of "sick buildings" and number of illnesses attributed to them, and number of accidents attributed to the design and maintenance of facilities.

Energy

As the cost of gas, oil, and electricity increases, assessors measure cost, reliability, and consumption of energy, always seeking ways to minimize use and costs. Assessment questions related to energy focus on quantity, cost, quality, reliability, and efficient use of energy. Assessors seek answers to the following performance questions pertaining to energy:

Does the organization have adequate energy to help it achieve its intended outcomes and move forward in relation to its vision and strategic goals?

How reliable is the organization's energy supply?

How much does energy cost? How much will it cost in the future?

Is the organization adequately funded to meet future energy costs?

To measure quality of energy, assessors query databases and analyze documents to collect data about the amount, cost, and reliability of energy used, by location, time of day, and season.

Information

Organizations in higher education require a great deal of different types of information to operate and succeed. For example, they require information about changing needs and requirements of the people they serve and the future direct of the institution. They also require information specific to the organization's mission. The measurement questions pertaining to information focus on accuracy, currency, timeliness, cost, and understandability. Assessors seek answers to the following performance questions pertaining to information:

> Does the organization have adequate information to achieve its intended outcomes and move forward in relation to its vision and strategic goals?
>
> Does the organization receive critical information in a timely manner?
>
> Is critical information accurate, current, appropriate, and easy to understand?
>
> How much does it cost to obtain critical information?

To measure quality of information, assessors determine which information the organization deems critical. Then they analyze documents to determine the accuracy, cost, timeliness, understandability, and currency of information received, by recipient of the information.

Exhibits 5.7 and 5.8 provide examples of performance indicators that measure Q_2: Quality of Inputs of an academic organization and of Information Services, respectively, using examples of inputs from Exhibits 2.3 and 2.4. Because some of the performance indicators in these exhibits are the same as in Exhibits 5.5 and 5.6, assessors can use some performance indicators to measure performance in both Q_1: Quality of Upstream Systems and Q_2: Quality of Inputs.

Worksheet 5.4 will help assessors assess the quality of their unit's inputs.

Q_3: Quality of Key Work Processes

The third dimension of quality that assessors measure is quality of key work processes. This is a measure of the design, flow, variation, value added, and compliance of work (tasks and activities). Sink and Tuttle (1989) define quality of key work processes as a measure of the organization's capacity to build quality into its products and services. This measure also reflects the extent to which work tasks and activities comply with established legal, administrative, and ethical standards.

The focus of measurement in this area of organizational performance is the process itself rather than goal achievement (which is effectiveness) or productivity (which is the ratio of outputs created to inputs consumed). Process quality is a measure of how well work is performed and the degree to which processes produce outputs that meet the specifications and requirements of the people who receive or experience them.

There are several purposes for measuring process quality. One is to understand the speed and cost of doing work. Processes that are slow and costly need to be improved. Another purpose is to understand how output quality is achieved. Much of the measurement of process quality is derived from a growing number of systematic approaches to process management, such as Six Sigma and benchmarking, that recognize the value of managing work processes as well as personnel performance. Another important purpose of measuring process quality is to uncover operations and work that are not in compliance with legal, administrative, and ethical standards.

When measuring process quality, assessors often begin by measuring cost and speed to see how well the process is working overall. Process cost is the cost of equipment, supplies, and personnel engaged in the work. Process speed is measured as cycle time, which is the amount of time the process takes from start to finish—from the moment a request is received by the process to the moment the process delivers the requested product or service. When initial results of cost and cycle time are poor, assessors seek more definitive measures of performance—measures that capture the amount of work in the process that adds no value. One way to measure non-value-adding work is to measure waste, scrap, and rework. Waste, according to John Oakland (1992), is unnecessary work resulting from errors, poor organization, and use of wrong materials. Scrap is defective outputs that cannot be repaired, used, or sold. Rework (or rectification) is the time and cost devoted to correcting defective materials or errors to meet requirements.

In addition to cost, cycle time, waste, scrap, and rework, assessors measure quality of work in terms of compliance—the extent to which work complies with guiding principles, laws and regulations, specific ethical codes of conduct, generally accepted practices, and requirements of specific assessment user groups.

Finally, assessors measure process quality by examining quality of inputs going into the process (discussed as Q_2: Quality of Inputs), quality of outputs going out of the process (Q_4: Quality of Outputs), and levels of satisfaction of the people who receive or experience those outputs (discussed under "Customer and Stakeholder Satisfaction"). Process quality is a crucial aspect of organizational performance for the long-term survival of both academic and administrative organizations. Measurement of this area of performance is therefore indispensable.

Academic Organizations

Assessors in academic organizations measure process quality in each of the four key work processes: teaching, research, service, and management.

Teaching. Assessors measure teaching quality in several ways. The most common method is to survey students on their evaluations of faculty. Assessors also examine course retention rates and student grade averages. They also analyze documents to learn results from peer reviews, number of teaching faculty nominated for and receiving teaching awards and honors from peers, percentage of undergraduate students involved in research, and percentage of tenure-track faculty involved in undergraduate classroom instruction.

Assessors also measure process quality in teaching by measuring cycle time and cost to develop new courses and programs and to conduct program reviews. Finally, assessors analyze documents to determine the number and types of allegations, citations, and sanctions of faculty and staff for noncompliance with laws, ethics codes, policies, procedures, and regulations. Barbara Walvoord (2004) provides a full discussion of the assessment of teaching quality.

Research. The process of research is assessed at the project level by external academic peers based on guidelines, protocols, and practices determined by professional associations, government entities, and institutions, among other groups. Some investigators review process quality at the end of a major research project to compare planned activities against actual activities to find ways to reduce waste, rework, and scrap in future research efforts.

Research quality is always measured in connection with research effectiveness; consequently, many of the same performance indicators used for measuring research effectiveness are used for measuring research process quality. For example, assessors measure quality of research process by determining the number of research faculty nominated for and receiving awards and honors from peers, number of articles accepted for publication in refereed journals, number of citations in other works, patents applied for and approved, and so forth. There are several additional dimensions, however, that process quality adds to the family of performance indicators used to measure research quality: cycle time and cost to prepare research proposals, percentage of research projects completed on time, percentage of research projects completed as specified in proposals, unanticipated and unfunded costs absorbed by the department, and organizational impact from sanctions attributed to work that did not comply with research protocols, laws, standards, and codes of ethics established by research sponsors and the discipline. Depending on the nature of misconduct, organizational sanctions can range from remedial actions imposed on individuals to full-blown organizational shutdowns, particularly with respect to support (including financial aid) for federally funded institutions, according to Eric Meslin of the Indiana University Center for Bioethics (personal communication, Mar. 9, 2002).

Service. Assessment of service quality is focused on the quality of service activities and not on service results, which is service effectiveness; however, many of the same performance indicators are used for both. Assessors measure service quality by determining cycle time and cost to prepare contract proposals, percentage of contracted services completed on time, percentage of contracted services completed as specified in proposals, unanticipated and unfunded costs absorbed by the department, and organizational impact from sanctions attributed to services that did not comply with research protocols, laws, standards, and codes of ethics established by research sponsors and the discipline.

Assessors also measure quality of service activities by measuring costs and cycle time of important internal service-related processes, such as selecting new partners and building new partnerships, creating and reviewing articulation agreements, and designing new outreach programs and services. Some assessors use service quality as a window into the true cost, cycle time, and collegiality of processes used by major committees to make decisions and frame recommendations.

Management. Measurement of process quality in management is focused on the way managerial tasks and activities are performed. For example, assessors look at cycle time and costs to develop budgets and facilities proposals, search for and orient new faculty, select new graduate students, conduct student appeals, develop class schedules, award scholarships, and schedule sabbaticals. Assessors also look at frequency of allegations and findings of misconduct.

Administrative Organizations

Assessors of process quality in administrative organizations use similar methods and performance indicators as academic organizations. As mentioned in Chapter Two, key work processes in administrative organizations are mission-specific.

In the admissions office, assessors use performance indicators such as cycle time and cost to measure quality of recruitment and application processes. In the registrar's office, assessors use the same performance indicators to measure quality of processes to prepare transcripts, verify enrollment, prepare and mail grades, and process student appeals; they also monitor frequency and timing of course drops and adds. In the purchasing office, assessors use similar performance indicators to measure quality of the requisition-to-purchase order process (with and without a bid) and the process for creating or renewing a contract; they also monitor the number of requisitions on backlog and examine the percentage of departments using online services. Assessors measure process quality in Information Services by measuring cycle time and costs of purchasing, installing, and repairing equipment; backing up systems; restoring networks and servers; completing programming requests; and so forth. Quality of management processes of administrative organizations are measured in the same ways as management processes of academic organizations.

Exhibits 5.9 and 5.10 provide examples of performance indicators that measure Q_3: Quality of Key Work Processes for an academic department and for Information Services, respectively, using examples of key work processes from Exhibits 2.5 and 2.6.

Worksheet 5.5 will help assessors evaluate the quality of their unit's key work processes.

Q_4: Quality of Outputs

The fourth dimension of quality in organizational performance is output quality. Chapter Two defined outputs as products, services, or information that customers receive or experience. High-performing organizations design outputs that meet or exceed the needs and requirements of the people they serve.

Sink and Tuttle (1989) define output quality as a measure of organizational performance that focuses on "assurance that what is coming out of the organizational system meets the specification, requirements, and expectations established" (p. 175). They also remind assessors that inspection of output quality, often referred to as quality control or quality assurance, does not ensure that quality is built in to the product or service; rather, quality outputs come from good design based on customer needs and requirements and good design and inspection of work processes. Inspection of output quality at the end of the line protects customers from receiving products and services that do not meet design specifications and requirements.

Measurement questions pertaining to output quality focus on conformance to standards, quantity, completeness, timeliness, price, accuracy, reliability, speed, alignment, defectiveness, availability, and convenience from the perspective of internal and external customers, stakeholders, faculty, and staff. Assessors monitor ever-changing customer needs and requirements and constantly measure the extent to which outputs meet or exceed those needs and requirements.

Academic Organizations

Assessors in academic organizations measure output quality in relation to each of the unit's four key work processes.

Exhibit 5.9
Examples of Performance Indicators for Q_3:
Quality of Key Work Processes in an Academic Department

Teaching

- Cycle time and cost to plan, change, and evaluate curriculum and instruction at the program and course levels
- Number of nominations for national awards
- Number of distinguished teaching awards and honors
- Percentage of undergraduate students involved in research
- Percentage of tenure-track faculty involved in undergraduate classroom instruction
- Number and types of allegations, citations, and sanctions for noncompliance with laws, ethics codes, policies, procedures, and regulations
- Total instructional costs as a percentage of total expenditures
- Number and types of allegations and sanctions for legal and ethical misconduct

Research

- Cycle time and cost to prepare proposals
- Percentage of funded projects completed on time and within specifications of proposals
- Number of publications, patents, and citations
- Number of faculty nominated for and receiving distinguished research awards and honors
- Unanticipated and unfunded costs absorbed by the department
- Number and types of allegations, citations, and sanctions for legal and ethical misconduct

Service

- Cycle time and cost to develop contracted service proposals
- Cycle time and cost to develop new business partnerships and to create articulation agreements
- Percentage of contracted services delivered on time that meet contractual requirements and specifications
- Cycle time and cost of committees to make major decisions and recommendations
- Number and types of allegations, citations, and sanctions for legal and ethical misconduct

Management

- Cycle time and cost to admit new graduate students and to award departmental scholarships
- Cycle time and cost to search, hire, and train new faculty and staff
- Cycle time and cost to develop annual budgets and capital requests
- Number and types of allegations, citations, and sanctions for legal and ethical misconduct (including AAUP sanctions)

Exhibit 5.10

Examples of Performance Indicators for Q_3:
Quality of Key Work Processes in Information Services

Desktop and Laptop Computer Support

- Cycle time and cost to purchase, receive, distribute, and install desktop and laptop computers and software
- Percentage and dollar value of equipment and supplies destroyed or stolen from the dock, storage, and other locations on campus as a result of poor security

Network Services

- Cycle time and cost to restore network
- Cycle time and cost to purchase, receive, and install network machines and equipment

Server Administration

- Cycle time and cost to restore servers
- Cycle time and cost to purchase, receive, install, and repair servers
- Cycle time and cost to complete system backups

Application Support

- Cycle time and cost to complete programming requests
- Amount of programming requests on backlog
- Number of programming and data entry errors
- Cycle time and cost to purchase, receive, distribute, and install new or upgraded administrative systems

Training, Consulting, and Problem Solving

- Cycle time and cost to design new end user training programs
- Cycle time and cost to evaluate training effectiveness
- Number of scheduling and registration errors in training programs

Management

- Percentage and dollar value of equipment and supplies damaged as a result of poor ventilation or dampness in storage areas
- Percentage and dollar value of equipment and supplies stolen from the dock, storage, or other locations within the department
- Cycle time and cost to develop annual budgets and capital requests
- Cycle time and cost to search for and train new IS technical staff
- Number and types of allegations, citations, and sanctions for legal and ethical misconduct

---

Teaching. To measure output quality from teaching, assessors measure alignment of course learning objectives with program-level learning objectives. They also examine currency of curricula to make sure they are responsive to emerging factors in the internal and external environment and changes in the discipline. Finally, assessors track program accreditation, numbers of classes scheduled compared to need, attendance patterns, and faculty no-shows.

Research.   Assessors measure research output quality by measuring numbers of proposals accepted and dollars awarded. They measure the extent to which researchers completed projects on time and within specifications of proposals. They also monitor the number of articles published in refereed journals, articles presented at conferences, books published, citations in other works, number of patent applications submitted, dollar value of intellectual property licensed for commercial use, and number of research faculty nominated for and receiving prestigious research awards.

Service.   Assessors measure output quality in service by measuring percentage of contract proposals accepted, total dollars generated from contracted services as a percentage of total revenues, and percentage of contracted services delivered on time and within contract specifications. They also measure quality of committee recommendations and reports.

Management.   Assessors measure management output quality by measuring quality of strategic and operational plans, annual and monthly reports, budget requests, course schedules, and the like.

Administrative Organizations

Assessors of administrative organizations measure output quality by monitoring output completeness, timeliness, price, accuracy, reliability, defects, convenience, and suitability. As mentioned in Chapter Two, outputs for administrative organizations are mission-specific. For example, in the admissions office, assessors measure timeliness and accuracy of admission decision letters, brochures, and flyers. They measure attendance at admissions-sponsored workshops and receptions and analyze feedback from participants. For the registrar's office, assessors measure timeliness and accuracy of the schedule of classes, grades, transcripts, and commencement brochures. In the purchasing office, assessors measure the completeness and accuracy of purchase orders and the clarity, accuracy, and completeness of service contracts. For Information Services, assessors measure accessibility, speed, accuracy, reliability and suitability of machines and software, and end user evaluation of the quality of training. Exhibits 5.11 and 5.12 provide examples of performance indicators that measure Q_4: Quality of Outputs for an academic department and for Information Services, respectively, using examples of outputs from Exhibits 2.7 and 2.8.

Worksheet 5.6 will help assessors determine the quality of their unit's outputs.

Exhibit 5.11

Examples of Performance Indicators for Q_4:
Quality of Outputs in an Academic Department

Teaching

- Alignment of courses and teaching methods with established learning outcomes
- Currency of curriculum
- Program accreditation status
- Program national ranking
- Program reputation
- Average class size
- Attendance rates in classes and other department-sponsored events open to the public
- Number of courses offered compared to student need
- Number of faculty no-shows, by course type

Research

- Percentage of proposals accepted
- Total dollars generated from sponsored research as a percentage of total revenues
- Number of articles published in refereed journals
- Number of citations in other works
- Number of patent applications submitted and approved
- Number of research faculty nominated for and receiving research awards and honors
- Dollar value of intellectual property licensed for commercial use

Service

- Percentage of contract proposals accepted
- Total dollars generated from contracted services as a percentage of total revenues
- Percentage of contracted services delivered on time that meet contractual requirements and specifications
- Percentage of committee recommendations approved and implemented

Management

- Departmental faculty and staff opinions about quality of strategic and operational plans, annual and monthly reports, budget requests, course schedules, assessment reports, and new hires resulting from search processes

Q_5: Quality of Leadership Systems

The fifth dimension of quality is a measure of the quality of services that the leadership system provides to the organization. Governing boards and other important outsiders with a stake in the success of leadership personnel have a keen interest in this area of organizational performance. Furthermore, everyone inside the organization is

Exhibit 5.12

Examples of Performance Indicators for Q_4:
Quality of Outputs in Information Services

Desktop and Laptop Computer Support

- Number of repeat service requests, by type of equipment serviced and type of service provided initially
- Percentage of end users giving positive responses when asked about the quality of new or repaired desktop and laptop computers and software in offices, classrooms, labs, and research centers
- Average response time from receipt of service request to completion of service
- Percentage of machines that meet current standards
- Percentage of machines with current versions of operating systems
- Number of inappropriate accesses to desktop and laptop computers

Network Services

- Network downtime as a percentage of total time
- Transmission time
- Network traffic statistics
- Collision counts
- Number of network-related service requests and complaints
- Number of inappropriate accesses to the network

Server Administration

- Server downtime as a percentage of total time
- Frequency and type of server crashes and repairs
- Frequency and nature of requests for data stored on backup tape
- Number of inappropriate accesses to key system files, by location and time of day
- Transaction time
- Number of steps required of end users to enter data and submit queries
- Server traffic statistics

Application Support

- Percentage of end users who are satisfied with system capabilities in terms accessibility, speed, accuracy, reliability, and availability
- Number of steps required to submit data
- Number of steps required to query data
- Number of error reports associated with programming errors
- Frequency and nature of requests for data stored on backup tapes
- Number of inappropriate accesses to major databases, per year

Training, Consulting, and Problem Solving

- Percentage of training participants reporting positive evaluations of training programs and consulting services

Management

- IS employee opinions about quality of strategic and operational plans, annual and monthly reports, budget requests, course schedules, assessment reports, and new hires resulting from search processes

---

interested in and has a stake in the quality of the leadership system because of its significant impact on organizational capacity, operations, performance, and assessment. Leadership system quality, like other aspects of quality, is crucial to organizational success. Without direction and support, long-term survival of the organization is in jeopardy.

The primary focus is on the performance of the leadership system as a process and not necessarily that of individual leaders. Assessors should recognize that the leadership system is made up of several individuals whose roles and contributions to the leadership system vary and change over time. Admittedly, it is difficult to separate personnel performance from process performance. Nevertheless, assessors should focus on the quality of services provided to the organization by the leadership system. More specifically, assessors should examine the quality of direction and support given to the organizational system and their impact on organizational performance.

Assessors have many avenues for measuring quality of a unit's leadership system available to them. For example, they can measure the following aspects of leadership:

- Follower and stakeholder perceptions about the quality of services provided to the organization
- Quality of external relations
- Quality of services that provide internal direction and support to the organization through organizational mission, vision, guiding principles, strategic goals, organizational structure, and resources
- Costs and benefits of the leadership system

Many of the performance indicators that measure quality of leadership systems are the same as those used to measure other areas of organizational performance, as described elsewhere in this chapter.

Follower and Stakeholder Perceptions of Service Quality

Measurement of leadership system quality begins by collecting data on follower perceptions regarding the quality of services provided to the organization by the leadership system. These data are gathered through self-reporting methods, such as surveys, interviews, and focus groups, which serve several purposes when done properly. Follower feedback provides valuable insights that can help leaders improve the system and at the same time provides opportunities for followers to contribute meaningful and constructive suggestions to system leaders.

To be successful, follower feedback should involve leaders in the design of the feedback process, be anonymous, and be clear in its purpose and consequences. One way to make follower feedback more

Exhibit 5.13

Examples of Performance Indicators for Q_5: Quality of Leadership Systems: Follower and Stakeholder Perceptions and External Relations

Follower and Stakeholder Perceptions

- Percentage of followers and selected stakeholders giving positive responses when asked about their satisfaction with services provided by the organization's leadership system
- Nature of comments from accreditation site visit teams and other mechanisms of peer review
- Nature and scope of administrative AAUP censure
- Percentage of sports leaders suspended or reprimanded by the NCAA or other athletic associations
- Sanctions for legal, administrative, and ethical misconduct of individuals and groups representing the leadership system

External Relations

- Strength of partnerships with upstream systems (see Exhibits 5.5 and 5.6)
- Perceptions of the general public and targeted groups about the image of the organization through image studies
- Newspaper clippings and other media reports describing or implying the organization's public image
- Percentage of local tax levies that pass the first time
- Dollar value of local donations and gifts
- Performance indicators for measuring satisfaction of external assessment user groups (see Exhibits 5.22 and 5.23 in this chapter and Exhibit 6.4 in Chapter Six)
- Percentage of followers and selected stakeholders giving positive responses when asked about their satisfaction with the organization's leadership system
- Nature of comments from accreditation site visit teams and other mechanisms of peer review
- Nature and scope of administrative AAUP censure
- Percentage of sports leaders suspended or reprimanded by the NCAA or other athletic associations
- Sanctions for legal, administrative, and ethical leader misconduct

meaningful for leaders is to compare actual follower perceptions with desired perceptions articulated by leaders prior to measurement. This sequence not only helps structure a successful feedback process but also focuses feedback on areas of service quality important to the leadership system. Sometimes leaders prefer to differentiate participant responses by respondent characteristic, such as by faculty, staff, administrators, gender, or longevity at the institution; others prefer to differentiate responses by organizational unit.

Leadership systems often receive follower feedback as part of larger organizational climate studies. They can also receive follower feedback as part of 360-degree performance management programs. Finally, they can glean stakeholder feedback from such documents as peer reviews, accreditation site visit team reports, censures from AAUP, reprimands and sanctions from NCAA, and sanctions for legal and ethical misconduct. Exhibit 5.13 provides examples of performance indicators that measure follower and stakeholder perceptions of leadership system quality.

External Relations

Assessors also measure quality of a leadership system by examining the quality of services directed toward enhancing relations with the organization's external environment. Chapter Two described the following external responsibilities of a leadership system, each of which provides opportunities for measuring leadership system quality:

- Building and maintaining strong partnerships with important upstream systems
- Creating positive images of the unit to targeted groups such as potential students, employees, and other external benefactors
- Identifying and serving major assessment user needs, expectations, and requirements

To measure quality of services provided in external relations, assessors measure quality of partnerships (in terms of costs and benefits) formed with important upstream systems, as described in our discussion of Q_1: Quality of Upstream Systems (see Exhibits 5.5 and 5.6). They also measure quality of the organization's public image held by members outside the organization through well-designed public image studies often conducted in conjunction with upcoming local tax levy campaigns or before and after changes in senior leaders. They analyze local newspaper clippings and other media reports suggesting an organization's local reputation. Finally, they monitor passage rates of local tax levies and other indicators of public support.

Assessors measure levels of user group satisfaction with the organization's actual performance and with the quality of assessment reports provided to them. Satisfaction of the unit's actual performance is reflected in decisions made by assessment user groups such as rank, category, and appropriations (see the discussion of customer and stakeholder satisfaction later in this chapter). Quality of assessment reports is measured in terms of accuracy, credibility, timeliness, usefulness, and readability. (A full discussion of how assessors measure overall performance of an assessment program, including user satisfaction and quality of assessment outputs, is provided in Chapter Six.) Exhibit 5.13 provides examples of performance indicators that measure leadership system quality in terms of external relations.

Worksheet 5.7 will help assessors assess their unit's leadership system in terms of both follower satisfaction and quality of services that enhance external relations.

Internal Direction and Support

Assessors also assess leadership system quality by measuring the quality of services that provide internal direction and support to the organizational system. Chapter Two identified the following internal responsibilities that provide direction and support to the organization. Each responsibility offers an opportunity for measuring leadership system quality:

- Clarifying and gaining support for the organization's mission
- Clarifying and gaining support for the organization's vision of performance excellence
- Clarifying guiding principles and building and sustaining an organizational culture reflecting those principles that maximizes organizational performance
- Establishing and gaining support for strategic goals that help the organization find its competitive advantage and place in the environment
- Creating organizational design and governance structures that maximize performance
- Acquiring and allocating necessary resources to achieve mission, vision, and strategic goals

Mission.   As discussed in Chapter Two, all organizational systems are open, customized systems created for a purpose. The role of the leadership system is to clarify the unit's purpose through its mission statement. Mission statements enable organizations in higher education to distinguish themselves from one another. They clarify what an organization is as well as what it is not. Mission statements also answer purpose-related questions: Whom does the organization serve? How does it serve them? What results does it seek as a result of that service? Mission statements also clarify important boundaries that limit or extend an organization's service area, customers, and products and services.

Not only does a mission statement inform measurement about whom and what to measure and present a context for evaluating alignment of programs, services, customers served, and intended outcomes, but it also provides an avenue for evaluating the quality of the leadership system itself. Assessors begin by measuring the quality and effectiveness of the organization's mission. First, they determine if the leadership system created and published a mission statement.

Then they use surveys, focus groups, interviews, participant observations, database queries, and document analyses to measure quality and effectiveness of the mission statement itself.

Assessors measure quality of the mission statement by determining the degree to which it characterizes the following:

- Distinguishes the unit from other organizations in higher education and clarifies what the unit is and is not

- Clarifies whom the unit serves, how it serves them, and what it seeks as a result of that service

- Aligns with the organization's vision, guiding principles, and strategic goals

- Is adequately communicated to all members of the organizational community

- Reveals whom to assess and what aspects of organizational performance are critical to success and therefore important to assess

Assessors measure effectiveness of an organization's mission statement by determining the degree to which it serves its purpose. They collect data on the percentage of faculty, staff, stakeholders, and to some degree students who understand and support the organization's mission. They also measure alignment of programs, services, customers served, and intended outcomes with mission. Too easily, organizations can become entangled in new programs and services inconsistent with mission, especially when they are driven by serious stakeholder pressure or supported by lucrative unrestricted funding. Exhibit 5.14 provides examples of performance indicators that measure quality and effectiveness of mission statements.

Vision.   Also discussed in Chapter Two is the leadership system's responsibility for providing a clear and shared vision of performance

Exhibit 5.14
Examples of Performance Indicators for Q_5:
Quality of Leadership Systems: Mission

- Clarity in the mission statement about what the organization provides, to whom, and why, determined through document analyses
- Alignment between mission and vision, guiding principles, and strategic goals
- Alignment between mission and current programs and services offered and customers served
- Percentage of faculty, staff, stakeholders, and (when appropriate) students who understand and support the mission

---

excellence. Such a vision, commonly expressed through a vision statement, is a shared mental model of what an organization desires to become. The purpose of the vision statement is to clarify the organization's future desired state in terms of performance results; it should also inspire and motivate. An organization's vision should be strategic and lofty while presenting a clear and exciting picture of what the unit seeks to become.

Assessors measure the quality and effectiveness of the organization's vision statement as a reflection of the quality of the leadership system. First, they determine if the leadership system created and published a vision statement. Then they use surveys, focus groups, interviews, participant observations, database queries, and document analyses to measure the quality and effectiveness of the vision statement itself.

Assessors measure quality of a vision statement by determining the degree to which it reflects the following:

- Is adequately communicated to all members of the organizational community
- Provides a clear mental picture of the unit's desired state
- Clarifies what "excellence" means to members of the organization
- Is presented as a long-term vision of performance excellence
- Translates the mission into meaningful intended results
- Is realistic given the organization's capacity
- Clarifies performance excellence for evaluation purposes

Assessors measure effectiveness of the vision statement by collecting data to determine the degree to which it accomplishes the following:

- Instills a common identity and sense of destiny for employees
- Builds consensus and support for the organization's future desired state in relation to performance excellence
- Inspires and motivates employees
- Influences major decisions regarding strategic goals
- Guides acquisition and allocation of resources
- Provides a context for evaluating performance findings in relation to performance excellence

Exhibit 5.15 provides examples of performance indicators that measure quality and effectiveness of vision statements.

Guiding Principles.   As described in Chapter Two, guiding principles lay the foundation for vision and mission. Therefore, the lead-

Exhibit 5.15

Examples of Performance Indicators for Q_5:
Quality of Leadership Systems: Vision

- Clarity in the vision statement about the future desired state in terms of performance excellence
- Percentage of faculty, staff, stakeholders, and (when appropriate) students who understand, share, and are motivated and inspired by the vision
- Percentage of employees who share a common identity and destiny expressed in the vision
- Alignment between vision and mission, guiding principles, and strategic goals
- Alignment between vision and current programs and services offered, customers served, and intended outcomes
- Alignment between vision and allocation of resources

ership system is also responsible for providing the organization with a set of guiding principles that present the basic truths and practices that guide how people behave, work, and relate to those they serve and to each other. Some guiding principles emanate from laws, legal codes, government regulations, and institutional policies and procedures; others derive from formal ethical codes of conduct and standards of behavior rooted in organizational traditions, values, and beliefs. Formal codes of ethics in higher education are created by many groups, including professional associations, unions, institutions, student organizations, and governmental agencies. Different codes of ethics frame acceptable behavior for different groups—for example, there are usually different codes of conduct for faculty and staff and for students.

Leadership systems use guiding principles to articulate desired cultural beliefs, values, and norms that leaders believe will help the organization achieve its mission and vision of excellence. Guiding principles, like mission and vision, also tell assessors what to measure and provide a context for evaluating organizational performance, particularly in terms of organizational culture.

Assessors measure leadership system quality in part by measuring quality and effectiveness of the unit's guiding principles. Sonja Sackmann (1991), who studies culture in organizations, advocates using an "issue focus" when measuring organizational culture because of its ubiquitous nature. An issue focus enhances comparisons by introducing "a specific context that forces respondents to draw on the same stock of knowledge" (p. 305). She advises that issues should be nonthreatening to respondents; some examples are leadership, compensation, reward systems, goals and objectives, and innovation.

Assessors begin by determining if the leadership system created and published guiding principles. Then they use surveys, focus groups, interviews, participant observations, database queries, and documentary analyses to measure quality and effectiveness of the guiding principles.

Assessors measure quality of guiding principles by determining the degree to which they reflect the following:

- Are adequately communicated to all members of the organizational community
- Are aligned with the organization's mission, vision, and strategic goals
- Clarify how people should behave, work, and relate to those they serve and to each other
- Provide standards (but not details) for doing things
- Invite rather than restrict creativity
- Balance needs and requirements of the corporate and scholarly cultures
- Lay an adequate foundation for vision and mission

Assessors measure effectiveness of guiding principles by determining the degree to which they accomplish the following:

- Instill in faculty, staff, and students the values, beliefs, and norms that leaders believe will bring the organization closer to its vision and strategic goals
- Provide standards against which people can hold themselves accountable
- Shape organizational design and major decision-making processes
- Guide everyday decisions, choices, and selection of strategic goals and objectives
- Bring coherence among diverse efforts
- Encourage harmony, balance, and respect among people embedded in the institution's corporate and scholarly cultures
- Provide a context for evaluating organizational culture, especially with respect to innovation

Finally, assessors measure quality of oversight processes that the organization uses to encourage behavior that conforms to established guiding principles and, when behaviors do not, processes the organization uses to impose sanctions for misconduct. Furthermore, assessors measure the impact those sanctions have on an organization's capacity to perform. Exhibit 5.16 provides examples of performance indicators that measure quality and effectiveness of guiding principles.

Exhibit 5.16
 Examples of Performance Indicators for Q_5:
 Quality of Leadership Systems: Guiding Principles

- Clarity in guiding principles about how people are expected to behave, work, and relate to those they serve and to each other
- Alignment between guiding principles and mission, vision, and strategic goals
- Performance indicators for measuring employee perceptions about quality of worklife (see Exhibit 5.21)
- Performance indicators for measuring employee perceptions about the quality of oversight processes
- Frequency and number of alleged and confirmed instances of faculty, staff, and student misconduct

Strategic Goals. As explained in Chapter Two, the leadership system is also responsible for setting direction through strategies they believe will help the organization find its competitive advantage and place in the environment. The leadership system is responsible for clarifying and prioritizing strategies through timetables, performance measures, and reference points; making clear who is responsible and accountable for performance results; supporting action plans with adequate resources; and setting high performance expectations that balance the often conflicting needs of organizational stakeholders, customers, faculty, and staff. Strategic goals also provide structural stability to organizational systems because they enable organizational constituencies to work together in the achievement of common goals.

Another way to measure leadership system quality is to determine the quality and progress toward achievement of the organization's strategic goals. Goal achievement, as described earlier, is a reflection of organizational effectiveness. Therefore, organizational effectiveness, like other areas of organizational performance, is one of the important measures of the quality of an organization's leadership system in relation to its strategic goals.

Assessors must also determine the quality of the strategic goals themselves. They begin by determining if strategic goals and high performance expectations were created and published. Then they use surveys, focus groups, interviews, participant observations, database queries, and documentary analyses to determine the quality and effectiveness of strategic goals.

Assessors measure quality of strategic goals by determining the degree to which they reflect the following:

- Are adequately communicated to all members of the organizational community

- Are understood, supported, and "owned" by faculty, staff, students, and stakeholders
- Align with and further the achievement of the organization's mission and vision
- Prepare the organization to meet future challenges presented by environmental, social, political, health, technological, and economic forces projected to affect future resources (human, financial, technology, energy, physical space), customer base, program mix, and so forth
- Are consistent and align with guiding principles
- Are realistic given the organization's capacity for implementation and supported with necessary resources
- Are aligned with functional and lower-level operational plans
- Are created through collaboration between members representing the corporate and scholarly cultures
- Are prioritized and clear in terms of responsibility, accountability, timetables, performance indicators, and reference points

Assessors measure effectiveness of strategic goals by determining the extent to which they accomplish the following:

- Provide structural stability to organizational systems by enabling organizational constituencies to work together in the achievement of common goals
- Ensure efficient and focused use of critical resources
- Influence decisions, actions, and allocation of time, energy, and resources
- Frame departmental operational plans and budgetary requests that align with strategic goals

Exhibit 5.17 provides examples of performance indicators that measure quality and effectiveness of strategic goals.

Organizational Structure.   Another internal responsibility of a leadership system is to create organizational structure. Leaders can specifically and intentionally design an organization's structure to optimize resources and improve organizational performance or, in the case of many small organizations, let it evolve as needs arise. As explained in Chapter Two, quality of organizational structure is measured along two dimensions: design and governance.

Design.   Assessors use surveys, focus groups, interviews, participant observations, database queries, and documentary analyses to determine quality and effectiveness of structural design.

Exhibit 5.17

Examples of Performance Indicators for Q_5:
Quality of Leadership Systems: Strategic Goals

- Alignment between strategic goals and mission, vision, and guiding principles
- Alignment between strategic and functional goals
- Alignment between strategic goals and local operational goals
- Clarity in accountability and responsibility for goal achievement
- Clarity in timetables, performance indicators, and reference points for goal assessment
- Percentage of employees who understand, support, and take ownership of strategic goals
- Percentage of employees who believe that strategic goals present the best route for achieving performance excellence and positioning the organization in its external environment
- Percentage of employees who believe that strategic goals are adequately supported with critical resources
- Percentage of employees who believe that strategic goals set high performance expectations that balance conflicting needs of organizational stakeholders, customers, faculty, and staff

Assessors measure quality of design by determining the degree to which it reflects the following:

- Aligns with mission, vision, and strategic goals
- Is linked to specific areas of organizational performance it will strengthen
- Represents specific values and beliefs expressed in guiding principles (such as collegiality)
- Is based on specific strategies to improve organizational performance
- Represents the most efficient use of critical resources

Assessors measure effectiveness of organizational design by determining the degree to which it accomplishes the following:

- Helps the organization achieve its purpose, vision, and strategic goals
- Improves specific areas of organizational performance it was intended to improve (and does not decrease performance in other areas)
- Generates appropriate amounts and levels of work for employees
- Provides easy service access for internal and external customers and reduces customer complaints related to service access

Exhibit 5.18

Examples of Performance Indicators for Q_5: Quality of Leadership
Systems: Organizational Structure: Design and Governance

Organizational Design

- Alignment between organizational design and mission, vision, guiding principles, strategic goals
- Supporting evidence that the design improves targeted areas of organizational performance
- Frequency and number of customer complaints about access to services
- Frequency and number of employee complaints about workload
- Employee turnover rates
- Employee absenteeism rates
- Other quality-of-worklife indicators (see Exhibit 5.21)

Governance

- Alignment with mission, vision, guiding principles, and strategic goals
- Percentage of faculty, staff, and students serving on important committees and task forces
- Percentage of faculty, staff, and students who support major decisions affecting the organization's future capacity to perform
- Percentage of faculty, staff, and students who believe that the governance structure produces decisions in a timely and cost-effective manner that improves organizational performance
- Other performance indicators for measuring quality of key work processes (see Exhibits 5.9 and 5.10)
- Alignment between strategic goals and mission, vision, and guiding principles
- Clarity in accountability and responsibility for goal achievement
- Clarity in timetables, performance indicators, and reference points for goal assessment
- Alignment of strategic and operational goals at the institution and departmental levels
- Percentage of employees who understand, support, and take ownership of strategic goals as the best route for achieving performance excellence and taking competitive advantage of its position in the external environment
- Percentage of employees who believe that strategic plans are adequately supported with critical resources
- Percentage of employees who believe that strategic goals set high performance expectations that balance the conflicting needs of organizational stakeholders, customers, faculty, and staff

---

Exhibit 5.18 provides examples of performance indicators that measure quality of organizational design.

Governance.   As explained in Chapter Two, an organization's governance structure, in assessment, is represented by its decision-making processes and practices. Decision-making practices vary among and within organizations in higher education, depending on their mission, size, history, culture, traditions, and guiding principles. Decision making can be systematic or ad hoc, centralized or decentralized, top-down or bottom-up, or some combination of these. However, most leaders in higher education strive for some level of collegiality in their governance structures because they believe that collegiality increases employee involvement through participation on ad hoc and standing committees, tasks forces, and improvement teams. They also believe that collegiality increases employee support for proposals and recommendations for change.

Assessors measure quality and effectiveness of an organization's governance structure by determining the quality of decision-making processes and practices and the decisions derived from them. They use surveys, focus groups, interviews, participant observations, database queries, and documentary analyses to identify formal and informal decision-making processes and to measure their quality and effectiveness.

Assessors measure quality of major decision-making processes by determining the degree to which they reflect the following:

- Are consistent with the organization's guiding principles
- Are robust, responsive, and cost-efficient
- Minimize cycle time, average cost, rework, and waste

Assessors measure effectiveness of decision-making processes by determining the extent to which they accomplish the following:

- Help the organization achieve its mission and vision
- Generate short- and long-term acceptance by the people affected by change
- Produce decisions in a timely and cost-effective manner that improves organizational performance by helping the organization move toward its vision and achievement of strategic goals

Exhibit 5.18 provides examples of performance indicators that measure quality and effectiveness of organizational structure in terms of design and governance.

Resources. An organization's leadership system is also responsible for acquiring and allocating resources necessary for the organization to achieve performance success as defined by its mission and vision. Assessors measure leadership system quality in terms of the quality of resources it acquires and quality of processes it uses to allocate resources.

Resources Acquired. Chapter Two described resources (called inputs in systems thinking) required of organizations to perform work and create outputs. These inputs are human resources, financial resources, equipment, supplies, physical space, energy, and information. Measurement of input quality is not only a measure of organizational performance but also a measure of leadership system quality. As a measure of leadership system quality, input quality (described as Q_2: Quality of Inputs) examines the following areas:

- Human resources in terms of levels of preparedness and qualifications, quantity, cost, levels of satisfaction, productivity, and success in relation to strategic execution
- Financial resources in terms of quantity, appropriateness, and timeliness
- Equipment and supplies in terms of quality, replacement and maintenance cost, quantity, currency, reliability, safety, and suitability
- Physical space in terms of quality, quantity, currency, healthiness, safety, maintenance cost, and accessibility of buildings and grounds
- Energy in terms of quantity, cost, and reliability
- Information in terms of accuracy, currency, timeliness, understandability, and quantity

Allocation Processes.   An assessment of the quality of resource allocation processes follows the same measurement practices of any key work process (described as Q_3: Quality of Key Work Processes). Assessors measure process design with performance indicators to determine if it is robust, responsive, and cost-efficient. More specifically, they seek indicators of cost, cycle time, rework, waste, and scrap as a measure of process quality. They also look at the quality of resource allocation decisions to determine if they help the organization move toward its mission, vision, and strategic goals. Exhibit 5.19 provides examples of performance indicators that measure quality of resources and resource allocation processes.

Exhibit 5.19
  Examples of Performance Indicators for Q_5:
  Quality of Leadership Systems: Resource Acquisition and Allocation

---

Resource Acquisition
  - Performance indicators for measuring quality of inputs (see Exhibits 5.7 and 5.8)

Resource Allocation
  - Performance indicators for measuring quality of resource allocation processes (see Exhibits 5.9 and 5.10)

Costs and Benefits. The last dimension of leadership system quality is a measure of the costs to operate a leadership system compared with benefits gained by the organization from services provided by the system. The costs of a leadership system are determined by salaries, benefits, and current expenses required by leaders and their staff to carry out their work. Benefits are measured in terms of quality of services provided, as discussed earlier, plus organizational performance in other areas such as financial durability, to be discussed shortly. Assessors also measure total leadership system costs as a percentage of total operating costs and compare leadership system salaries with faculty and staff salaries. Exhibit 5.20 provides examples of performance indicators measuring costs and benefits of leadership systems as well as other aspects of Q_5: Quality of Leadership Systems for both academic and administrative organizations, using examples from Exhibits 2.1 and 2.2.

Worksheet 5.8 will help assessors evaluate the quality of services that provide direction and support to the organization.

Q_6: Quality of Worklife

The sixth and last dimension of quality is quality of worklife, which is a measure of employees' perceptions and attitudes about the quality of their organization, work experiences, and workplace. Sink and Tuttle (1989) define quality of worklife as the affective response of the workforce to the workplace. Figure 5.4 illustrates that Q_6: Quality of Worklife is linked to a system's inputs and key work processes.

Quality of worklife is also a reflection of the quality of organizational culture. Therefore, it is not only an important area of overall organizational performance to measure but also another avenue for

Exhibit 5.20
    Examples of Performance Indicators for Q_5:
    Quality of Leadership Systems: Costs and Benefits

- Ratios of administrator FTE to faculty FTE or staff FTE (or both)
- Salaries of administrators (or senior leaders) compared with salaries of faculty or staff or both
- Total leadership system costs as a percentage of total departmental costs
- Total leadership system costs compared with quality of services provided (see Exhibits 5.14 to 5.19)
- Total leadership system costs compared to improvements in other areas of organizational performance such as financial durability (see Exhibits 5.27 and 5.28)

---

measuring quality of services provided by the organization's leadership system.

Employees perceive quality of worklife differently, depending on their demographic and socioeconomic characteristics, specific positions, scope of responsibilities, and longevity with the organization. Therefore, it is wise to segment perception results by types of employees relevant to assessment users. For example, senior leaders typically prefer to differentiate responses of faculty from administrators and staff and by department; administrators and managers typically prefer to differentiate responses by gender, longevity, and job description.

Employees determine quality of worklife by considering the following aspects of their work experiences and workplace: adequacy of resources and quality of the workplace environment; treatment by supervisors and others in the organization; job design, rewards, incentives, and recognition programs; and organizational reputation and success.

With respect to adequacy of resources and quality of the workplace environment, employees consider the following questions:

- Is equipment adequate to do the work?

- Are people trained sufficiently to use equipment and perform new work?

- Are the costs of continuing education required by the organization adequately covered by tuition reimbursement programs?

- Is child care available? If so, is it adequate?

- Are recreational facilities available? If so, are they adequate?

- Does a wellness program exist? If so, is it adequate?

- Is the workplace safe and secure?

- Is the work environment comfortable?

- Do interdepartmental wars interfere with work?

- Are work hours flexible enough?

Regarding treatment by supervisors and others, employees consider the following questions:

- Are people treated in a fair and equitable way?

- Are people treated with respect, dignity, and trust?

- Do people believe they are part of a supportive team?

- Do people receive clear directions, guidance, and advice from supervisors?

- Do people receive appropriate feedback in a timely manner?

- Do people respect leaders as competent and inspirational?

With respect to job design, rewards, incentives, and recognition programs, employees consider the following questions:

- Are people given appropriate authority along with assigned responsibility?
- Are jobs in keeping with people's skills and abilities?
- Are people given opportunities to grow, be creative, and take risks?
- Are compensation and benefits competitive and comparable with the work and with others who perform similar work?
- Are people recognized and rewarded for accomplishments?
- Do people have opportunities for promotion and time off?

Regarding organizational reputation and success, employees consider the following questions:

- Does the organization enjoy an excellent reputation and public image?
- Does it offer only high-quality programs and services?
- Does it set high standards for moral and ethical behavior?
- Does it demonstrate good citizenship and protect the local environment?

Assessors collect data about quality of worklife through self-reporting methods (surveys, interviews, and focus groups) to determine employee perceptions and attitudes. They also query databases and analyze documents to collect data about employee turnover, absenteeism, sick leave, complaints, grievances, crime rates, lawsuits, injury rates, and frequency and types of noncompliance citations from OSHA and other organizations that set workplace standards. Exhibit 5.21 offers examples of performance indicators that measure Q_6: Quality of Worklife in both academic and administrative organizations.

Worksheet 5.9 will help assessors determine their unit's quality of worklife.

Customer and Stakeholder Satisfaction

Customer and stakeholder satisfaction is the fourth major area of organizational performance. Unlike effectiveness, productivity, and quality, this area of performance focuses on the extent to which the organization's internal and external customers are satisfied with system outputs, and internal and external stakeholders (including assessment

Exhibit 5.21

Examples of Performance Indicators for Q_6: Quality of Worklife

- Employee perceptions about adequacy of resources and quality of the workplace environment
- Employee perceptions regarding treatment by supervisors and others in the organization
- Employee perceptions about job design, rewards, incentives, and recognition programs
- Employee perceptions of organizational reputation and success
- Employee turnover rates
- Employee absenteeism rates
- Frequency and duration of sick leave
- Number of grievances and formal complaints
- Campus crime rates
- Number of lawsuits
- Number of injuries, by type
- Employee participation rates in committees and attendance at social events sponsored by the organization
- Number and types of noncompliance citations from OSHA and other organizations that set workplace standards
- Degree of decision acceptance among employees significantly affected by major organizational changes

users) are satisfied with organizational performance. Generally, administrators and managers are interested in customer satisfaction and senior leaders are interested in stakeholder satisfaction, but it depends on the specific stakeholder group and what aspect of performance is under consideration. Figure 5.5 illustrates that customer and stakeholder satisfaction is linked to a system's outputs and outcomes.

Customer Satisfaction

Chapter Three defined customers, for purposes of assessment, as people and organizations who directly receive or experience the organization's outputs. Customers can be potential or current, external or internal. Exhibits 3.7 and 3.8 provided examples of external and internal customers of academic and administrative organizations.

Customer satisfaction is crucial to organizational success because customers are the reason organizations exist. The needs and preferences of customers (and to some extent faculty, staff, and stakeholders) define what and how the organization creates and how it delivers its products and services. The experiences of customers as they interact with products and services determine the degree to which an organization achieves its intended outcomes. Defining customers as

Figure 5.5

Customer and Stakeholder Satisfaction

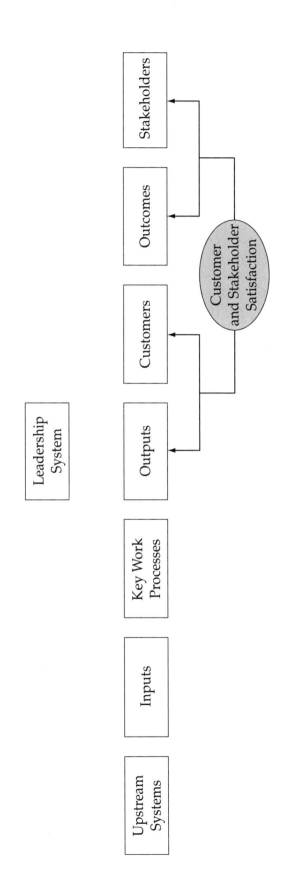

Source: Adapted from Sink and Tuttle, 1989.

persons and organizations who directly receive or experience an organization's products and services is important in assessment because it identifies those whose needs, preferences, and perceptions serve as reference points for evaluating areas of organizational performance such as Q_3: Quality of Key Work Processes, Q_4: Quality of Output, and customer satisfaction.

Colleges and universities have always competed with one another for critical resources. They compete for faculty and financial support, including grants and contracts. They compete for reputation and rank. They also compete for the best students. When students are unsatisfied, they go elsewhere for service, when they can. Unsatisfied customers also influence choice decisions of future customers, potential donors, and stakeholders. Without customer satisfaction, organizations lose customer loyalty, and lost customer loyalty translates into lost customers. Organizations without customers cannot achieve their purpose and therefore cannot survive.

As discussed earlier, Q_6: Quality of Worklife is a measure of organizational performance from the perspective of employees. Similarly, customer satisfaction is a measure of organizational performance from the perspective of customers. The key to good measurement of customer satisfaction is knowledge of what customers need, prefer, and require. Unfortunately, these characteristics change constantly, so assessors must continuously check their assumptions. For example, staff from a registrar's office at a large state-supported institution assumed that undergraduate students hated waiting in line to register. As it turned out, many new students enjoyed the social interactions that occurred while waiting in line. So along with shortening the wait time, staff began serving coffee and donuts to waiting students and introducing subtle activities to increase social interactions. Assessors must always maintain up-to-date knowledge and understanding of customer needs, preferences, and requirements so that they can frame their measurement of customer satisfaction within the right context for evaluation. Chapter Four described the use of gap analysis in analyzing customer satisfaction by measuring discrepancies between actual performance and customer preferences and perceptions.

The number of methods available to assessors seeking customer satisfaction data is constantly increasing. The most common ones are self-reporting methods such as surveys (student evaluations of faculty, for example) and focus groups and interviews used to determine customer attitudes and opinions, including preferences and perceptions. Assessors also collect data on application rates, attendance rates, retention rates, participation rates, and traffic patterns. Several innovative methods are available to assessors as well: customer listening posts, complaint management, and cycle of service. Each is described in turn.

Customer Listening Posts

One way to capture feedback from customers is through so-called customer listening posts. These are feedback opportunities created whenever the organization interacts with its customers. Some listening posts, such as customer surveys, toll-free telephone numbers, and suggestion boxes, are deliberately created to collect customer feedback. Other listening posts are the result of direct, face-to-face interactions with customers during meetings and interviews, customer councils, focus groups, and visits by ombudsmen and organizational leaders. Face-to-face listening posts are also created whenever employees meet directly with customers on a daily basis, as when employees answer phones, work at help desks, serve as receptionists, or work behind counters in the bookstore, cafeteria, housing office, admissions office, registrar's office, or bursar's office. All listening posts present wonderful opportunities for obtaining current and spontaneous customer feedback, and they require little extra effort on the part of assessors beyond designing data collection check sheets and phone logs.

Complaint Management

Another way to capture customer feedback is through analysis of complaints. Assessors analyze documents to determine the frequency and patterns of customer complaints, which provide a wealth of information about the nature of customer interactions with system outputs from the customers' point of view.

Cycle of Service

Karl Albrecht and Lawrence Bradford (1990) offer an innovative approach to understanding how and when customers decide on their degree of satisfaction in service-based organizations. They suggest that assessors map "moments of truth" as they are experienced by customers in a "cycle of service." Moments of truth is a metaphor for defining the "precise instant when the customer comes into contact with any aspect of your business and, on the basis of that contact, forms an opinion about the quality of your service and, potentially, the quality of your product" (p. 30). Moments of truth do not necessarily have to involve human contact. Customers driving into an organization's parking lot can experience a moment of truth. Customers might ask, Is the lot convenient? Are there enough parking spaces? Has recent snow been plowed? Are there sufficient signs to help find their way? Is there sufficient lighting to make it safe?

Albrecht and Bradford (1990) argue that leaders of all service-based organizations should identify and manage moments of truth, or else quality of service "regresses to mediocrity" (p. 32). One way to identify moments of truth is to brainstorm, from the perspective of customers, a list of brief encounters during which customers form an opinion about quality of service. Because moments of truth usually occur in a logical and measurable sequence, assessors can build a circular map of those moments—a map Albrecht and Bradford call a "cycle of service" (p. 33). Furthermore, assessors can identify moments of truth in the cycle of service that, if not managed positively, will almost certainly lead to customer dissatisfaction or a loss of customer confidence. Albrecht and Bradford call these "critical moments of truth" (p. 35). The true value of mapping moments of truth in a cycle of service is that it encourages assessors not only to view service from the customer's perspective but also to recognize how one aspect of service is related to other aspects and how combinations of experiences affect customer satisfaction. And it helps frame components of customer satisfaction feedback mechanisms as well.

Worksheet 5.10 will help assessors identify performance indicators to measure their unit's customer satisfaction.

Stakeholder Satisfaction

Chapter Three defined stakeholders as individuals and groups who benefit from organizational effectiveness—the achievement of intended outcomes and strategic goals. At the institutional level, stakeholders refer to the general public along with local, state, and national governments, organizations, and businesses that benefit from an educated public, a skilled workforce, and the creation and transfer of new knowledge. At the academic or administrative department level, stakeholders are specific groups who directly benefit from departmental goal achievement.

In general, academic departments have more stakeholders than administrative organizations. External stakeholders of academic departments are people and organizations outside the institution who benefit from an educated public, an educated workforce, and the creation and transfer of new knowledge. Internal stakeholders of academic departments are people and organizations inside the institution, like other academic departments, who benefit from service courses provided to their majors that meet general education requirements.

Stakeholders of administrative organizations are generally internal stakeholders just like their primary customers are generally internal customers. In fact, most stakeholders of administrative organizations are customers of their internal customers. For example, internal stakeholders of Information Services are customers of the registrar's office who benefit from IS-supported technology the office uses to increase the productivity and quality of the services it provides.

Not all stakeholders are critically important to the performance success of an organization. But those that are important present another opportunity to assess organizational performance in terms of stakeholder satisfaction. Sometimes stakeholders, like state governing boards, also operate as upstream systems when constraining resources. This does not present problems in assessment so long as assessors recognize the proper relationship between external elements and the organizational system at the time they are collecting data about organizational performance.

Stakeholder satisfaction is an important area of organizational performance. Assessors generally measure satisfaction of external and internal stakeholders differently. For example, assessors measure satisfaction of external stakeholders, such as employers, through surveys and observation of employment patterns. They rarely measure satisfaction of internal stakeholders directly; rather, they depend on their internal customers to measure customer satisfaction and convey that feedback back to them as a measure of stakeholder satisfaction. For example, it is unlikely that Information Services would directly survey the registrar's office's customers about their satisfaction with IS-supported technology used by that office. Instead, they would ask the registrar's office to measure customer satisfaction pertaining to IS-supported technology as part of the office's overall measurement of customer satisfaction and to convey that feedback to Information Services as a measure of stakeholder satisfaction. It is unlikely that Information Services would directly survey student satisfaction with Blackboard, a Web-based classroom management tool used by faculty. Instead, they would ask faculty to measure student satisfaction with Blackboard and convey that feedback to IS as a measure of stakeholder satisfaction. It should be noted, however, that Information Services is likely to survey students to measure customer satisfaction with e-mail, a service IS provides directly to end users.

Exhibits 5.22 and 5.23 provide examples of performance indicators that measure customer and stakeholder satisfaction of an academic department and Information Services, respectively, using examples of external and internal customers and stakeholders from Exhibits 3.7 through 3.10.

Worksheet 5.11 will help assessors identify performance indicators to measure their unit's stakeholder satisfaction.

Exhibit 5.22

Examples of Performance Indicators for Customer
and Stakeholder Satisfaction in an Academic Department

External Customer Satisfaction
- Percentage of patrons reporting positive responses to performance events sponsored by faculty and students
- Percentage of research sponsors funding future requests

(continued on the next page)

Exhibit 5.22, *continued*
Examples of Performance Indicators for Customer and Stakeholder Satisfaction in an Academic Department

Internal Customer Satisfaction

- Percentage of students responding positively in student evaluation of faculty surveys
- Summary of documented customer complaints and compliments
- Number of course drops and adds
- Retention rates
- Attendance rates
- Customer responses recorded in phone logs and check sheets from customer listening posts

Stakeholder Satisfaction

- Percentage of employers responding positively in employer surveys
- Student placement rates
- Percentage of alumni responding positively in alumni follow-up studies
- Dollar value of donations and gifts from alumni
- Percentage of department graduates admitted to graduate programs of their choice
- Retention and graduation rates of program completers as graduate students and undergraduate students at transfer institutions
- Percentage of institutional revenues generated from research
- Percentage of institutional revenues generated from contracted services
- Number of positions funded by research and contracts

Exhibit 5.23
Examples of Performance Indicators for Customer and Stakeholder Satisfaction in Information Services

External Customer Satisfaction

- Percentage of external organizations contracting for IT services responding positively in customer satisfaction surveys
- Dollar value of new business generated from external organizations contracting for IS services

Internal Customer Satisfaction

- Percentage of end users responding positively on end user satisfaction surveys
- Summary of documented customer complaints and compliments
- Customer responses recorded in phone logs and check sheets from customer listening posts

Stakeholder Satisfaction

- Percentage of students and staff responding positively to IS customers on surveys of customer satisfaction related to IS-supported technology

Efficiency

Efficiency is the fifth important area of organizational performance to measure. Efficiency reflects how well an organization optimizes use of its scarce resources. Sink and Tuttle (1989) define efficiency as "resources expected or predicted or forecasted or estimated to be consumed divided by resources actually consumed" (p. 172). Assessment user groups use efficiency data to determine what efficiency gains are critical to organizational success. Generally, senior leaders, administrators, and managers are interested in this area of organizational performance. Figure 5.6 illustrates that efficiency is linked to a system's inputs.

Assessors measure two dimensions of efficiency: resource utilization and costs and benefits of quality management.

Resource Utilization

One method assessors use to measure efficiency is to compare actual use of people's time, equipment, supplies, physical space, energy, and financial resources against budgeted or planned use. For example, at the institutional level, assessors measure efficiency by comparing actual expenditures to budgeted estimates or actual expenditures to total resources available against the institution's strategic goals. Assessors monitor the overall expenditure structure to determine how expenditures, by category, compare to total expenditures or to budgeted estimates. Assessors monitor these expenditures to answer a number of performance questions: What percentage of dollars were spent on each category (such as instruction and academic support)? To what extent do actual expenditures compare favorably with planned and budgeted estimates? To what extent do expenditures align with and help the organization achieve its strategic goals?

Because higher education is a labor-intensive endeavor, efficient use of faculty, staff, and student time is an important aspect of efficiency. One way to measure efficiency, therefore, is to compare actual to planned labor costs for specific activities. Activity-based costing is done by multiplying amount of time spent on an activity by the average hourly rate of individuals engaged in the activity. Assessors often use activity costs to measure efficiency of self-study and program review committees and to determine the true cost of their work.

Assessors also measure efficiency by measuring percentage of time employees spend directly serving customers as compared to time they spend in staff meetings, training sessions, planning workshops, employee recruitment activities, assessment, self-studies, and program reviews. Assessors in organizations with nonexempt employees measure efficiency by comparing actual to budgeted labor costs (using time

Figure 5.6
Efficiency

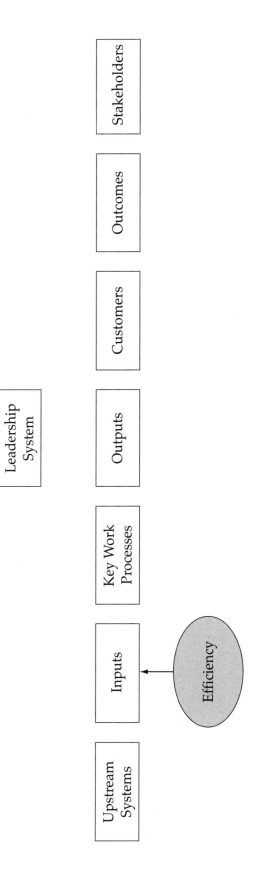

Source: Adapted from Sink and Tuttle, 1989.

and attendance data) as a form of quality control of overtime—they compare intended versus unintended overtime to learn who earned how much overtime, when, where, and why.

In addition to labor costs, assessors track number and dollar value of expensive new equipment that goes unused waiting for distribution or installation; utilization rates of classrooms, computer labs, research labs, and libraries; working hours lost due to energy outages; and network and equipment downtime.

Costs and Benefits of Quality Management

Another important aspect of organizational efficiency involves the assessment of costs and benefits of quality management. Higher education has a long history of making sure that programs and services meet quality standards. It is wise for assessors to monitor quality management costs continuously to ensure that they stay within intended parameters and lead to anticipated benefits.

As explained in our discussion of quality, poor quality can be fatal to an institution or program. Any cost incurred to assure and control quality of programs and services thus pales in comparison to the true cost of poor quality, reflected in loss of enrollments, accreditation, and jobs; reduced appropriations, donations, and gifts; and lower national rankings. However, just as for any other costs, assessors must analyze costs and benefits of quality management in their overall measurement of efficiency.

According to John Oakland (1992), many quality management costs are hidden or intangible. To help assessors find and track those costs, he offers three types of costs assessors should measure: failure costs (internal and external), appraisal costs, and prevention costs.

Failure Costs
According to Oakland (1992), failure costs are the costs of "getting it wrong." There are many hidden failure costs in higher education. For example, there are failure costs associated with replacing students lost through attrition. These include costs to recruit, admit, orient, advise, register, and house new students who replace lost students. There are failure costs in poorly designed processes resulting in refunds and reimbursements and in repeating paperwork that was incorrectly submitted or processed. There are failure costs in faculty and staff searches that yield no viable offers or acceptances the first time around. There are failure costs to repeated repairs and services not done properly the first time. There are failure costs to defend lawsuits and pay damages. There are failure costs to manage customer complaints and process employee grievances.

Appraisal Costs

According to Oakland (1992), appraisal costs are the costs of "making sure it is right." Appraisal activity has been a common form of quality control in higher education for years. There are large appraisal costs in conducting self-studies and program reviews and for managing and implementing performance appraisal systems. There are appraisal costs in building, deploying, and maintaining a high-quality assessment system. There are appraisal costs in inspecting equipment, furnishings, and supplies at the receiving dock and taking periodic inventories. There are appraisal costs in purchasing and maintaining software that tracks computer problems and requests for repair, computer and network usage and outages, equipment and energy reliability, donor activities, breaches of security, prospective student inquiries, and yield rates. There are appraisal costs in preparing monthly budget and annual reports tracking revenues and expenditures and in preparing and analyzing assessment reports conveying organizational performance.

Prevention Costs

According to Oakland (1992), prevention costs are the costs of "doing it right the first time." He describes prevention costs as planned costs incurred prior to operations. There are prevention costs in higher education associated with the development of quality standards and other reference points against which measured performance is evaluated as part of the evaluation process. For example, there are prevention costs in staffing committees that set standards for general education, computer competencies, professional licensing, and other program requirements. There are prevention costs in developing strategic plans, operating and capital budgets, assessment plans, and course schedules. There are prevention costs in developing campus master plans and creating specifications for construction bids, training personnel, funding professional development activities, and so forth.

Exhibits 5.24 and 5.25 offer examples of performance indicators that measure efficiency of an academic department and Information Services, respectively.

Worksheet 5.12 will help assessors evaluate their unit's efficiency.

Innovation

Innovation is the sixth area of organizational performance. Innovation is a measure of an organization's creative changes put into place to improve organizational performance. Sink and Tuttle (1989) define innovation as "the creative process of changing what we are doing, how we are doing things, structure, technology, products, services, meth-

Exhibit 5.24
Examples of Performance Indicators for
Efficiency in an Academic Department

- Percentage of unfilled seats in scheduled classes
- Usage rate of departmental classrooms and labs
- Circulation of departmental library holdings
- Percentage of students in good academic standing who do not return
- Activity cost and percentage of total time of faculty and staff conducting teaching, research, program reviews, self-studies, and peer reviews and performance appraisals
- Activity cost and percentage of total time of faculty and staff engaged in professional development, attending general meetings (by type and faculty rank), scheduling courses, and creating budgets, capital requests, and annual reports
- Actual student credit hours generated as a percentage of budgeted student credit hours
- Dollar value of overtime, intended and unintended, as a percentage of total budgeted salaries and wages

Exhibit 5.25
Examples of Performance Indicators for
Efficiency in Information Services

- Activity cost and percentage of total time of staff spent consulting end users, training end users, engaged in professional development and training, attending general meetings (by type and employee salary range), inventorying equipment, repeating service on desktop machines, developing budgets and capital requests, scheduling and marketing training classes, and conducting performance appraisals
- Dollar value of equipment unused, waiting for distribution or installation
- Number of days new and repaired equipment waits for distribution or installation
- Working hours lost due to energy outages and network or equipment downtime
- Projected IS fees generated compared with actual fees collected
- Dollar value of overtime, intended and unintended, as a percentage of total budgeted salaries and wages

ods, procedures, policies, etc., to successfully respond to internal and external pressures, opportunities, challenges, threats" (p. 183). Their operational definition has several key words. First, innovation involves change—without change, an organization cannot be innovative. Second, innovation involves creativity—without creativity, an organization cannot change in innovative ways. Finally, innovation involves a successful response to environmental forces—without responding successfully to environmental forces, organizations may change creatively but not in ways that improve performance. In general, senior leaders, administrators, and managers who seek innovation in their organization's practices, products, and services are most interested in this area of organizational performance. Figure 5.7 illustrates that innovation is linked to all system elements.

Innovative organizations typically reflect a leadership system that supports risk taking and change. Organizations that are innovative have a leadership system that clearly articulates innovation as part of the organization's vision and guiding principles. Leaders also incorporate innovation into strategic goals. Finally, leaders create and implement institutional rewards and incentive systems that encourage innovation over maintenance of the status quo.

Leaders of innovative organizations also ensure that change is not implemented merely for change's sake. Innovative organizations implement change as part of strategic initiatives designed to respond to environmental forces. Depending on the organization's mission, vision, and strategic goals, most organizations are capable of demonstrating change in almost every aspect of organizational operations. However, organizations that change for change's sake are not necessarily innovative. Innovative organizations not only change but also improve strategically. Innovation is always measured in relation to improvements in specific areas of organizational performance linked to strategic and operational goals.

According to Senge (1998), innovation reflects an organization's learning culture. As mentioned in Chapter One, Senge expanded on Drucker's "discipline of innovation" by incorporating the need for organizations to work together and learn from one another's efforts. Without a culture of organizational learning, Senge argues, organizations stifle their ability to be innovative. Assessment is a core research initiative for all learning organizations that are innovative. And for purposes of innovation, assessment for learning is much more powerful than assessment for evaluation. For leaders seeking a culture of organizational learning, measurement of innovation is also a measure of organizational learning.

Assessors begin their measurement of innovation with a listing of major changes implemented during a given period of time. Then they analyze those changes in several ways. First, they determine the scope and creativity of changes listed for that time period. Second, they analyze the link between changes and requirements of strategic goals. Finally, they determine the impact changes made on specific areas of organizational performance as a measure of an institution's ability to successfully respond to environmental factors in a timely, appropriate, and results-driven manner.

Figure 5.7
Innovation

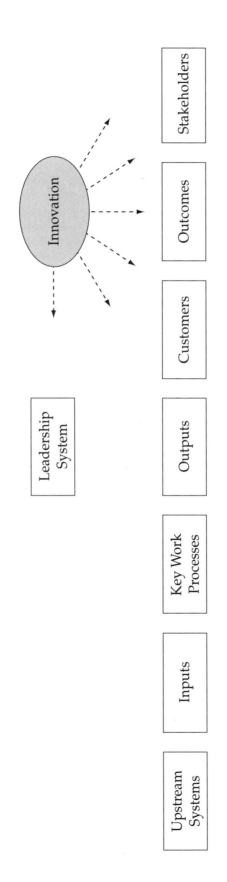

Source: Adapted from Sink and Tuttle, 1989.

Exhibit 5.26
Examples of Creative Changes Supporting Innovation

- New technology to increase productivity and customer satisfaction
- New organizational structures to improve efficiency, productivity, customer satisfaction, and financial durability
- Reengineered work processes to improve quality, efficiency, and productivity
- New programs and services to improve effectiveness, customer satisfaction, and financial durability
- New pricing structures to strengthen financial durability

Measurement of innovation also includes analyses of organizational culture described as Q_5: Quality of Leadership Systems and to some extent analyses of employee attitudes and perceptions described as Q_6: Quality of Worklife.

Exhibit 5.26 offers examples of creative changes that affect areas of organizational performance that could be linked to strategic initiatives and serve as indicators of organizational innovativeness.

Worksheet 5.13 will help assessors evaluate their unit's innovation.

Financial Durability

The seventh area of organizational performance is financial durability, a mission-specific measure of the financial health and well-being of the organization under review. It is an essential bottom-line financial measure of an organization's overall performance. Sink and Tuttle (1989) call this area of organizational performance "profitability" for profit centers and "budgetability" for cost centers.

For organizations within the institution whose mission is "to make a profit," such as auxiliary enterprises, assessors measure financial durability by comparing costs to revenues and other measures of liquidity and financial performance. For nonprofit organizations whose mission is goal achievement, assessors measure financial durability by comparing total operating costs to revenues or total operating costs to benefits (as measured by goal achievement). Figure 5.8 illustrates that financial durability is linked to a system's inputs, outputs, and outcomes. Senior leaders and external stakeholders are primarily interested in this area of organizational performance.

Senior leaders use financial durability data in several ways. They use financial durability data to monitor stability and reliability of institutional revenues and expenditures to discover trends that might

Figure 5.8
Financial Durability

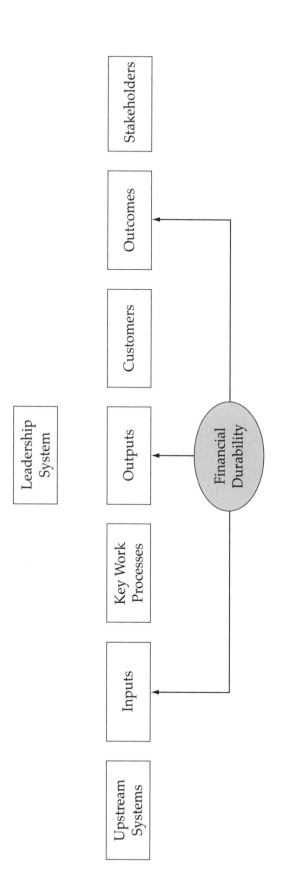

Source: Adapted from Sink and Tuttle, 1989.

have a deleterious effect on the financial situation. They also use financial durability data as a basis for allocating resources in incentive-based, responsibility-based, and program-based budgeting processes. Finally, they use financial durability data to support decisions to sustain, downsize, expand, outsource, or privatize all or some of an institution's operations. In general, financial durability data help senior leaders answer the assessment question of whether maintaining a unit is worthwhile: Do benefits from the unit compare favorably with its total operating costs?

To measure financial durability at the institutional level, assessors measure operating surpluses and deficits, proportion of long-term debt to total liability, asset-to-liability ratios, size of endowment and its yield, total return and growth, and sources of gifts and diversity of gift giving. At the academic department level, assessors measure instructional costs as compared to tuition and fees collected, student financial aid dollars generated as percentage of total tuition and fees collected, and student credit hours generated per faculty FTE. Finally, they compare total operating costs of the unit to benefits achieved in terms of effectiveness, quality, and customer or stakeholder satisfaction.

Exhibits 5.27 and 5.28 offer examples of performance indicators that measure financial durability of an academic department and Information Services, respectively.

Worksheet 5.14 will help assessors evaluate their unit's financial durability.

Critical Success Factors

The final aspect of measuring organizational performance is comparing an organization's performance in areas deemed critical to its success and its long-term survival. As discussed in Chapter Four, critical success factors are unique to each unit of analysis; factors critical to the success of one unit may not be critical to another. Critical success factors are also mission-specific. Once assessors have identified their organization's critical success factors, they identify performance indicators and reference points for evaluating performance for each success factor.

Worksheet 5.15 will help assessors measure organizational performance in relation to their unit's critical success factors.

Exhibit 5.27

Examples of Performance Indicators for
Financial Durability in an Academic Department

- Tuition and fees generated by the department as a percentage of total departmental expenditures
- Student credit hours generated compared to total departmental expenditures
- Student credit hours generated per faculty FTE
- Total dollars generated from sponsored research as a percentage of total departmental expenditures
- Total dollars generated from sponsored research as a percentage of total departmental revenues
- Endowment ranking
- Total departmental expenditures compared with the following measures of benefits: effectiveness (see Exhibit 5.1), quality of outputs (see Exhibit 5.11), and customer and stakeholder satisfaction (see Exhibit 5.22)
- Research support staff salaries as a percentage of total departmental expenditures
- Administrator salaries as a percentage of total departmental expenditures
- Administrator salaries compared with faculty salaries
- Total leadership system expenditures as a percentage of total departmental expenditures
- Total leadership system costs as a percentage of total departmental revenues

Exhibit 5.28

Examples of Performance Indicators for
Financial Durability in Information Services

- IS fees generated as a percentage of total IS departmental expenditures
- Total IS expenditures compared to total number of campus employees served
- Total IS expenditures compared to total number of students served
- Total IS expenditures compared with current fund surplus (or deficit), effectiveness (see Exhibit 5.2), quality of outputs (see Exhibit 5.12), and customer and stakeholder satisfaction (see Exhibit 5.23)
- Administrator salaries compared with technical staff salaries
- Total leadership system expenditures as a percentage of total departmental expenditures
- Total leadership system costs as a percentage of total departmental revenues
- Percentage and dollar value of computing services outsourced

Assessment Users' Preferred Areas of Organizational Performance

Worksheet 5.16 will help assessors identify areas of organizational performance important to their unit's major assessment user groups identified on Worksheet 1.1.

Interrelationships in Organizational Performance

Sink and Tuttle (1989) point out that interrelationships exist among the seven areas of organizational performance. For example, effectiveness incorporates quality attributes, and productivity incorporates efficiency. Sink and Tuttle note, in demonstrating the overlap, that an organizational system that is effective, efficient, and has high-quality outputs and processes will likely be productive but will have to maintain a certain quality of worklife and level of innovation in order to maintain financial durability and achieve excellence, survival, and growth.

Another way of viewing interrelationships in organizational performance uses systems thinking. From this perspective, assessors look at the effect the performance of one unit has on the performance of other units in the same institution. For example, suppose senior leaders allocated additional resources to unit A at the expense of unit B in the same institution. Most likely, unit A's performance will improve due to increased resources. However, increases in unit A's performance may be offset by decreases in unit B's performance due to its reduced resources. In other words, achievement of one goal may be at the expense of achievement of another goal. It is important, therefore, that assessors monitor performance changes across units when change is introduced into the larger system, particularly resource allocation changes.

Yet a third way of viewing interrelationships among performance also uses systems thinking. Assessors look at how changes in one area of performance affect performance in other areas within the same unit of analysis. For example, suppose senior leaders told an academic department to accommodate a 10 percent increase in enrollment by increasing productivity (measured as course credit hours taught per faculty FTE). To accomplish this, the department had to increase faculty workload from four to five courses for each of six faculty members who regularly taught introductory-level courses. Assessors for this unit now face several performance questions:

What happened to the quality of teaching in these courses (defined as Q_3: Quality of Key Work Processes)?

What happened to sponsored research projects under way for three of the six faculty members (defined as effectiveness and Q_4: Quality of Outputs)?

What happened to student learning in these courses (defined as effectiveness)?

What happened to the department's efficiency ratings measured by classroom utilization rates and unfilled seats (defined as efficiency)?

What happened to the department's financial stability (defined as financial durability)?

Using systems thinking, it is safe to say that one major change in one area of organizational performance has the potential of affecting other areas of performance within the same system. It is important, therefore, that assessors understand the nature, complexity, and interrelationships of organizational performance and always seek ways to measure unintended performance results caused by intentional changes introduced into the system.

Kaplan and Norton (1996) hint at another set of interrelationships among areas of performance. Using their differentiation of leading indicators (performance drivers) and lag indicators (outcomes measures) discussed in Chapter Four, assessors could consider effectiveness, customer and stakeholder satisfaction, and possibly financial durability as lag indicators of performance, while treating productivity, quality, efficiency, and innovation as leading performance drivers. Both leading and lag indicators are important when measuring performance of organizations in higher education and should be represented in the unit's family of performance indicators.

Summary

This chapter operationally defined seven areas of organizational performance assessors can measure: effectiveness, productivity, quality (of upstream systems, inputs, key work processes, outputs, leadership systems, and worklife), customer and stakeholder satisfaction, efficiency, innovation, and financial durability. Links between areas of organizational performance and system elements were illustrated and explained. Examples of performance indicators were given in each area of organizational performance for both academic and administrative organizations. Worksheets were also provided to help assessors identify performance indicators and reference points in each area of organizational performance for organizations whose performance they intend to measure.

Worksheet 5.1
  Assessing Effectiveness

Unit of Analysis: _____ *(Example: Chemistry Department)*

Date: _____

Use this worksheet to assess the unit's effectiveness. Effectiveness is a measure of the extent to which the unit achieves its intended outcomes. List major outcomes identified on Worksheet 2.8 in column A. Identify performance indicators that measure achievement of each outcome in column B. Identify reference points for evaluating goal achievement in column C. Name sources of data in column D, and indicate due dates (day and month) for reporting assessment findings in column E.

Major Outcomes (A)	Performance Indicators (B)	Reference Points (C)	Data Sources (D)	Assessment Report Due Date (E)
Example: Chemistry graduates looking for immediate employment are hired by reputable companies in chemistry-related jobs	*Example:* Percentage hired within three months, six months, and one year after graduation	*Example:* 100 percent hired within three months after graduation	*Example:* Employer surveys; Alumni surveys	*Example:* August 1 (annually)

Worksheet 5.2
   Assessing Productivity

Unit of Analysis: _____ (*Example: Chemistry Department*)

Date: _____

Use this worksheet to assess the unit's productivity. Productivity is the ratio of outputs created to inputs consumed. In column A, list outputs created (from Worksheet 2.8). In column B, list inputs consumed (from Worksheet 2.7). In column C, identify ratios expressed as outputs created divided by inputs consumed. In column D, identify reference points for evaluating results. List sources of data in column E and indicate due dates for reporting performance findings in column F.

Outputs Created (A)	Inputs Consumed (B)	Ratios (C)	Reference Points (D)	Data Sources (E)	Due Date (F)
Example: Total number of course credit hours taught each term	*Example:* Total teaching faculty FTE used to teach those credit hours	*Example:* Course credit hour per teaching faculty FTE	*Example:* 12 course credit hours per teaching faculty FTE	*Example:* University course master; HR system	*Example:* August 1 (annually)

Worksheet 5.3
     Assessing Q_1: Quality of Upstream Systems

Unit of Analysis: _____ (*Example: Chemistry Department*)

Date: _____

Use this worksheet to assess the quality of the unit's upstream systems. In column A, list the unit's important upstream systems (from Worksheet 3.1), with suppliers first, then constraining systems, and finally service providers. In column B, name the products and services each upstream system provides to the unit. Identify performance indicators that measure quality in column C and reference points to evaluate quality in column D.

Upstream Systems (A)	Product or Service Supplied or Constrained (B)	Performance Indicators (C)	Reference Points (D)
Example: Chemistry lab equipment manufacturers	*Example:* Equipment delivered, installed, and maintained for teaching and research labs	*Example:* • Number of manufacturer service calls • Percentage of price discounted on the purchase, installation, and maintenance of equipment • Percentage of on-time deliveries and installation of purchased equipment • Response time to repair specialized lab equipment	*Example:* • 15 percent or greater discount of purchase and maintenance price • 100 percent on-time deliveries and installation • No service calls within first three years • Three-hour response time for repairs

Worksheet 5.4
Assessing Q_2: Quality of Inputs

Unit of Analysis: _____ (*Example: Chemistry Department*)

Date: _____

Use this worksheet to assess the quality of a unit's inputs. List the unit's important inputs (from Worksheet 2.7) in column A, giving consideration to the unit's human resources, financial resources, equipment and supplies, physical space, energy, and information. Identify performance indicators that measure quality in column B and reference points to evaluate quality in column C.

Inputs (A)	Performance Indicators (B)	Reference Points (C)
Example: Tenure-track teaching faculty	*Example:* • Percentage with terminal degrees • Demographic profile	*Example:* • 100 percent • 25 percent female

Worksheet 5.5
   Assessing Q_3: Quality of Key Work Processes

Unit of Analysis: _____ (*Example: Chemistry Department*)

Date: _____

Use this worksheet to assess quality of the unit's key work processes. In column A, list the unit's key work processes (from Worksheet 2.8). Identify performance indicators that measure quality in column B, and reference points to evaluate quality in column C.

Key Work Processes (A)	Performance Indicators (B)	Reference Points (C)
Example: Recruit new faculty	*Example:* ▪ Cycle time ▪ Cost per search ▪ Percentage of offers accepted the first time	*Example:* ▪ Less than six months ▪ $2,500 or less per search ▪ 100 percent of offers accepted the first time

Worksheet 5.6
   Assessing Q_4: Quality of Outputs

Unit of Analysis: _____ *(Example: Chemistry Department)*

Date: _____

Use this worksheet to assess quality of the unit's outputs. In Column A, list the unit's outputs (from Worksheet 2.8). Identify performance indicators that measure quality in column B and reference points to evaluate quality in column C.

Outputs (A)	Performance Indicators (B)	Reference Points (C)
Example: A new polymer to be used in dentistry	*Example:* • Actual delivery time of new polymer • Comparison of polymer features with specification in proposal • Number of research articles published in refereed journal • Number of national awards and other recognition for principal investigators • Future research funding	*Example:* • Actual delivery of new polymer meets or exceeds delivery date specified in project proposal • New polymer meets 100 percent of specifications • All articles submitted are published by refereed journals • Principle investigator receives national award

Worksheet 5.7
   Assessing Q$_5$: Quality of Leadership Systems:
   Follower Satisfaction and External Relations

Unit of Analysis: _____ (*Example: Chemistry Department*)

Date: _____

Use this worksheet to assess the quality of the unit's leadership system in relation to follower satisfaction and quality of external relations. In column A, identify performance indicators and reference points for assessing overall follower satisfaction with quality of the leadership services to the organization. In column B, identify performance indicators and reference points for assessing the strength of the unit's partnerships with important upstream systems. In column C, identify performance indicators and reference points for assessing quality of the unit's public image.

	Overall Follower Satisfaction with the Leadership System (A)	**Strength of Partnerships with Upstream Systems (B)**	**Quality of Public Image (C)**
Performance Indicators	*Example:* Percentage of surveyed employees indicating that they are satisfied or very satisfied with the quality of the leadership system	*Example:* Quality of entering students from feeder schools	*Example:* National ranking
Reference Points	100 percent of respondents are satisfied or very satisfied	Top 10 percent of high school graduating class	#1 ranking

Worksheet 5.8

Assessing Q_5: Quality of Leadership Systems: Direction and Support

Unit of Analysis: _____ (*Example: Chemistry Department*)

Date: _____

Identify performance indicators and reference points, as indicated, for assessing quality of the unit's leadership system in relation to its mission statement, vision statement, guiding principles, strategic plans, organizational design, governance structure, and organizational resources.

	Quality of Mission (A)	Quality of Vision (B)	Quality of Guiding Principles (C)	Quality of Strategic Plans (D)	Quality of Organizational Design (E)	Quality of Governance Structures (F)	Quality of Organizational Resources (G)
Performance Indicators	*Example:* Percentage of faculty, staff, stakeholders, and (when appropriate) students who understand and support the Chemistry Department's mission	*Example:* Percentage of faculty, staff, stakeholders, and (when appropriate) students who understand, share, and are motivated and inspired by the Chemistry Department's vision	*Example:* Frequency and number of allegations of faculty, staff, and student misconduct	*Example:* Clarity in timetables, performance indicators, and reference points for goal assessment	*Example:* Frequency and number of employee complaints about workload	*Example:* Percentage of senior faculty participating on important university-wide committees and task forces	*Example:* Percent increase in dollar value of departmental funding from all sources
Reference Points	100 percent	100 percent	Zero allegations or punishments	100 percent clarity	Zero complaints	60 percent of senior faculty	10 percent increase over last budget cycle

Worksheet 5.9
     Assessing Q_6: Quality of Worklife

Unit of Analysis: _____   (*Example: Chemistry Department*)

Date: _____

Use this worksheet to assess the unit's quality of worklife. Quality of worklife reflects an organization's employees' perceptions, attitudes, and opinions about organizational quality and levels of satisfaction with the workplace. Identify performance indicators that measure quality of worklife and reference points to evaluate it.

	Adequacy of Resources (A)	**Quality of the Workplace Environment (B)**	**Treatment by Others and Supervisors (C)**	**Job Design, Rewards, Incentives, and Recognition Programs (D)**	**Organizational Reputation and Success (E)**
Performance Indicators	*Example:* Percentage of employees giving positive responses	*Example:* Percentage of employees giving positive responses	*Example:* Percentage of employees giving positive responses	*Example:* Percentage of employees giving positive responses	*Example:* Percentage of employees giving positive responses
Reference Points	100 percent of employees are Satisfied or very satisfied	100 percent of employees are satisfied or very satisfied	100 percent of employees are satisfied or very satisfied	100 percent of employees are satisfied or very satisfied	100 percent of employees are satisfied or very satisfied

Worksheet 5.10
  Assessing Customer Satisfaction

Unit of Analysis: _____ *(Example: Chemistry Department)*

Date: _____

Use this worksheet to assess the unit's customer satisfaction. List important customers from Worksheet 3.2 in column A. State their needs and expectations in column B. Identify performance indicators to measure satisfaction in column C and reference points to evaluate satisfaction in column D.

Customers (A)	Customer Needs and Expectations of Output Quality (B)	Performance Indicators (C)	Reference Points (D)
Example: Students enrolled in chemistry courses	*Example:* • Courses cover material required to pass the chemistry exit exam • Faculty start and end classes on time • Classrooms and labs are well equipped, comfortable, and conducive to learning • Faculty are prepared for class • Faculty grade exams, homework, and papers in a fair and timely manner	*Example:* Percentage of students reporting positive responses in student evaluation of faculty	*Example:* 100 percent of students indicate that they are satisfied or very satisfied.

Worksheet 5.11
  Assessing Stakeholder Satisfaction

Unit of Analysis: _____ (*Example: Chemistry Department*)

Date: _____

Use this worksheet to assess the unit's stakeholder satisfaction. In column A, list important stake-holders cited on Worksheet 3.3. State their needs and expectations in column B, performance indi-cators in column C, and reference points in column D.

Stakeholders (A)	Stakeholder Needs and Expectations (B)	Performance Indicators (C)	Reference Points (D)
Example: Ace Chemicals, Inc., an employer who regularly hires Chemistry Department graduates	*Example:* A knowledge-able, skilled, and capable workforce	*Example:* ▪ Survey results measuring employer satisfaction with new hires from the Chemistry Department ▪ Number of graduates Ace Chemicals, Inc., hires annually ▪ Dollar value of equipment donated by Ace Chemicals	*Example:* ▪ 100 percent of respondents indicate that they are satisfied or very satisfied ▪ 5 percent increase in number of graduates hired by Ace Chemicals ▪ $250,000 in donations averaged over three years

Worksheet 5.12
  Assessing Efficiency

Unit of Analysis: _____ (*Example: Chemistry Department*)

Date: _____

Use this worksheet to assess the unit's efficiency. Efficiency is a measure of how well the unit optimizes its use of scarce resources. In column A, list performance indicators to measure efficiency of the unit. In column B, identify reference points to evaluate efficiency. List sources of data in column C and due dates (month and day) for reporting performance findings in column D.

Performance Indicators (A)	Reference Points (B)	Data Sources (C)	Assessment Report Due Date (D)
Example: Number of empty seats in scheduled chemistry classes and labs	*Example:* Zero empty seats	*Example:* Class master	*Example:* July 1 (annually)

Worksheet 5.13
    Assessing Innovation

Unit of Analysis: _____ *(Example: Chemistry Department)*

Date: _____

Use this worksheet to assess the unit's innovation. Innovation is a measure of the unit's ability to creatively change in response to internal and external pressures, opportunities, challenges, and threats. In column A, list creative changes intentionally put into place over the past two to three years. In column B, cite environmental forces causing this change. Note intended results in column C and actual results in column D. Finally, list data sources in column E.

Intentional Changes (A)	Environmental Forces (B)	Intended Results (C)	Actual Results (D)	Data Sources (E)
Example: Curricular changes in lab courses	*Example:* New research equipment in teaching and research labs	*Example:* Students will be able to use state-of-the-art chemistry lab equipment	*Example:* Students were somewhat more capable of using new lab equipment as demonstrated in lab exercises; however, more curricular changes are needed	*Example:* Grades on lab exercises Survey results from students enrolled in labs Survey results from lab instructors and faculty who teach in updated labs

Worksheet 5.14
Assessing Financial Durability

Unit of Analysis: _____ (*Example: Chemistry Department*)

Date: _____

Use this worksheet to assess the unit's financial durability. Financial durability is a mission-specific bottom-line measure of the financial health and well-being of a unit. In column A, list performance indicators to measure financial durability, and in column B, reference points to evaluate financial durability. In column C, describe sources of data, and in column D, due dates (month and day) for reporting performance findings.

Performance Indicators (A)	Reference Points (B)	Data Sources (C)	Assessment Report Due Date (D)
Example: Tuition and fees generated by the Chemistry Department as percentage of total departmental expenditures	*Example:* Tuition and fees generated by the Chemistry Department exceed total departmental expenditures by 5 percent	*Example:* Accounting system; Course master	*Example:* August 1 (annually)

Worksheet 5.15
  Assessing Critical Success Factors

Unit of Analysis: _____ (*Example: Chemistry Department*)

Date: _____

Use this worksheet to assess the unit's performance in relation to its critical success factors. In column A, list the unit's critical success factors identified on Worksheet 4.1. Identify performance indicators in column B and reference points for each factor in column C.

Critical Success Factors (A)	Performance Indicators (B)	Reference Points (C)
Example: High national ranking	*Example:* Actual rank published by *U.S. News and World Report*	*Example:* Ranked as #1 in our classification

Worksheet 5.16
Organizational Performance Areas Important to Assessment Users

Unit of Analysis: _____ (*Example: Chemistry Department*)

Date: _____

Use this worksheet to describe areas of organizational performance important to each major assessment user group. In column A, list major assessment user groups identified on Worksheet 1.1; then check the columns representing the areas of organizational performance that are important to each group.

Assessment User Groups (A)	Effect-iveness (B)	Produc-tivity (C)	Quality (D)	Customer and Stakeholder Satisfaction (E)	Effici-ency (F)	Inno-vation (G)	Financial Durability (H)
Example: Self-Study Committee	✔		✔	✔			✔
Example: Organic Chemistry Program Review Committee	✔	✔	✔	✔	✔		✔

CHAPTER 6

Creating and Maintaining Assessment Programs

This chapter explains how to build, deploy, and assess an institution's new or existing assessment program.

Building Assessment Programs

Every organization has a preferred and traditional method for launching new initiatives. The launching of a new assessment program should follow local institutional customs and practices so long as they allow leaders to clarify the purpose of assessment and specify requirements of assessment user groups, build a supportive organizational culture, create a strong leadership structure for the assessment program, identify and reach consensus on assessment program elements, make visible direct and indirect costs of assessment, avoid information overload, manage risk, and build an ongoing two-way communication plan.

Clarifying Purpose and Specifying Assessment User Groups

Chapter One explained how external and internal user groups generally use assessment. With the help of senior leaders, assessors must decide who the unit's important assessment users are and areas of organizational performance important to each group so that they can design an assessment program that meets all their needs. Assessors can use Worksheet 1.1 to help them identify assessment user groups and Worksheet 5.15 to identify areas of performance important to each group.

Building a Supportive Organizational Culture

The success of any assessment program requires broad employee involvement and support. Whenever an organization launches a new assessment initiative or formalizes existing assessment practices into an organized assessment program, members of the community naturally become concerned for a variety of reasons, all of which must be addressed by assessment leaders. Sink and Tuttle (1989) call some of these concerns "measurement paradigms": measurement is threatening; measurement has a single-indicator focus; subjective measures are sloppy; standards operate as a ceiling on performance; if you can't measure it, you can't manage it; and language isn't important. Each of these is discussed in turn.

Measurement Is Threatening

Sink and Tuttle (1989) argue that measurement per se is not threatening; the use of measurement is what is threatening. They argue that people generally like to get feedback on how they are doing. What they actually fear is misuse of measurement data by someone else.

Wheatley (2005) argues that measurement is threatening but feedback is not. Feedback is also more useful in encouraging organizational vitality. Unlike measurement, she argues, people see feedback as something they generate themselves, not something imposed externally; they also see feedback as more adaptable than measurement.

In an organizational culture characterized by little or no fear, assessment is a welcomed activity because of the valued feedback it provides. The truth is, however, few organizations enjoy a fear-free culture, and assessors must therefore move cautiously when introducing assessment initiatives. One way assessors can reduce fear about assessment in the workplace is to encourage two-way communication between assessment user groups and members of units under review early in the assessment design process. Leaders and members of the unit should be forthright about how they intend to use assessment findings. Senior leaders of institutions migrating to incentive-based budgeting systems should be particularly sensitive to and aware of growing concerns of unit members who are apprehensive about how performance results conveyed through a new assessment program will affect their unit's future funding. Ongoing two-way communication between assessment users and other members will go a long way toward reducing fear, minimizing misuse of data, and strengthening support for assessment, all of which are critical for assessment to succeed and survive in the long run.

Kaplan and Norton (1996) argue that another way of building a supportive culture for assessment is to include the parties most affected by change in the process of identifying strategic goals, performance indicators, and reference points. This not only increases support for assessment but also builds support for future changes.

Measurement Has a Single-Indicator Focus

According to Sink and Tuttle (1989), organizational performance is complex, and measurement should therefore reflect that complexity.

A good assessment program provides multiple indicators because organizational performance is complicated, organizational missions in higher education are multifaceted, information needs of assessment users are varied, and organizations have numerous critical success factors. Furthermore, multiple indicators are needed because assessors must monitor unintended outcomes that may result from intentional changes introduced into the system.

Subjective Measures Are Sloppy

Sink and Tuttle (1989) argue that as the focus of measurement shifts to knowledge work and service organizations, there is an increasing "need to measure softer dimensions of performance . . . such as employee morale and customer perceptions" (p. 59). They contend that measurement of attitudes and perceptions is not necessarily sloppy. In fact, it is well established in the field of industrial psychology and can lead to highly reliable and valid indicators. Good measurement of organizational performance does not require as much precision as engineers, scientists, and accountants require in laboratories, they argue. The basic purpose of organizational performance measurement, according to Sink and Tuttle, is to "tell the organization whether it is headed in the right direction" (p. 59). Performance indicators used as examples throughout this book are both subjective and objective. Questions about validity associated with any performance indicator should be raised and tested by everyone affected by assessment findings.

Standards Operate as a Ceiling on Performance

This paradigm is rooted in the belief that standards act as a ceiling when they imply absolute desired levels. This paradigm most likely emerged in the 1980s after W. Edwards Deming insisted that leaders eliminate work standards that cap the amount of improvement to be achieved (Scherkenbach, 1986); such caps, Deming argued, confuse a person's understanding of the job. Sink and Tuttle (1989) contend that standards are less likely to operate as a ceiling when they are viewed as targets or benchmarks linked to and derived from strategic goals that are understood and accepted as a means for the organization to achieve its competitive position in the environment. However, Thor (1993) warns assessors to use care when generating competitive benchmarks because organizations do not operate in identical environments, nor do they conduct work in exactly the same ways. Thor suggests that continuous improvement should be stressed everywhere in the organization regardless of its position in the industry and the benchmark.

If You Can't Measure It, You Can't Manage It

According to Wheatley (2005), organizations today are crazy about numbers. "The search for measures has taken over the world as the primary means to control systems and people. We depend on numbers to know how we're doing for virtually everything" (p. 156). She claims that organizations are driven by a prevailing belief that if you can't measure it, you can't manage it. Too many organizations have "lost the path to quality because they have burdened themselves with unending measures" (p. 158). But measurement is critical, she concedes, because it provides essential feedback required of organizations (as open, living systems) to survive and grow. And feedback, as explained earlier, is different from measurement because it is viewed as self-generated and adaptable.

Language Isn't Important

Benjamin and Hersh (2002) warn assessment designers not to import assessment or efficiency rhetoric from business and K–12 education. The culture of higher education is unique, they argue, because of the nature of teaching, learning, and scholarship in the context of college and university cultures.

Scholars in higher education have always resisted rhetoric (and practices) invented by others, particularly those from the business world. For example, in the late 1980s, institutions began struggling with concepts and rhetoric associated with "marketing" borrowed from the business world. Even though most institutions desired increased enrollment and improved institutional reputation, they struggled with the notion that marketing, regarded as a business practice, was appropriate in higher education. Some of the struggle pertained to acknowledgment that institutions needed to market themselves at all. Some of the struggle pertained to language embedded in marketing itself. Possibly the most difficult struggle was articulating quality in terms meaningful to people outside the academy.

Possibly even greater resistance to language came soon thereafter with the introduction of Total Quality Management (TQM). TQM, much like marketing, came from the business world. TQM had a whole new set of terms (process management, quality, empowerment, customer) that many scholars in the academic world still find offensive today. Early TQM advocates, who saw themselves as change agents, found it necessary to literally translate the language of TQM into more acceptable terminology for members of the scholarly community.

Assessors in institutions where assessment is new or becoming more formalized are serving their institutions as change agents. They must recognize that language is important and use language that fits the organizational culture. Many of the terms and definitions in this book do not fit some organizational cultures. For example, the term *customer*, when applied to currently enrolled students, is still a volatile term in the higher educational community. However, the concept behind the term customer and the definition used in this book (anyone who receives or experiences the system's outputs) is important in assessment because it presents two opportunities for measuring organizational performance: customer satisfaction and quality of outputs. Needs, preferences, and perceptions of students and other customers, such as organizations that sponsor research and contract for services, are used as reference points for evaluating customer satisfaction and output quality. *Productivity* is another controversial and emotionally loaded word. To some people, the mere mention of the word implies job losses and decreased quality. Nevertheless, productivity is an important area of organizational performance to measure, particularly in comparison with other areas. As explained in Chapter Five, a highly productive organization may or may not be very effective.

Because language is important in assessment, many assessors find it helpful to return to language embedded in the organization's mission statement and guiding principles. For example, assessors might use the term *students* and *end users* in lieu of customers.

Building a Strong Leadership Structure for the Assessment Program

Most senior leaders agree that the success of any new initiative requires the skilled leadership of one or more qualified persons. Launching a new initiative in assessment requires such leadership in the form of assessment coordinators and steering committees.

Assessment Coordinator

The assessment coordinator organizes and supervises the overall assessment program. The institution should have a single assessment coordinator, who has direct access to senior leaders. The coordinator should be a person who enjoys a high level of respect and who possesses strong skills as a communicator and project manager. The coordinator should also be knowledgeable about assessment practices in higher education and skilled in database management, qualitative and quantitative research design, statistical analysis, and other aspects of educational research. However, it is not uncommon for effective coordinators to rely heavily on the technical and research skills of institutional researchers and willing faculty members.

The role of the assessment coordinator is to serve as a staff consultant and trainer to unit personnel engaged in assessment activities.

The coordinator is responsible for auditing, coordinating, and monitoring all assessment activities that take place throughout the institution. The coordinator is also responsible for building and maintaining strong partnerships with the assessment program's upstream systems.

As a staff consultant, the assessment coordinator provides advice, clerical support, and data collection and analysis assistance. As a trainer, the assessment coordinator offers both formal training through workshops and meetings and informal training through one-on-one interactions to help unit personnel develop assessment skills. The goal is for unit personnel to ultimately become proficient in conducting their own assessment without the help of the assessment coordinator. Assessment is ultimately the responsibility of the unit's leadership system, not the assessment coordinator.

Assessment Steering Committee

Assessment also needs a steering committee made up of representatives from various units in the organization. The committee should include someone familiar with the institution's mission, vision, guiding principles, and strategic plans. It should also include people with technical knowledge of current administrative systems, databases, and other computing resources; academic program review and accreditation standards, schedules, and procedures; human resource policies and procedures; and institutional planning and budgeting processes, particularly if the institution is migrating to an incentive-based budgeting system. The committee should also include selected representatives from units currently and formerly under review. Steering committee members should be appointed by the president for at least a three-year term initially.

The purpose of the assessment steering committee is to provide credibility to the assessment program. The committee's primary responsibilities are as follows:

- To clarify purposes and goals of assessment
- To formulate assessment policies, procedures, practices, and schedules
- To identify resources required to build and maintain assessment across the institution
- To measure and evaluate the performance of the assessment program

Decision Making

Many decisions are made in the design, deployment, and evaluation of assessment. Decisions are made about who should coordinate assessment efforts, what policies and procedures are best, what areas of performance are critical to success, how to measure and evaluate performance, and who should know about performance results and when.

The best decision-making process in assessment is based on decision rules and criteria established long before decision making begins. Decision rules make visible the criteria for correct decisions. They encourage decision makers to debate and reflect on desired results before engaging in specific decisions. Decision rules help decision makers minimize the political aspects of decision making or at least move political considerations to the discussion of decision rules and criteria. For example, before selecting an individual to coordinate assessment efforts, decision makers should decide what qualifications the person needs: required levels of technical expertise, prior experience in assessment, level of respect among peers and the institution's leadership team, ability to work well with technical experts, and so forth. When the time comes to actually select the person for the position, decision makers merely have to decide which candidate best fits the decision criteria. Another example is the application of decision rules to selected performance indicators and reference points. For example, decision makers might consider decision rules that require that performance indicators and reference points be aligned with and support accreditation standards, program ranking criteria, NCAA eligibility requirements, and so forth.

Identifying and Reaching Consensus on Assessment Program Elements

When building an assessment program, planners must clarify and reach consensus on the program's internal and external system elements as described in Chapters Two and Three. Clarification of system elements is required to measure the program's performance.

Exhibit 6.1 provides examples of mission, vision, guiding principles, strategic goals, and organizational structure for an assessment program at the institutional level.

Making Visible Direct and Indirect Costs of Assessment

Assessment costs can be a measure of assessment effort but not a measure of assessment effectiveness. The total cost of assessment is a combination of direct and indirect costs. Direct costs are outlays for assessment personnel, equipment, supplies, travel, professional development, and other line-item expenses. Indirect costs are infrastructure costs (electricity, heating and cooling, parking, office and lab space), activity costs of campus personnel engaged in assessment activities, and opportunity costs of work not being performed because people are engaged in assessment. Exhibit 6.2 provides examples of

Exhibit 6.1

Examples of Mission, Vision, Guiding Principles, Strategic Goals, and Organizational Structure for an Assessment Program

Mission	The mission of the assessment program is to provide coordination, consulting, and training services to university personnel engaged in assessment activities that will enhance the institution's ability to account to others and improve its programs and services.

Vision of Performance Excellence

- Assessors in all organizations, including the institution as a whole, are actively and appropriately engaged in effective, productive, and high-quality assessment activities.
- Assessment users are extremely satisfied with the quality of assessment reports they receive.
- All assessment users fully and accurately understand the performance of their organizations.
- The overall campus environment is supportive of assessment.

Guiding Principles

Beliefs
- We believe that assessment is a core research initiative for learning organizations that are innovative.
- We believe that assessment for learning is much more powerful than assessment for evaluation.
- We believe that organizational performance is complex and should be measured through a family of performance indicators.
- We believe that a supportive organizational culture is essential to the long-term survival and success of assessment.

Values
- We respect the concerns and talents of the people we work with and serve.
- We value the talents and diversity of each other and the people we serve.
- We prefer to agree on decision criteria before making difficult decisions.

Norms
- We will respect the talents and diversity of each other and the people we serve.
- We will hold all assessment findings in confidence.
- We will honor important decisions made by unit leaders about what and how to assess performance and who receives what information and when.
- We will engage in ongoing professional development to constantly expand our knowledge, skills, and abilities in assessment.
- We will be professional in our work, as explained in the institution's code of ethics.

Strategic Goals (First Year)

- To create an organizational culture supportive to assessment
- To strengthen senior leaders' role and necessary skills required to successfully build, deploy, and assess a new assessment program

Organizational Structure

The institutional assessment program is staffed by a full-time coordinator classified as an administrator who is aided by two full-time classified support staff. The institutional assessment coordinator reports directly to the president and regularly participates in meetings of the president's cabinet and the academic council. The institutional assessment coordinator works closely with the provost and other vice presidents, the director of institutional planning and research, and the chief information officer. The institution's full-time assessment staff are served by and work closely with an assessment steering committee whose members are appointed by the president for a three-year term. All important decisions about what and how to assess a unit's performance and who receives what information and when rests within the authority of the leadership system of the unit under review

Exhibit 6.2

Examples of Direct and Indirect Assessment Costs

Direct Costs	**Indirect Costs**
• Personnel costs (compensation and benefits) of assessment coordinators and support staff	• Infrastructure costs (electricity, heating and cooling, parking, office and lab space)
• Equipment purchase and maintenance costs (including computer hardware, software, printers, scanners, phones, and fax and copy machines that assessment staff primarily use)	• Costs of employees engaged in assessment-related tasks and activities (academic personnel administering standardized tests or reviewing student portfolios, steering committee members discussing policies and reviewing results, institutional research staff gathering and reporting data, computer programmers writing programs related to assessment)
• Office and assessment supply costs (such as standardzed tests and test readers)	• Opportunity costs or costs of work not performed because people are engaged in assessment activities
• Travel costs	
• Professional development costs	

direct and indirect assessment costs. Exhibit 6.3 offers examples of internal and external elements of an assessment program at the institutional level.

In an era of declining resources, assessment leaders should make assessment costs as visible as possible in the institution's budgeting process. Visibility increases awareness of the scope of assessment effort and gives organizational leaders another opportunity to make their support (or lack of support) of assessment visible. Visibility also provides another opportunity for analyzing the costs and benefits of assessment investments.

Avoiding Information Overload

One common criticism of assessment programs is they are data-rich but information-poor. Assessors can use several strategies to address this common problem. First, assessors can focus measurement

Exhibit 6.3

Internal and External Assessment Program Elements

Internal and External Assessment Program Elements

Upstream Systems	▪ Strategic planners ▪ Institutional researchers ▪ Senior leaders ▪ Departmental assessors ▪ Information Services Department ▪ State Board of Regents ▪ Local governing board ▪ Accreditors ▪ Governmental agencies ▪ Assessment test manufacturers
Inputs	▪ Human resources ▪ Financial resources ▪ Equipment and supplies ▪ Physical space: offices, conference and work rooms, storage ▪ Energy ▪ Information
Key Work Processes	▪ Consulting ▪ Training ▪ Data collection and analysis ▪ Report preparation and dissemination ▪ Communications ▪ Program management
Outputs	▪ Reports (written and oral) ▪ Assessment policies and procedures ▪ Advice and support ▪ Training workshops and consults ▪ Guest speaker program
Customers	▪ Senior leaders ▪ Administrators and managers ▪ Faculty and staff ▪ Departmental assessors ▪ External assessment user groups
Stakeholders	▪ All external and internal assessors and assessment user groups

Competitors

Students and alumni	▪ Taxpayers
Outcomes	▪ External assessment users achieve their goals of holding organizations accountable and supporting policy, resource, affirmation, and choice decisions. ▪ Internal assessment users achieve their goals of accounting to others, managing strategy, managing organizational culture, allocating resources, controlling quality, improving programs and services, and supporting personnel decisions.

efforts on critical success factors. Second, they can focus on performance areas that have the greatest impact on strategic execution. Third, they can be careful about selecting performance indicators that measure what is important, not just what is easy to measure. And finally, assessors can develop processes for obtaining prompt feedback from assessment users about quality, quantity, and distribution of assessment reports.

Managing Risk

Assessment designers should also anticipate all the possible unintended and potentially dysfunctional consequences that can occur from program deployment. The assessment coordinator and members of the steering committee should be prepared for possible negative or unintended consequences and take every precaution to avoid them. This prevention task is known as risk management.

When designing assessment programs, designers should set aside time to brainstorm, as a group, answers to the following questions, in the following order:

1. What can possibly go wrong?
2. What contingencies can we put into place to prevent those things from happening?
3. What can possibly go wrong with these contingencies?
4. What contingencies can we put into place if those contingencies fail?

This approach to assessment design not only prevents some problems from occurring but also increases the leadership team's readiness to deal with problems when they do occur.

Building an Ongoing Two-Way Communication Plan

As stated earlier, ongoing two-way communication between organizational leaders, assessment leaders, assessors, assessment users, and everyone else affected by assessment is crucial to the success of all assessment programs. Communication should be planned and two-way; it should also take place before, during, and after assessment is deployed. With assistance from the assessment steering committee, the assessment coordinator should develop and execute a good communication plan.

The assessment communication plan should identify all important players involved in and affected by assessment. It should identify all the needs of important assessment users, including what information is needed, when and where, and how it is to be obtained.

Chapter Four offered suggestions on various formats and channels for disseminating assessment findings. Assessors must recognize that the needs of assessment users can change at any time during the development and deployment of the assessment. The coordinator must therefore continually adapt the communication process to the changing needs of all its important players.

The communication plan should also incorporate two-way mechanisms for leaders to receive information as well as disseminate it. Two-way communication is essential if the assessment system is to continually improve. A good communication plan identifies what is needed to improve assessment, from whom, and when. It also provides structure for receiving feedback from important users after reports are disseminated.

Worksheet 6.1 will help assessors build their unit's assessment communication plan.

Deploying Assessment Programs

When deploying assessment programs, assessors should consider ways to encourage broad involvement, be systematic, adopt an experimental approach, and rigorously monitor strategic partnerships.

Encouraging Broad Involvement

Because the assessment steering committee is basically a policy-making body and the assessment coordinator is mostly a consultant and trainer, much of the day-to-day assessment work is generally performed by a broad range of people, most of whom work in the unit under review. Leaders of successful assessment programs understand that people engaged in and affected by assessment must believe they have a say in what is important to measure, how it should be measured, when it should be measured, and how and to whom results should be conveyed. Furthermore, they must support the goals assessment is trying to achieve.

Being supportive of assessment is not enough, however. People actively engaged in assessment tasks and activities must feel confident in their skills and abilities as assessors. They must believe that they are making a difference, are being recognized for their assessment work, and are being rewarded in ways that are meaningful to them. Finally, they must be made aware, on a regular basis, of the quality of their work and the extent to which it is helping the assessment program achieve its purposes for both the institution and the unit under review.

Being Systematic

When deploying a new or more formalized assessment program in a unit, assessors, with the guidance and assistance of the assessment coordinator, should be systematic in their deployment approach. In fact, the following sequential deployment steps are recommended:

1. Using Worksheets 1.1 and 5.15, identify all important assessment user groups and areas of organizational performance important to each group.

2. Using Worksheets 2.1 through 3.3, define this unit's internal and external system elements as described in Chapters Two and Three. Reach consensus on the accuracy and completeness of each definition.

3. Using Worksheet 4.1, determine critical success factors and reach consensus on their priorities.

4. Using Worksheets 5.1 through 5.16, identify a family of performance indicators that measure selected areas of organizational performance needed for the assessment users identified on Worksheet 5.15. Reach consensus on the validity, reliability, and priority of each performance indicator.

5. Also using Worksheets 5.1 through 5.16, identify reference points for each performance indicator, and reach consensus on the appropriateness of each reference point.

6. Determine who will gather data, how data will be gathered, and what sources will be tapped for each performance indicator and reference point; then decide who will compile the data into assessment reports and who will distribute what reports to whom and when. When all this is completed, using Worksheet 4.2, build an assessment report schedule.

7. Decide how organizational performance results will be stored and who will be responsible for maintaining and securing the records.

8. Using Worksheet 6.1, develop an assessment communication plan.

Adopting an Experimental Approach

There are several approaches for deploying new assessment programs, but one of the best is experimental. Using this approach, leaders start small and experience some inevitable mistakes before expanding the program. Deming (1993) calls this approach the "PDSA cycle" (PDSA stands for "Plan, Do, Study, Act"). According to Deming, the PDSA cycle is a tool for learning and improving a product or process. The PDSA cycle calls for leaders to develop a plan of action, do it (or parts of it), then systematically study it to see how things are going, and finally take actions to make it even better before expansion.

Monitoring Strategic Partnerships

Assessment is a program that capitalizes on the skills and knowledge of many people throughout the institution. One of the important responsibilities of the assessment coordinator is to manage partnerships with important upstream systems. Exhibit 6.3 gives examples of important upstream systems to an institutional assessment program. Three partnerships are particularly important to the success of assessment: partnerships with strategic planners, institutional researchers, and senior leaders.

Strategic Planners

It is important that leaders engaged in strategic planning and those engaged in assessment foster strong partnerships. The outputs or deliverables from strategic planning, as described in Chapter Two, are strategic goals typically stated within the context of a set of planning assumptions, performance indicators, and performance expectations defined in reference points. Strategic goals, by definition, are derived from careful consideration of factors in the organization's external and internal environments. Their purpose is to move the organization toward a more competitive place in the external environment. Assessment, by contrast, is an analysis of an organization's past performance. One of the main purposes of assessment is to provide feedback on progress toward the achievement of an organization's strategic goals. It measures progress through performance results framed as performance indicators evaluated within the context of reference points aligned with organizational mission, vision, and guiding principles.

Institutional Researchers

It is equally important that assessors forge partnerships with institutional researchers. According to Brenda Rogers and Karen Gentemann (1989), institutional research offices play important roles in assessment, particularly when supporting assessment activities such as faculty evaluations, program and curriculum reviews, self-studies, and analyses of faculty workload and salary comparisons.

Institutional researchers are generally skilled at research design, data collection, statistical analysis, policy analysis, and report writing. They are also familiar with databases existing throughout the institution. These are critical skills and knowledge necessary for assessment.

If a formalized program of assessment is a new initiative for an institution, the workload, goals, and resource requirements of critical partners, such as institutional researchers, will be greatly affected. It is wise for assessors to build and closely monitor the strength of these important partnerships.

Senior Leaders

Senior leaders are important partners in assessment. Without their leadership and visible support, assessment will not succeed and survive over the long term. Senior leaders are important assessment users who, as described in Chapter One, use assessment to account to others, manage strategy, support resource allocation decisions, and manage organizational culture. They are also partners in the design and deployment of new and more formalized assessment programs. Their job is to help the community understand how it can use assessment for learning as well as evaluation. Their job is to open doors for assessors; to encourage administrators, managers, faculty, and staff to participate in assessment activities; and to provide meaningful recognition and rewards for their contributions. Finally, their most important job is undoubtedly to demonstrate their visible support for assessment. Their beliefs, values, and behaviors communicate support (or lack of support) for assessment. Another visible demonstration of support is their funding (or lack of funding) of assessment initiatives. Finally, they demonstrate support in their day-to-day use (or misuse) of assessment data in reaching many difficult decisions they make that affect the lives and future success of the institution's employees, customers, and stakeholders.

As new and more formalized assessment programs emerge, senior leaders need to recognize their evolving assessment-related leadership roles and responsibilities. They must carry out their roles and responsibilities in ways that are visible to assessors and other members of the organizational community while simultaneously maintaining their constructive use of assessment as end users. It is wise for assessment leaders to garner support from their senior leader partners and to build strong partnerships that clarify and recognize senior leaders' evolving roles, responsibilities, and contributions as the assessment program develops and matures on campus.

Assessing Assessment Programs

Assessors must constantly assess the performance of the assessment program. Furthermore, they must follow the same assessment principles and practices they would in assessing any unit of analysis, beginning with the identification of system elements, critical success factors, performance indicators, reference points, assessment users, and so forth. Exhibit 6.1 offers examples of mission, vision, guiding principles, and strategic goals of an institutional assessment program. Exhibit 6.3 provides examples of internal and external system elements of an institutional assessment program. Exhibit 6.4 gives examples of factors critical to the success of assessment that inform selection of areas of performance to measure.

Exhibit 6.5 presents examples of a wide range of performance indicators for measuring performance of an assessment program. Actual selection of critical success factors, performance indicators, and reference points depends, of course, on the mission of the institution, intended purposes of the assessment program, longevity and history of assessment at the institution, and specific requirements of assessment user groups.

Exhibit 6.4
Examples of Critical Success Factors for
an Institutional Assessment Program

- Clarity in assessment goals and a campus culture supportive of assessment and those goals
- Confidentiality of assessment findings
- Quality of assessment data housed in systems controlled outside the assessment program
- Quality of assessment findings (reliability, validity, timeliness, accuracy, usefulness, readability) as perceived by assessors and assessment user groups
- Extent and appropriateness of assessment user group's use of assessment findings
- Quality of the assessment program's leadership system
- Quality of consultation and training services provided by the assessment coordinator and support staff
- Customer satisfaction with consulting and training services and assessment processes and reports
- Quality of support (visible and ongoing) demonstrated by senior leaders
- Quality of support and direction provided by the assessment steering committee
- Quality of two-way ongoing communication between unit members and leaders about the design and use of the assessment program and credibility of assessment findings
- Quality of cooperation of unit personnel engaged in assessment activities
- Currency of technology

Exhibit 6.5

Examples of Performance Indicators for
Measuring Assessment Program Performance

Effectiveness (see Exhibits 5.1 and 5.2)	*Intended Outcome Achievement* ▪ Percentage of selected external assessment user groups giving positive responses when asked if their use of assessment helped them achieve their goals of holding organizations accountable; supporting policy and resource allocation decisions; imposing sanctions for noncompliance; supporting choice decisions; affirming accreditation, rank, and so forth; and validating research ▪ Percentage of selected internal assessment user groups giving positive responses when asked if their use of assessment helped them achieve their goals of accounting to others, managing strategy, managing organizational culture, allocating resources, controlling quality, improving programs and services, and supporting personnel decisions ▪ Percentage of actively engaged assessors at the department level giving positive responses when asked if they had sufficient assessment-related knowledge, skills, and abilities required to conduct assessment activities *Strategic Goal Achievement* ▪ Percentage of organizational constituents reporting positive attitudes toward assessment at the institution ▪ Working hours senior leaders spend discussing and learning about their leadership role in assessment ▪ Percentage of senior leaders reporting they are comfortable with and understand their leadership role in assessment
Productivity (see Exhibits 5.3 and 5.4)	▪ Average cost per unit served ▪ Number of units served per assessment staff FTE ▪ Number of universitywide assessment reports published each year per assessment office staff FTE ▪ Average cost to prepare and disseminate routine universitywide assessment reports
Quality (see Exhibits 5.5 to 5.21)	▪ Quality of the assessment program's leadership system ▪ Quality of inputs used in the assessment program ▪ Percentage of assessment user groups giving positive responses when surveyed about quality (credibility, accuracy, timeliness, readability) of assessment reports ▪ Number of incorrect reports conveyed to assessment users that had to be redone ▪ Average cycle time and cost to prepare and disseminate routine universitywide assessment reports
Customer and Stakeholder Satisfaction (see Exhibits 5.22 and 5.23)	▪ Percentage of customers giving positive responses in regard to quality of advice, support, training workshops, guest speakers, and written instructions in end-of-service surveys ▪ Percentage of new academic and administrative organizations seeking support from the assessment office because of positive feedback from previous customers ▪ Attendance at assessment training workshops

(continued on the next page)

Exhibit 6.5, *continued*
Examples of Performance Indicators for Measuring Assessment Program Performance

Efficiency (see Exhibits 5.24 and 5.25)	■ Percentage of assessment coordinator time spent with individual units as compared against target goals ■ Percentage of assessment coordinator time spent planning assessment program goals and objectives ■ Percentage of assessment coordinator time spent marketing services of assessment program to potential departmental assessors ■ Percentage of assessment coordinator time spent assessing and communicating assessment program costs and benefits ■ Percentage of departmental assessors' time spent conducting assessment-related activities as compared with non-assessment-related departmental activities ■ Percentage of departmental assessors' time spent conducting assessment-related activities as compared with target time goals
Innovation (see Exhibit 5.26)	■ Improved quality and efficiency in data collection and analysis due to acquisition and use of new technology ■ Improved dissemination of assessment reports to assessment users through new Web-based reporting mechanisms ■ Increased productivity and quality of training due to new Web-based training programs and discussion boards ■ Increased communication between and among assessors due to new Web-based discussion boards
Financial Durability (see Exhibits 5.27 and 5.28)	■ Total operating costs of the assessment office compared to actual benefits achieved as perceived by internal assessment user groups ■ Total operating costs of the assessment office as a percentage of the institution's total operating costs

Summary

This chapter described many issues and offered several recommendations about building, deploying, and assessing a new or formalized assessment program. In the building phase, it was recommended that assessors clarify the program's purpose, build a supportive culture, clarify assessment user groups and their specific needs, build a leadership structure for administering the program, clarify system elements of an assessment program, identify and make visible direct and indirect assessment costs, build an ongoing two-way communication plan, design the program so as to avoid information overload, and conduct risk management to prepare for and minimize the impact of unexpected negative consequences. In the deployment phase, it was recommended that the assessment program's leadership system encourage broad involvement, be systematic, use an experimental approach, and develop partnerships with important upstream systems. In the assessment phase, it was recommended that assessors use the same process and practices they would use for any unit of analysis. Examples of system elements, critical success factors, and performance indicators for measuring performance of an assessment office were offered.

Worksheet 6.1
   Communication Planning

Unit of Analysis: _____ (*Example: Chemistry Department*)

Date: _____

Use this worksheet to build a communication plan for the unit's assessment program. In column A, decide who needs to be informed, and in column B, describe what this person (or office) needs to know. In column C, indicate when this person (or office) should receive the information, and in column D, state how information will be disseminated to this person (or office). Finally, in column E, indicate who is responsible for disseminating the information.

Who Needs to Be Informed? (A)	What Do They Need to Know? (B)	When Do They Need to Receive It? (C)	How Will Information Be Disseminated? (D)	Who Is Responsible for Disseminating This Information? (E)
Example: Dean of the College of Arts and Sciences	*Example:* Updates on timeliness and problems finalizing assessment reports (such as Student Placement Report) important to the dean for developing the college's annual budget request	*Example:* One month prior to budget request deadlines	*Example:* E-mail and hard copy through campus mail	*Example:* Department chair

GLOSSARY

administrators and managers   One of three categories of internal assessment users. These are people who manage the operations of organizations, programs, and processes whose performance is under review. They are directors, coordinators, managers, and department chairs who use assessment results to account to important stakeholder groups for the organization's overall performance, to manage goals, to support resource allocation decisions, and to manage organizational culture. They also use assessment to monitor and control operations; to improve programs, services, and processes; and to support personnel decisions.

appraisal costs   One of three types of costs of managing quality. Appraisal costs are the costs of "making sure it is right." Appraisal (inspection, review) activity has long been a common form of quality control in higher education.

assessment   The measurement of organizational performance that assessment users evaluate in relation to reference points to support their needs, expectations, and requirements.

assessment coordinator   Coordinator of the institution's overall assessment program, whose role is to serve as a staff consultant and trainer to unit personnel engaged in assessment activities and to coordinate and monitor all assessment activities throughout the institution. As a staff consultant, the assessment coordinator provides advice, clerical support, and data collection and analysis assistance. As a trainer, the assessment coordinator offers both formal training such as workshops and informal training such as one-on-one interactions to help unit personnel develop assessment skills.

assessment costs   A measure of assessment effort (but not of organizational effectiveness). Assessment costs can be direct or indirect.

assessment data   Data collected for use in assessment of organizational performance. Assessors collect three types of data: attitudinal (knowledge, opinions, beliefs, values, and so forth), behavioral (including skills and abilities), and demographic (characteristics or traits). Assessors collect descriptive data about institutional resources from internal databases and comparable and benchmark data from external databases, as well as performance data from internal and external documents.

assessment steering committee   A committee intended to provide credibility to the assessment program whose primary responsibilities are to clarify purposes and goals of assessment; to formulate assessment policies, procedures, practices, and schedules; to identify resources required to build and maintain assessment across the institution; and to measure and evaluate the performance of the assessment program.

assessment user groups   Groups inside or outside an institution that use assessment to support decisions that have the potential of affecting the organization's future capacity to perform.

constraining systems   One of the three types of upstream systems that impose operational constraints on organizations, programs, and processes. Constraining systems establish parameters for what an organization can provide, resources it can use, prices it can charge, methods it can employ, customers it can serve, and other similar matters.

costs of quality   An organization's costs for quality control of its processes, programs, and services. Three types of costs are associated with quality management: failure costs (internal and external), appraisal costs, and prevention costs.

critical success factors   Unique, mission-specific performance factors assessors measure that are critical to the success and long-term survival of an organization.

customers   People and organizations that directly receive or experience the organization's outputs (products and services). Customers can be potential or present, external or internal, or some combination of these. Customers' needs and requirements (and to a lesser extent those of stakeholders and employees) define what products, services, and information the organization produces and how it creates and delivers them. Customers' experiences as they interact with the system determine the degree to which an organization achieves its intended outcomes.

customer satisfaction   The extent to which the organization's internal and external customers are satisfied with outputs they receive or experience; one of the seven crucial areas of organizational performance.

data collection methods   Procedures assessors use to collect performance data at the organization, program, and process levels. The methods they use are based on the sources available to them, the types of data needed, and the overall design of the research approach. Assessors collect data about organizational performance from three main sources: people, directly or indirectly; databases, internal or external to the institution; and documents, internal or external to the institution.

data credibility   A critical success factor for any assessment program. Factors that determine credibility of assessment data include reliability, validity, proper selection of participants, and timeliness.

direct assessment costs   Expenses that contribute directly to the total cost of an assessment program, including line-item costs such as personnel costs (compensation and benefits) of assessment coordinators and support staff, equipment purchase and maintenance costs (for such things as computer hardware, software, printers, scanners, phones, and fax and copy machines that assessment staff use), office and assessment supply costs (such as office supplies, books, and assessment standardized tests), and travel costs.

effectiveness   The extent to which the organization achieves its intended outcomes as a result of customers' receiving or experiencing the organization's outputs; one of the seven crucial areas of organizational performance.

efficiency   One of several crucial areas of organizational performance that measures how well an organization optimizes use of its scarce resources. It compares actual use of people's time, equipment, supplies, physical space, energy, and financial resources against budgeted or planned use. Assessors measure two dimensions of efficiency: resource utilization and the costs and benefits of quality management.

executive guide   A report assessors use to disseminate assessment findings. It is an expansion of the report card and often preferred by senior leaders.

experimental approach   One way to implement a new assessment program. Leaders start small, documenting and correcting their mistakes before fanning out to encompass the entire institution. W. Edwards Deming (1993) calls this approach a PDSA cycle in which leaders develop a plan of action, do it (or parts of it), systematically check to see how things are going, and finally take actions to make it even better.

external academic peers   Scholars who assess the quality and effectiveness of research submitted for publication in refereed journals.

external assessment users   Groups outside the institution that use assessment findings for decision support. Each external assessment user group has a unique interest in assessment results based on its function and relationship to the organization. Each group requires different assessment information and uses it for different purposes. Some of the major external assessment user groups in higher education are governing boards; governmental agencies; potential students, donors, and contractors; organizations that affirm accreditation, rank, classification, and so forth; and external academic peers.

external customers   People and organizations outside the institution and the unit of analysis that directly receive or experience the organization's outputs (products, services, and information).

external stakeholders   Individuals and groups outside the institution who have a stake in, depend on, and benefit from an organization's achieving its intended outcomes.

evaluation   The act of judging the worth of measured performance within the context of reference points.

faculty and staff   One of the three categories of internal assessment user groups. Like senior leaders, administrators, and managers, they use assessment results for accountability, decision support, and improvement. However, they also use assessment results to support the work of committees and task forces conducting self-studies for accreditation and institutional program reviews, faculty personnel decisions, and other important universitywide functions. Faculty and staff can be owners of the assessment process as well as assessors who collect, analyze, and disseminate assessment findings.

failure costs   One of the three types of costs of managing quality. Failure costs are the costs of "getting it wrong." There are many hidden failure costs in higher education. One example is the cost to repeat repairs and services not done properly the first time.

financial durability   The financial health and well-being of an organization, one of the seven crucial areas of organizational performance. Financial durability is mission-specific and a critical, bottom-line financial measure of an organization's overall performance.

governance   An organization's decision-making processes and practices, executed in a structure devised by the organization's leadership system. Decision-making processes can be systematic or ad hoc, centralized or decentralized, top-down or bottom-up, or some combination of these.

governing board   An external assessment user group that governs, coordinates, and advises institutions and programs at the local and state levels and uses assessment to support decisions that have the potential of affecting an organization's capacity to perform.

governmental agencies   An external assessment user group representing federal, state, and local governmental and quasi-governmental organizations, commissions, task forces, and legislative delegations that uses assessment to support decisions that have the potential of affecting an organization's capacity to perform.

guiding principles   The foundation for an organization's vision and mission, presenting the basic truths and practices that guide how people within the organization behave, work, and relate to the people they serve and to each other. Some guiding principles emanate from laws, legal codes, government regulations, and institutional policies and procedures, while others are drawn from formal ethical codes of conduct and generally accepted behavior rooted in organizational traditions, values, and beliefs. Formal codes of ethics in higher education are established by many groups, including professional associations, unions, institutions, student organizations, and governmental agencies. Assessors often use an organization's guiding principles as a reference point against which to evaluate current organizational performance such as quality of worklife and quality of organizational culture.

indirect assessment costs   Expenses that contribute indirectly to the cost of an assessment program, including hidden costs such as infrastructure costs (for electricity, heating and cooling, parking, and office and lab space) and opportunity costs or costs of work not performed in other organizational systems when staff are engaged in assessment-related work.

innovation   Creative changes put into place to improve specific aspects of organizational performance as a successful response to environmental factors; one of the seven crucial areas of organizational performance.

inputs   Internal system elements that reflect the resources organizations require to perform work and create products and services for their customers. Upstream systems housed outside the organization provide inputs to the organization. Organizational inputs include human resources, financial resources, equipment, supplies, physical space, energy, and information.

internal assessment users   Groups within the institution that use assessment findings to account to others and to support decisions. In higher education, there are three types of internal assessment user groups: senior leaders, administrators and managers, and faculty and staff.

internal customers   External system elements consisting of people and organizations within the institution that directly receive or experience the unit's outputs. Internal customers are the primary customers of most administrative organizations. Students are internal customers of academic and administrative organizations that directly serve them.

internal stakeholders   Individuals and groups inside the institution but outside the unit under review who have a stake in the performance of the organization. Internal stakeholders are distinguished from customers in that they do not directly receive or experience the organization's products or services.

IPEDS   The Integrated Postsecondary Education Data System, an assemblage of survey components used to collect data from postsecondary educational institutions that receive federal dollars through aid, grants, and contracts. IPEDS data are often used in assessment for comparisons and benchmarks.

key work processes   The work done by people and machines performing tasks that create outputs. Work in most organizations is organized into four to eight key work processes central to the organization's mission. Key work processes transform inputs to outputs for customers, enabling the organization to achieve its purpose.

leadership system   An internal system element that provides direction and support to a unit under review. A unit's leadership system has external and internal responsibilities and is ultimately accountable for the overall performance of the unit.

measurement   The determination of how performance is operationalized, permitting its evaluation. Assessors use performance indicators to measure seven areas of organizational performance.

mission statement   An organization's statement of purpose, clarifying whom the organization serves, how it serves them, and what results it seeks as a consequence of that service.

organizational design   The formal relationships among people in an organization, specifying their roles and responsibilities (Autry, 1998). It divides work into units such as departments or divisions and defines hierarchy, scope of control, and centralization or decentralization of decision making (Davis and Weckler, 1996).

organizational structure   An organization's governance setup and design, established by the leadership system.

organizations that affirm   Any outside group that uses assessment to determine an institution's accreditation, censure, classification, rank, or eligibility and that bargains with the institution.

outcomes   Intended or desired results an organization seeks to achieve as a consequence of customers' receiving or experiencing the organization's outputs. Organizational outcomes are mission-specific. Achievement of intended outcomes, an area of organizational performance called effectiveness, is critical to organizational survival.

outputs   Deliverables from an organization's key work processes intended for customers who receive or experience them; products, services, and information designed and created for the purpose of meeting or exceeding the needs and requirements of targeted customers.

performance indicators   Statistics used to measure organizational performance. They can be quantitative or qualitative, direct or indirect, soft or hard, objective or subjective. Performance indicators are similar to descriptive statistics in that they lack worth when viewed by themselves (Borden and Bottrill, 1994). Performance measured through performance indicators is compared to reference points. Performance indicators do not necessarily convey information about causation.

prevention costs   One of the three types of costs of managing quality. Prevention costs are the costs of "doing it right the first time." They are planned and incurred prior to operations.

productivity   The ratio of outputs created (such as products, services, and information) to inputs consumed (such as faculty FTE); one of the seven crucial areas of organizational performance.

quality   One of the seven crucial areas of organizational performance, measured in six dimensions: Q_1: quality of upstream systems, Q_2: quality of inputs, Q_3: quality of key work processes, Q_4: quality of outputs, Q_5: quality of leadership systems, and Q_6: quality of worklife.

Q_1: Quality of Upstream Systems   The strength and effectiveness of an organization's partnerships with critical internal and external upstream systems.

Q_2: Quality of Inputs   The qualifications, quantity, cost, adequacy, reliability, restrictiveness, timeliness, currency, reliability, safety, age, and suitability of an organization's human resources, financial resources, equipment, supplies, physical space, energy, and information. Quality of inputs is also a form of quality assurance for upstream systems.

Q_3: Quality of Key Work Processes   A unit's capacity to build quality into its products and services, a measure of cycle time, cost, rework, waste, and scrap in the design, flow, and value added of work (tasks and activities). It is also a measure of the extent to which processes create quality outputs and procedures comply with legal and ethical laws and standards.

Q_4: Quality of Outputs   A measure of products, services, and information in terms of quantity, completeness, timeliness, price, accuracy, reliability, defectiveness, convenience, and appropriateness as perceived by internal and external customers who receive or experience them.

Q₅: Quality of Leadership Systems A measure of the quality and effectiveness of services provided by the system in an organization that sets direction and acquires and allocates organizational resources.

Q₆: Quality of Worklife An organization's employees' perceptions, attitudes, and opinions about organizational quality and levels of satisfaction with their work experiences and the workplace.

reference points Performance expectations that provide the context for evaluation as measured by performance indicators.

reliability The extent to which measurement data present the same results, regardless of when measurement occurs or who performs it. Reliability is a necessary but not a sufficient condition for validity.

report card A means for disseminating assessment findings that presents performance results in selected areas of importance to the organization and conveys a picture of the overall health and well-being of the organization at the time of publication.

risk management The process of anticipating and preparing for all possible unintended and potentially dysfunctional consequences that can result from implementation and use of a new or more formalized assessment program.

senior leaders An internal assessment user group consisting of presidents, vice presidents, chancellors, vice chancellors, deans, and others who operate at the institutional level (or, in certain large organizations, at the college or school level). Senior leaders use assessment results mainly to account to important external stakeholders, manage strategy, support resource allocation decisions, and manage organizational culture.

service partners One of the three types of upstream systems that complement an organization's performance by serving the organization's customers. Service partners provide services to customers before or during their experience in the system.

sources of assessment data Information providers from whom assessors collect assessment data about organizational performance. The main sources assessors consult are people, either directly or indirectly through others; databases, either inside or outside the institution; and documents, either internal or external.

stakeholders Individuals and groups who have a stake in, depend on, and benefit from the organization's achieving its intended outcomes.

stakeholder satisfaction The extent to which an organization's internal and external stakeholders are satisfied with the unit's effectiveness; one of the seven crucial areas of organizational performance.

strategic goals   Goals that help an organization find its competitive advantage and place in its greater environment, as determined by the leadership system.

students   People receiving or experiencing the outputs of organizations in higher education. Students function not only as customers but also as inputs and stakeholders.

supplier systems   One of the three types of upstream systems that represent the sources of essential resources the organization needs to perform its work and create and deliver products and services to its customers.

system elements   Components of organizational systems that present opportunities for measuring performance. Organizations in higher education have two types of system elements: internal elements (leadership systems, inputs, key work processes, outputs, and outcomes) and external elements (upstream systems, external and internal customers, and external and internal stakeholders).

systems thinking   A philosophy or perspective that enables organizational leaders, stakeholders, assessors, and other constituents to recognize organizations as customized systems created for a purpose, complex systems composed of interdependent internal and external system elements, and open systems that interact with their environment.

unit of analysis   An organization, program, or process whose performance is under review. In higher education, a unit of analysis can be an entire institution, a college, a school, a department, a program, or an administrative office. A unit of analysis can also be a key work process within an organizational unit or a cross-functional process that spans organizational boundaries.

upstream systems   External system elements either inside or outside the institution that support or influence the unit's capacity to perform. There are three types of upstream systems: suppliers, constraining systems, and service partners.

validity   The extent to which performance indicators actually measure what they are intended to measure.

vision statement   A statement of an organization's description of its desired future state in terms of performance excellence.

REFERENCES

ABET Engineering Accreditation Commission. "Criteria for Accrediting Engineering Programs." [http://www.abet.org/the_basics.shtml]. 2006.

Albrecht, K., and Bradford, L. J. *The Service Advantage: How to Identify and Fulfill Customer Needs.* Homewood, Ill.: Dow Jones/Irwin, 1990.

American Association of University Professors. "1940 Statement of Principles on Academic Freedom and Tenure with 1970 Interpretive Comments." [http://www.aaup.org/statements/Redbook/1940stat.htm]. 2004.

American Association of University Professors. "Academic Freedom for a Free Society." [http://www.aaup.org/aboutaaup/description.htm]. 2005a.

American Association of University Professors. "What Is Censure?" [http://www.aaup.org/COM-a/prcenback.htm]. 2005b.

Aronson, D. "Introduction to Systems Thinking." [http:www.thinking.net/Systems_Thinking/Intro_to_ST/intro_to_st.html]. 1996.

Autry, R. H. "What Is Organizational Design?" [http://www.inovus.com/organiza.htm]. 1998.

Banta, T. W. "Preface." In T. W. Banta and Associates, *Building a Scholarship of Assessment.* San Francisco: Jossey-Bass, 2002.

Benjamin, R., and Hersh, R. H. "Measuring the Difference College Makes: The RAND/CAE Value-Added Assessment Initiative." *peerReview*, 2002, 4(2/3), 7–10.

Borden, V.M.H., and Bottrill, K. V. "Performance Indicators: History, Definitions, and Methods." In V.M.H. Borden and T. W. Banta (eds.), *Using Performance Indicators to Guide Strategic Decision Making.* New Directions for Institutional Research, no. 82. San Francisco: Jossey-Bass, 1994.

Carnegie Foundation for the Advancement of Teaching. "Carnegie Classification of Institutions of Higher Education." [http://www.carnegiefoundation.org/Classification/2005.htm]. 2005.

Carr, C. "Task-Based Systems." *Performance and Instruction*, Jan. 1991, pp. 42–46.

Chun, M. "Looking Where the Light Is Better: A Review of the Literature on Assessing Higher Education Quality." peerReview, 2002, 4(2/3), 16–25.

Creswell, J. W. *Qualitative Inquiry and Research Design: Choosing Among the Five Traditions.* Thousand Oaks, Calif.: Sage, 1998.

Davis, M. R., and Weckler, D. A. *A Practical Guide to Organization Design.* Menlo Park, Calif.: Crisp, 1996.

Deming, W. E. *The New Economics for Industry, Government, and Education*. Cambridge: Massachusetts Institute of Technology, Center for Advanced Engineering Study, 1993.

Drucker, P. F. "The Discipline of Innovation." *Drucker Foundation News*, Mar. 1998.

Drucker, P. F. *Management Challenges for the 21st Century*. New York: Harper Business, 1999.

Eaton, J. S. "An Overview of U.S. Accreditation." Council for Higher Education Accreditation. [http://www.chea.org/pdf/overview_US_accred_8-03.pdf]. 1999.

Erwin, T. D., and Wise, S. L. "A Scholar-Practitioner Model for Assessment." In T. W. Banta and Associates, *Building a Scholarship of Assessment*. San Francisco: Jossey-Bass, 2002.

Ewell, P. T. "An Emerging Scholarship: A Brief History of Assessment." In T. W. Banta and Associates, *Building a Scholarship of Assessment*. San Francisco: Jossey-Bass, 2002.

Gray, P. J. "The Roots of Assessment: Tensions, Solutions, and Research Directions." In T. W. Banta and Associates, *Building a Scholarship of Assessment*. San Francisco: Jossey-Bass, 2002.

Huselid, M. A., Becker, B. E., and Beatty, R. W. *The Workforce Scorecard: Managing Human Capital to Execute Strategy*. Boston: Harvard Business School Press, 2005.

Kaplan, R. S., and Norton, D. P. *The Balanced Scorecard*. Boston: Harvard Business School Press, 1996.

Karash, R. "Learning-Org Dialog on Learning Organizations." [http://www.learning-org.com]. 2001.

Knight, J. "The AAUP's Censure List." American Association of University Professors. [http://www.aaup.org/publications/Academe/2003/03jf/03jfkni.htm]. 2003.

Kofman, F., and Senge, P. M. "Communities of Commitment: The Heart of Learning Organizations." *Organizational Dynamics*, 1993, 22, 5–23.

Lewis, P. S., Goodman, S. H., and Fandt, P. M. *Management: Challenges in the 21st Century*. St. Paul, Minn.: West, 1995.

McNamara, C. "Basic Guidelines for Reorganizing a Small Business (For-Profit or Nonprofit)." [http://www.managementhelp.org/orgnzing/basics.htm]. 1999a.

McNamara, C. "Strategic Planning (in Nonprofit or For-Profit Organizations)." [http://www.managementhelp.org/plan_dec/str_plan/str_plan.htm]. 1999b.

McNamara, C. "Thinking About Organizations as Systems." [http://www.managementhelp.org/org_thry/org_sytm.htm]. 1999c.

National Academies. "About the National Research Council." [http://www.nationalacademies.org/nrc]. 2006.

National Center for Educational Statistics. "About IPEDS." [http://nces.ed.gov/ipeds/AboutIPEDS.asp]. 2005.

National Collegiate Athletic Association. "NCAA-APR Questions and Answers." [http://www2.ncaa.org/academics_and_athletes/education_and_research/academic_reform/faq.html]. 2005a.

National Collegiate Athletic Association. *2005–06 NCAA Division III Manual: Constitution Operating Bylaws*, Administrative Bylaws. Indianapolis, Ind.: National Collegiate Athletic Association, 2005b.

National Collegiate Athletic Association. "Division I Athletics Certification Program: Benefits." [http://www1.ncaa.org/membership/membership_svcs/athletics_certification/benefits]. 2006a.

National Collegiate Athletic Association. "Division I Athletics Certification Program: Purpose." [http://www1.ncaa.org/membership/membership_svcs/athletics_certification/purpose]. 2006b.

National Education Association. "About NEA." [http://www.nea.org/aboutnea/index.html]. 2006.

Newton, R. "The Two Cultures of Academe: An Overlooked Planning Hurdle." *Planning for Higher Education*, 1992, 21(1), 8–14.

Oakland, J. S. *Total Quality Management*. Oxford: Butterworth-Heinemann, 1992.

Ostriker, J. P., and Kuh, C. V. (eds.). "Assessing Research-Doctorate Programs: A Methodology Study." National Research Council. [http://www7.national academies.org/resdoc/index.html]. 2003.

Palomba, C. A., and Banta, T. W. *Assessment Essentials*. San Francisco: Jossey-Bass, 1999.

Patton, M. Q. *Qualitative Research and Evaluation Methods*. (3rd ed.). Thousand Oaks, Calif.: Sage, 2002.

Pike, G. R. "Measurement Issues in Outcomes Assessment." In T. W. Banta and Associates, *Building a Scholarship of Assessment*. San Francisco: Jossey-Bass, 2002.

Princeton Review. "FAQs About the Best 361 Colleges and the Princeton Review College Rankings." [http:www.princetonreview.com/college/research/articles/find/rankingsFAQ.asp]. 2006.

Rogers, B. H., and Gentemann, K. M. "The Value of Institutional Research in the Assessment of Institutional Effectiveness." In B. H. Rogers and K. M. Gentemann (eds.), *Research in Higher Education*, vol. 30, no. 3. New York: Human Sciences Press, 1989.

Sackmann, S. A. "Uncovering Culture in Organizations." *Journal of Applied Behavioral Science*, 1991, *27*(3), 295–317.

Schein, E. H. *Organizational Culture and Leadership*. (2nd ed.) San Francisco: Jossey-Bass, 1992.

Scherkenbach, W. W. *The Deming Route to Quality and Productivity*. Milwaukee, Wis.: ASQC Quality Press, 1986.

Senge, P. M. *The Fifth Discipline: The Art and Practice of the Learning Organization*. New York: Currency/Doubleday, 1990.

Senge, P. M. "The Practice of Innovation." *Leader to Leader*, Summer 1998, pp. 16–22. [http://pfdf.org/leaderbooks/L2L/summer98/senge.html].

Seymour, D. T. *Causing Quality in Higher Education*. Phoenix, Ariz.: Oryx Press, 1993.

Shermis, M. D., and Daniels, K. E. "Web Applications in Assessment." In T. W. Banta and Associates, *Building a Scholarship of Assessment*. San Francisco: Jossey-Bass, 2002.

Sink, D. S., and Tuttle, T. C. *Planning and Measurement in Your Organization of the Future*. Norcross, Ga.: Engineering and Management Press, Institute of Industrial Engineers, 1989.

Southern Association of Colleges and Schools Commission on Colleges. *Principles of Accreditation: Foundations for Quality Enhancement*. Decatur, Ga.: Southern Association of Colleges and School Commission on Colleges, 2004.

State Council of Higher Education for Virginia. "Institutional Performance Standards." [http://www.schev.edu/Reportstats/InstitutionalPerformanceStandards.pdf]. 2005.

Taylor, B. K, and Massey, W. F. *Strategic Indicators for Higher Education, 1996*. Princeton, N.J.: Peterson, 1996.

Thor, C. G. "Ten Rules for Building a Measurement System." In W. F. Christopher and C. G. Thor (eds.), *Handbook for Productivity Measurement and Improvement*. Cambridge, Mass.: Productivity Press, 1993.

Tritelli, D. "From the Editor." *peerReview*, 2002, *4*(2/3), 3.

U.S. News and World Report. "America's Best Colleges 2005, Methodology: Best Values." [http://www.usnews.com/usnews/edu/college/rankings/about//05bymeth_brief.php]. 2005.

U.S. News and World Report. "America's Best Colleges 2005, Undergraduate Ranking Criteria and Weights." [http://www.usnews.com/usnews/edu/college/rankings/about/weight_brief.php]. 2006.

Walvoord, B. E. *Assessment: Clear and Simple*. San Francisco: Jossey-Bass, 2004.

Wheatley, M. J. *Finding Our Way: Leadership for an Uncertain Time*. San Francisco: Berrett-Koehler, 2005.